Action Learning in Practice

Action Learning
in
Practice

Second Edition

Edited by
Mike Pedler

Gower

First published 1983
Second edition published 1991 by
Gower Publishing Company Limited
Gower House
Croft Road
Aldershot
Hants GU11 3HR
England

Gower Publishing Company
Old Post Road
Brookfield
Vermont 05036
USA

British Library Cataloguing in Publication Data
Action learning in practice.–2nd. ed.
  1. Managers. Training. Teaching methods: Action learning
  I. Pedler, Mike *1944–*
  658.40712404

ISBN 0 566 02859 X

Phototypeset by Input Typesetting Ltd, London

Printed in Great Britain by
Billing & Sons Ltd, Worcester

Contents

List of Figures

Foreword

Don Young, Director, Young, Samuel, Chambers, formerly Director of Personnel, Thorn EMI plc

Early in my career as a manager, making a transition from being a Production Manager to an appointment as Training Officer, I first encountered the disturbing phenomenon of being viewed by ex-colleagues as moving from the 'real' world of making things to a peripheral role which seemed to be seen as a combination of scoutmaster and school teacher. It also occurred to me that still further distant from this 'real' world was the infrastructure of management education, in this case represented by the local Technical College, seemingly regarded by my ex-colleagues as being outside the real world altogether. My first personal breakthrough from this disturbing role of outsider happened when, on being asked to develop a training programme for fish filleters by a kindly colleague, who probably wished to make me feel wanted, it occurred to me to ask why he wanted a training programme. 'Because we're losing £500 000 a year on standard yield and throughput,' he replied. 'So,' I continued, 'the *problem* is to recover the £500 000 and to find out what might be done, including training, to achieve this.' 'Yes,' he answered simply; and we were away with a project which involved supervisors, the fish filleters themselves, factory accountants, the work study department, myself and a large cast of others, to crack the problem.

The second significant thing that happened to me, in the same factory some weeks later, was a chance remark by a colleague that he had never thought he would want to learn Dutch, but that his impending transfer to the factory in Holland had proved to be a remarkable motivator.

These two experiences – which might be summarized as 'How can those of us, not directly involved in the core processes of an organisation, directly help those who are, in order to make things better?' and 'If learning is vital to individual and organisation survival, how can we motivate people to want to learn?' have been experiences I have struggled with in a variety of organisations for 30 years. Had I known about it earlier, my struggles would have been made more productive by Reg Revan's triad: 'Who knows about this problem? Who cares about it? Who can do anything about it?'

More recent experience has brought me much closer to institutions which offer management education, and to many of the products (including people) of those institutions. The dilemma here is the same – how to get close to the real world of managers struggling with real management problems. Experience has taught me that many of these institutions (and often the most prestigious) have ducked out of addressing this question by pretending to themselves and their students that whatever they teach is 'management' when patently it is not. The main issue, therefore, still seems to me to be how to help managers, and in my latter working years it has been General Managers, to be able to improve, adapt and develop the practice of management through learning applied to the 'real world' challenges which they face. Focusing the problem in this way enables us to regard providers and potential providers of help as useful people, who can be brought into the managers' world to help them both to define and solve real problems and also to secure the base of improvement through learning which sticks. This simply has to be much more effective generally than the process of sending the manager into the world of the provider of learning in the hope that theory might be converted into practice back home.

All this indicates, I hope, that I am a strong advocate, through experience, of many of the principles of Action Learning as a vehicle for impacting on the growth and effectiveness of individuals, and as an invaluable provider of perspectives which will enable improvement to be embedded in the organisational infrastructure.

This book seems to me to provide a very rich series of such perspectives. It has provoked my own thinking, and I am sure will motivate many readers into a wider and deeper understanding of what is hopefully becoming something of a way of life.

Notes on contributors

Doris Adams (*Action Learning at Digital Equipment*) is an Assistant Professor at Trinity College in Burlington, Vermont. The focus of her teaching and consulting has been on development in the workplace. Dr Adams's recent dissertation from the University of Texas researched problem-solving approaches of small groups utilizing the concepts of Argyris, a framework she has continued to explore in her consulting and teaching.

Richard Baker (*Helping US human resource professionals into Action Learning*) is the president of Baker & Company, a Dallas based management consulting firm specializing in working with clients to strengthen their competitive positions. Mr Baker's firm has worked with recognized leaders in their industries including American Airlines, General Motors Corp., Xerox Corp., American National Can Co., Rockwell International, and AT & T.

David Boddy (*Supervisory development*) is head of department of Management Studies at Glasgow Business School. He has used Action Learning in a wide variety of management development designs, with supervisors, senior managers and with those responsible for introducing major technological changes. He is co-author of *Organisations in the Network Age*, Routledge, 1990.

Norman Brown (*Improving management morale and efficiency*) is founder of Management in Action, a consortium of consultants. He studied electronic engineering and progressed to general management via manufacturing, financial control and marketing. He has a strong interest in management and organisational development, and advises on marketing strategy, culture change and management training. He firmly believes that successful management is founded on integrity rather than 1980s materialism.

John Burgoyne (*Action Learning: an evaluation*) is Professor in Management Learning at the Centre for the Study of Management Learning in the University of Lancaster. He graduated in psychology and has long been concerned with the evaluation of management education, the design of programmes and the nature of managerial behaviour and competencies. In recent years his interests have broadened into the areas of career management and management development policy.

David Casey (*The role of the set adviser; The shell of your understanding*) has been fascinated by how people learn ever since, as a member of the first XI, he was asked to coach the under–14s. He has been a schoolteacher, an R & D manager and a personnel director; but the persistent attractions of teaching have always drawn him back. Since 1972 he has been a consultant in management learning using Action Learning with a variety of people including chief executives.

Nelson F. Coghill (*A bibliography of Action Learning*), a medicine and science graduate, spent six years in the RAMC during the war, and then 30 years as a consultant physician. A Fellow of the Royal College of Physicians, he was involved in higher medical training for consultants. From 1965 he worked with Reg Revans using Action Learning to improve patient care and staff relationships in hospitals. He has worked for the Action Learning Trust (now IFAL) since its foundation, being chairman for two years.

Ian Cunningham (*Action Learning for Chief Executives*) is Director of Roffey Park Management College and has previously been managing director of a management consultancy, Senior Research Fellow at Ashridge Management College, a polytechnic lecturer, a local government management trainer, a line manager and a chemist. He is the author of over 60 papers, articles and book chapters.

Nancy M. Dixon (*Helping US human resources professionals into Action Learning; Action Learning at Digital Equipment*) is an Associate Professor of Human Resource Development at The George Washington University in Washington DC. Dr Dixon has established (with Larry Hales) The Action Learning Network in the United States to promote the ideas of Action Learning in that country. Dr Dixon has had a long-term interest in the role experience plays in the learning and development of individuals within organizations. Her current work has broadened that focus to organizational learning, the processes whole organizations use to learn from their experiences and to adapt to their changing environments.

Mark Easterby-Smith (*Action Learning: an evaluation*) has been at the Centre for the Study of Management Learning at Lancaster University since 1978. He has worked on the evaluation of management development for more years than he cares to remember and has published much on this theme, including *Evaluation of Management Education, Training & Development*, Gower, 1986. He has recently been appointed director of the Management Teacher Development Centre at Lancaster.

Bob Garratt (*The power of Action Learning*) is an international consultant specializing in business strategy and the simultaneous development of top managers. He moved from architectural education to industry by joining the GEC senior managers programme with Reg Revans and others and has since worked on action learning projects in the UK and elsewhere. He is chairman of the Association for Management Education and Development, chairman of Media Projects International and Visiting Fellow at the Management School, Imperial College.

Larry Hales (*Helping US human resources professionals into Action Learning*) is the Manager of Advanced Learning at General Motors Corporate Education and Training in Warren, Michigan. His responsibilities include the identification, development and transfer of innovative learning processes into organizational change strategies, leadership development programmes and furthering a corporate learning culture.

J M Harries (*Developing the set adviser*) is a Senior Training Adviser with the Local Government Training Board. He spent 16 years in the RAF as an Education & Training Officer and attained the rank of Squadron Leader. Currently he heads the

Strategic Management project at LGTB which seeks to help local government to shape future service provision in the community. He is co-author of *Making Sense of Management Jargon: An A to Z guide to Management & Organisation Development*, Granary Press, 1984.

Martin Hughes (*The mixed set*) has had a varied career including management positions in textiles, recruitment consultancy and engineering. In 1980 he established Development Resources Ltd, his own management consultancy, operating in the UK and internationally. He uses Action Learning and self-development methods for management development and organizational change.

Alan Lawlor (*The components of Action Learning*) co-founded Action Learning Associates in 1978 to earn his living from applying the principles of Action Learning. He worked with many different management groups in large and small organizations and also with unemployed managers. He was a chartered engineer and had previously been head of department of Management Studies at Redditch College. He died in 1988.

Jean Lawrence (*Continuity in Action Learning*) is a managing partner in the Development Consortium and an Honorary Fellow of Manchester Business School. She was previously a production manager at Cadbury's and staff member at MBS. She is chairman of the International Foundation for Action Learning and a vice-president of the Association for Management Education & Development. She bases all her organization and management development work on action learning principles and works regularly at Henley, The Management College and Templeton College, Oxford, as well as on regular assignments overseas.

Ronnie Lessem (*A biography of Action Learning*) is Reader in International Management at City University Business School and manager of the consortial MBA. He has used Action Learning all over the world with small and large concerns to facilitate self, organization and business development. He has written eight books, the most recent of which is *Global Management Principles*, Prentice-Hall, 1989.

Alec Lewis (*An in-company programme*) has been an independent management consultant since 1984 and concentrates his Action Learning endeavours in the insurance and banking sectors. After graduating in economics he worked in sales and market research with Cadbury-Fry before joining Bristol Polytechnic in 1968 where he was Principal Lecturer in the South West Regional Management Centre.

Charles Margerison (*Learning from action in Australia*) is chairman of Team Management Systems and a vice-president of the International Management Centre from Buckingham. He was previously Professor of Management at the University of Queensland and Cranfield School of Management. He has written ten books and is the editor of the Journal of Management Development and Executive Development.

John Morris (*Minding our Ps and Qs*) is a Managing Partner of the Development Consortium, a management consultancy specializing in Action Learning within and between organizations. From 1970 to 1982 he was Professor of Management Development at the Manchester Business School, where he pioneered various forms of project-based learning.

David Pearce (*Getting started: an action manual*) is a consultant in management and organization development working in the UK and Europe. He was previously management development adviser with GEC where he worked on the introduction of Action Learning to the senior management development programme. With David Casey, he edited *More Than Management Development: Action Learning at GEC*, Gower, 1977.

Mike Pedler (*Management development as moral art; Questioning ourselves; Another look at set advising*) is a consultant in management and organizational learning. He has previously been a market researcher, a tutor with the Workers Educational Association and a polytechnic lecturer. He is editor of Management Education & Development, as associate and non-executive director of Transform Ltd., and a visiting fellow at the Centre for the Study of Management Learning at the University of Lancaster.

Reg Revans (*Action Learning: its origins and nature; The enterprise as a learning system*) wrote his first paper on Action Learning in 1938 and as an education officer in Essex was asked by the County Medical Officer why so many girls were abandoning hospital training that wards were threatened with closure. From this pre-war study he moved to the coal industry where he recommended the first non-expert-directed staff college on record and has since developed the Action Learning idea of concentrating upon the talents and motivations of the managers themselves in fifty countries. He has long forecast the uselessness of traditional 'management education' and is now concerned that, because this forecast is verified, genuine Action Learning will be replaced by 'established futilities being marketed at still higher fees as "advanced Action Learning" and under scores of different names, such as "quality assurance" and "clinical evaluation" '.

Warwick Rowell (*Applying Action Learning in several Australian settings*) is an independent management consultant, working in the area of ethical investment and in the counselling of senior managers. He has used Action Learning for management education and social issues for the last 15 years and received a Master's Degree for his work in this field. One of his current projects is attempting to address the pressing problems of the Aborigines in northern Western Australia.

Eric Schlesinger (*Quality service in New Zealand*) is an independent management consultant with 20 years of experience of developing people and organizations in engineering, local government and financial services in the UK and Australasia. He focuses upon Action Learning and 'action thinking' as major routes to reality, and is convinced that Western, Northern and Eastern ways of thinking about management have much to learn from each other and even more to learn from Southern ways.

David Sutton (*A range of applications*) who died in 1990, realised as a works manager that he had only had the most ineffective and pedestrian training for his job. Later as a principal lecturer at Manchester Polytechnic he embraced Action Learning enthusiastically when he became aware of it in 1968. By 1972 he was a freelance consultant and involved with Reg Revans in founding Action Learning Projects International. Ever since he practised and wrote about Action Learning and was Treasurer of the International Foundation for Action Learning.

Maggie Taylor (*Action Learning in an academic context*) is Senior Lecturer in Management Development at Manchester Polytechnic and a course team member of the MSc in Management by Action Learning. Previously her career has centred on personnel management as a practitioner, lecturer, consultant and course manager in the UK and the USA. She is a member of the IPM and has served on national committees and working parties in education.

Richard Thorpe (*Action Learning in an academic context*) is Principal Lecturer in Management Development at Manchester Polytechnic and a course team member of the MSc in Management by Action Learning. After ten years in industry he worked at Strathclyde and Glasgow Universities and Blackburn College. His interests in 'motivation and reward' and small firms led to collaboration in *Payments Systems and Productivity*, Macmillan, and *Management Research: An Introduction to the Process and Context of Inquiry*, Sage.

Tony Winkless (*Doctors as managers*) is a chartered psychologist and runs his own business, providing management assessment and development services to the private and public sectors. His previous career was in personnel and training in industry and included five years with Kodak and ten with the Geest Organization.

Zhou Jianhua (*Self-improvement in Chinese joint venture companies*) is a lecturer in China's National Centre for Management Development at Wuxi. He has ten years experience as personnel manager of Wuxi Electric Equipment Company and joined the China-EEC Management Programme for three years. His recent interest has focused upon Sino-foreign enterprises on which he has published several papers including 'The Cultural Discrepancy and Mixtures in Joint Ventures' and 'China's Joint Ventures and Their Environment.'

Introduction

Mike Pedler

Since the first edition of this book appeared in 1983, the Action Learning idea has become widely known amongst management developers in many parts of the world including the UK, Europe and Australasia. As David Sutton says in his chapter, it was easy at that time to select a range of applications because there were only a few programmes and practitioners, but now the 'numbers who actively follow the Action Learning banner can be numbered in their cohorts and platoons'.

Allowing for some 'talking up' by a well-known practitioner, there is evidence that the idea has entered the mainstream. The six-month management development programme which has a 'start-up module, monthly learning sets, occasional workshops and a final workshop' has almost reached the status of a new orthodoxy in some quarters. However, the term 'Action Learning' does not always appear on such designs, which is why it sometimes seems as if it is the idea and not the trade name which has become widely known. For example, here is an extract from a letter sent by the management development centre in a 'Blue-chip' British corporation to its internal customers:

> Let me list some of the practical changes in this new phase of management training. First, nothing is longer than a week – the two-week courses have gone, replaced by a single week together with some supplementary days. These shorter events should help overcome the problems of releasing staff from work.

Second, these supplementary days of preparation and follow-up are an integral and not optional part of the course. They help to make the training more related to the individual workplace, the time between them and the main module being used for specific projects or research.

Is this Action Learning? Perhaps. Has this design, and many others like it, been influenced by the action idea? Probably. Does it matter? Well, yes and no. No, because if Action Learning has made a contribution to improving management development practice, which in turn has helped improve the quality of managing and organising, then that should be enough. But yes, if, in all the diffusion, the idea of Action Learning has become empty technique.

There is a dilemma here. The first edition began with the desire to produce a 'practical guide to Action Learning' for the frustrated manager who said 'Going around I've realised that there is nothing that I can give people that shows them how to do Action Learning: nothing that shows them how to get on with it'. Ask Reg Revans and he will say with some justice that 'it's all in the ABC' (Revans 1983). Yet still people ask for 'practical guidance'. Perhaps this siren song should be resisted? This second edition therefore confronts the same question as the first – 'How do you communicate Action Learning without packaging it and reducing it to mere technique?'

The three parts of this book set out to address the related questions:–

1. What is Action Learning?

2. How does Action Learning work?

3. How can I get started on Action Learning?

Accordingly, Part I attempts the first and most difficult question. The contributors here each address the problem in a different and personal way. Action Learning is not susceptible to the 100 word definition, and one's efforts to do this, for example in brochures, always seem unsatisfactory. Here is one of my recent efforts:

> Action Learning is an approach to the development of people in organisations which takes the task as the vehicle for learning. It is based on the premise that there is no learning without action and no sober and deliberate action without learning. On the whole our education system has not been based upon this principle. The method has been pioneered in work organisations and has three main components – people, who accept the responsibility for taking

action on a particular issue; problems, or the tasks that people set themselves; and a set of six or so colleagues who support and challenge each other to make progress on problems. Action Learning implies both self-development and organisation development. Action on a problem changes both the problem and the person acting upon it. It proceeds particularly by questioning taken-for-granted knowledge.

This seems pretty unobjectionable stuff, but I was stopped in my tracks once by Revans for making a similar statement. On the Hospital Internal Communication Project, for example (Revans 1972), there were no 'sets' but a much larger group of doctors, nurses, porters and so on, who met on a regular basis to share information, ask questions and plan action. Sets are a splendid and by now widespread social invention, but neither they, nor any other form which programmes may take, can be said to define Action Learning. Many other aspects of the above 'definition' could be challenged – for example, that people set themselves tasks. In the book which most pretends definition, *The ABC of Action Learning*, it is significant that Revans does not address the simple question 'What is Action Learning?', but only the reciprocal 'What Action Learning is not'. As he says in Chapter 1, 'Action Learning takes so long to describe . . . because it is so simple'!

What is Action Learning?

One way in which this book differs from the first edition is that whereas the earlier book consisted entirely of newly commissioned papers this book includes some reprints of what are, in my opinion, classics which have appeared over the years. Two of these appear in Part I. Chapter 2 is Ronnie Lessem's hymn to Revans and Action Learning which first appeared, along with Revans's 'The enterprise as a learning system' (chapter 7) in what amounts to Revans's collected works to 1982, *The Origins and Growth of Action Learning*. I have long admired Lessem's essay, which brings together some of the key elements of Action Learning and illustrates how these have been forged from Revans's successive encounters with the world.

Chapter 7 sets out some deceptively simple guidelines to developing organizations as learning systems. I have included this partly as a reminder that Action Learning is more than management development, but also to represent Revans's approach to organization development. This seems relevant once again in the light of the recent interest in 'Learning Organizations'.

Of the other chapters, 1, 4 and 5 appeared in the first edition, while 3 and 6 were newly written for this edition. Chapter 3 explores the moral philosophy of Action Learning and draws out some of the implications for management development. John Morris elegantly minds his P's and Q's in Chapter 6, picking his way through a range of problems from personal to organizational to matters of national and international concern.

Part I, then, consists of some practitioners trying to express the essence of Action Learning for themselves. Perhaps sometimes at a cost of mastery, action learners are holistic by inclination. They are no respecters of boundaries, organizational or academic. When the essence is captured we are confronted one minute with the depths of the individual psyche and the next with the intricacies of some vast organizational system. Such entanglement is part of the definition; problems concerning marketing are not separated out from production matters, nor those concerning individuals from those facing nations. Such breadth can lead to a loss of focus and a countervailing particularity and pernicketiness is called for.

In terms of what Action Learning may be, there are a number of issues which appear to be common to the process whether the discussion is taking place at the level of the person or at the collective – organizational or even national – level. The model below is a spiral rather than a cycle and depicts what I take to be the key issues.

First it is a 'problem' which starts the learning spiral (not a puzzle). Our ability to 'problematize' the world – constructing appropriate vehicles which are not so small as to be puzzles or too big to engender helplessness – is critical for our subsequent action and learning.

An important qualifying point is the recognition of the inner and outer nature of problems; that all problems are personal *and* public, and that 'those unable to change themselves are unable to change the world around them'. A third issue is the building up of an action and learning system. Revans has called this the 'Structure d'acceuil' – the structure of welcome. To tackle problems worthy of the name we need help – allies, comrades, colleagues and resources. Working in a set or small group can provide for mutual empowerment.

A fourth issue is to do with learning as development over time, involving our past, present and future. Action Learning involves reconstructive learning, or re-framing, as well as simple

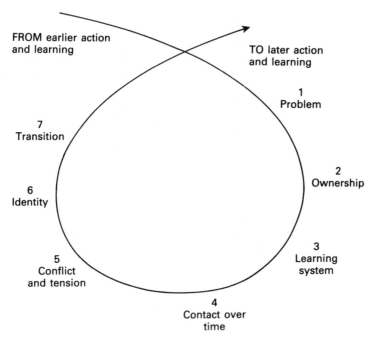

Figure I.1   The learning spiral

additive learning or error-correction. We can only learn when we are ready to do so, and what we have learned in the past, including the 'professional deformation' which comes from long practice, can take a long time to loosen and transform.

Fifthly, action and learning involve the application of power, and sooner rather than later produce conflict. Acting and learning produce a necessary tension within the person and within the organisation – 'when you are attacked or ridiculed or opposed you know you are getting somewhere'. This cannot be avoided, and the skills of confrontation, handling negative feedback and managing conflict for creative outcomes, are important here.

All significant learning, whether individual or organizational, involves a shift in identity. We and our problems are in transition; pursuing the spiral we move on to the next (and bigger?) problem.

How does Action Learning work?

Parts II and III contain case studies and applications from the UK, Australia, New Zealand and China. Here are examples of work with supervisors and chief executives, with doctors and students on a Master's programme, with in-company groups and with mixed sets. Much variety of form is evident, yet this is only a sample of the richness of designs which Action Learning has engendered.

Five chapters – by David Sutton who sadly died whilst the book was in press, Martin Hughes, Alec Lewis, David Boddy and Norman Brown – stand the passage of time (with varying degrees of revision) from the first edition. The other eight chapters are new. Tony Winkless draws on his experience working in the National Health Service to illustrate that Action Learning continues to be put to good use there, whilst Richard Thorpe and Maggie Taylor describe the MSc in Management by Action Learning at Manchester Polytechnic. Nancy Dixon and her colleagues contribute two very welcome case studies from the USA. It is particularly pleasing to hear that Action Learning has started to make an impact in North America. Charles Margerison and Warwick Rowell provide contrasting but appropriately biographical accounts of their use of Action Learning in Australia. It is particularly pleasing that Rick should appear here as he was to have been one of the editors of this book when it was first mooted in 1979. Eric Schlesinger harnesses Action Learning to quality management in New Zealand and Zhou Jianhua describes how Action Learning is being used to create joint ventures in China.

There is a rapid evolution and turnover of forms of Action Learning. This selection is intended to provide enough width to encourage rather than constrain innovations while illustrating some underlying commonalities.

How to get started

There is only one way to find out about Action Learning. Like many of the good things in life Action Learning is best approached through personal experience and not via second hand accounts. The purpose of this book is not to satisfy but to stimulate. It is meant to encourage you to make your own efforts. An important aspect of Action Learning is the possibility of failure. Failure in resolving an intractable problem is no disgrace, though in these image-conscious days it may often be unwise to demonstrate it. What we call 'success' or 'problem-solving' may often be more to do with personal PR than with a sober assessment of affairs. That is what it means to deal with problems rather than puzzles, however diverting. We have the power to decide whether we have 'succeeded' or 'failed'; but they do say that we learn from our failures – mainly because failure means that questions will be asked, by me or by you. If truth is the first casualty in war, then admitting failure is the first victim of the unforgiving organization.

With this caveat, Part IV is intended to help you to get started in Action Learning. This part retains five original chapters from the first edition and adds three new ones. The first contributor here, Alan Lawlor, died in 1988. His chapter has a special value for me, for it was he who introduced me to some of the magic of Action Learning in practice when he came to Sheffield to help set up an 'Action Learning Clinic' with the Institute of Works Managers in 1976. I can remember vividly how I felt when he taught us Reg's famous triad of key questions for action learners – 'Who knows (about the problem)?' 'Who cares?' and 'Who can (do something)?'

To David Casey's splendidly enduring paper on the role of the set adviser is added another fine piece of writing by him 'The shell of your understanding'. It is also David's work which Ian Cunningham discusses in a specially shortened version of his research paper 'An Evaluation of an Action Learning Programme for Chief Executives'. This is one of the best pieces of evaluative work done on Action Learning to date. Jean Lawrence contributes a thoughtful Chapter 24 on how to keep 'Q' – the essence of Action Learning – alive in the face of all the normalizing pressures in organizations. The other papers by J. M. Harries, myself, Mark Easterby-Smith and John Burgoyne remain unchanged from the earlier edition.

In the Appendices can be found even more practical advice. David Pearce's 'Manual' is as near to P on Action Learning as we want to get (perhaps nearer than some of us want to get). However, here are all sorts of useful tips and hints culled from David's wide experience in the GEC Programme and elsewhere. Nelson Coghill has prepared an extended and updated bibliography of sources on Action Learning which makes up Appendix 2. As the archivist of the Action Learning idea Nelson's knowledge is unparalleled. Finally, Appendix 3 contains the names of some people and organizations known to be active in this field. This appendix is the one most liable to offend (by missing people out who should be in) and most liable to decay. It is included to provide starting points for people who have no convenient local source of information and advice.

Bibliography

Revans, R. W. (1972) *Hospitals: Communications, Choice and Change*, London: Tavistock.

Revans, R. W. (1982), *The Origins and Growth of Action Learning* Bromley, UK: Chartwell-Bratt.

Revans, R. W. (1983) *The ABC of Learning*, Bromley, UK: Chartwell-Bratt.

PART I

WHAT IS ACTION LEARNING?

1 Action Learning: its origins and nature

Reg Revans

In 1971 Action Learning circumnavigated the globe; in the summer of that year I visited New York (to discuss the publication of *Developing Effective Managers*, where it had appeared), Dallas (where Southern Methodist University was initiating a programme), Sydney (to lay the foundations of future programmes), Singapore (where discussions about starting a programme continue), Delhi (now the headquarters of a programme run by the Government of India) and Cairo (to follow up the Nile Project).

In this chapter I try to explain what Action Learning may be, but this is not easy when those who read my lines have not tried Action Learning themselves. There is nothing in this chapter about what teachers of management ought to do about getting started, for that is dealt with by others. My only suggestion to those running the management schools is, over and above what they are already teaching, they should set out to contrive the conditions in which managers may learn, with and from each other, how to manage better in the course of their daily tasks.

Action Learning takes so long to describe, so much longer to find interesting, and so much longer still to get started because it is so simple. As soon as it is presented as a form of *learning by doing* the dismissiveness pours forth. 'Not unlike *learning by doing?* . . . But that's precisely what everybody here has been up to for donkeys' years! Anybody in management education can tell you that lectures and bookwork alone are not sufficient for developing people who have to take decisions in the real world. We all know that practice alone makes perfect, and ever since our first programmes were set up we've made all our students, however senior, do a lot of case studies. Some we fit into practical projects, and others do job rotation in their own firms. What's more, all our staff have been managers themselves, averaging over ten years of business experience, so they can get in on local problems to write up as our own cases. Quite often the initiative for this comes from the firms down on the industrial estate; one man has a quality problem, another is trying to cut his stock levels, and they ask us if we'd like to help both them and our own students. . . . So, what with one thing and another going on here, we don't see what this excitement is about. Action learning? Learning by doing? What's so new? And who wants another book about it?

We may all agree that learning by doing is, in many forms, nothing very new. It is one of the primary forces of evolution, and has accompanied mankind since long before our ancestors came down from the trees. Even the most primitive creatures must have learnt from their own experience, by carrying on with what they found good for them and by refraining from what they found to be harmful. The earliest living things, without any memory worth mentioning, also learnt by doing; if it was fatal to their life style they died, and if it was agreeable they flourished. Their behaviour was self-regulatory and its outcomes either 'Yes' or 'No'. But, as evolution went forward and the brain developed, the results of more and more experiences were remembered and the organisms grew more and more discriminating: outcomes were no longer just black or white, life or death, go or no-go. They took on more subtle differences of interpretation, like 'good' or 'bad'; 'try again' or 'that's enough for now'; 'carry on by yourself' or 'ask someone to help you'. These experiences are enshrined in our proverbs: 'The burned child dreads the fire'; 'Once bitten, twice shy'; and (Proverbs ch. xiv, v. 6) expresses clearly the regenerative nature of learning, knowledge building upon knowledge in a true desire to learn: 'A scorner seeketh wisdom and findeth it not: but knowledge is easy unto him that understandeth'. Once the first point has been grasped the others readily follow: 'Nothing succeeds like success' is, perhaps, a more modern way of saying the same thing. Even the failure to learn has its aphorism: 'There's no fool like an old fool' tells of those to whom experience means little, and who go on making the same mistakes at 70 that might have been excused at 17. With so much common testimony to learning by doing, therefore, what can be said for Action Learning that we find it necessary to keep on about it?

One reason is that it is a social process, whereby those who try it learn with and from each other. The burned child does not need to be told by its mother that it has been hurt, nor that the fire was the agent of pain. Action Learning has a multiplying effect throughout the group or community of learners. But this effect has also long been known: 'Iron sharpeneth iron; so a man sharpeneth the countenance of his friend' (Proverbs ch. xxvii, v. 17) expresses well one aspect of Action Learning today. The best way to start on one's really difficult problems is to go off and help somebody else with theirs. To be sure, the social strength of Action Learning (as I believe it to be) has a subtlety of its own: it is more than mutual growth or instruction, whereby each partner supplies the manifest deficiencies of the others with the knowledge or skill necessary to complete some collective mission. Lending a hand to the common cause may well be part of any Action Learning project – but it remains incidental, rather than central, to it. Nor is Action Learning the essence of the mutual improvement societies so morally essential to the Victorians and still, to some degree, the contract tacitly uniting all communities of scholars. We must applaud the free exchange of what is known between the experts who know it; the sophisticated approach of operational research, in which teams of scientists, engineers and mathematicians work together on the complexities of vast undertakings, such as international airports, new towns, atomic energy plants and so forth, demands that one professional shall learn with and from the other. Nevertheless, what they are doing, for all its intricate teamwork, may be far from Action Learning – and may even be flatly opposed to it. For in true Action Learning, it is not what a man already knows and tells that sharpens the countenance of his friend, but what he does not know and what his friend does not know either. It is recognized ignorance not programmed knowledge, that is the key to Action Learning: men start to learn with and from each other only when they discover that no one knows the answer but all are obliged to find it.

In practice, we find small groups are more effective at learning than simple pairs, provided that every member can describe his need to learn to the others in his set. The explanation of our paradox – that the learning dynamic is the recognition of a common ignorance rather than of some collective superfluity of tradeable knowledge – is both simple and elusive. Action

Learning, as such, requires questions to be posed in conditions of ignorance, risk and confusion, when nobody knows what to do next; it is only marginally interested in finding the answers once those questions have been posed. For identifying the questions to ask is the task of the leader, or of the wise man; finding the answers to them is the business of the expert. It is a grave mistake to confuse these two roles, even if the same individual may, from time to time, occupy them both. But the true leader must always be more interested in what he cannot see in front of him, and this is the mark of the wise man; the expert's job is to make the most of all that is to hand. To search out the meaning of the unseen is the role of Action Learning; to manipulate to advantage all that is discovered is the expression of programmed teaching. Action Learning ensures that, before skills and other resources are brought to bear in conditions of ignorance, risk and confusion, some of the more fertile questions necessary to exploring those conditions have been identified: there is nothing so terrible in all human experience as a bad plan efficiently carried out, when immense technical resources are concentrated in solving the wrong problems. Hell has no senate more formidable than a conspiracy of shortsighted leaders and quickwitted experts. Action Learning suggests that, only if a man, particularly the expert, can be persuaded to draw a map of his own ignorance, is he likely to develop his full potential. In an epoch of change, such as that in which the world now flounders, there is no handicap to exceed the misconception of past experience – particularly that on which present reputations are founded. The idolization of successes established in circumstances unlikely to recur may well guarantee one's place in The Dictionary of National Biography, but it is of little help in the fugitive present; there are times when we do well to put our fame aside:

> At the same time came the disciples unto Jesus, saying, Who is the greatest in the kingdom of heaven? And Jesus called a little child unto him, and set him in the midst of them and said, Verily I say unto you, Except ye be converted and become as little children, ye shall not enter into the kingdom of heaven. Whosoever therefore shall humble himself as this little child, the same is greatest in the kingdom of heaven. (Matthew ch. xviii, v. 1)

In times such as now, it is as imperative to question the inheritance of the past as it is to speculate upon the uncertainties of the future. As indicated in the quotation above Jesus warns of the need to be converted, to become once more as little children, since there is little hope for those who cannot unclutter their memories of flattery and deceit. It is advice most worthy of attention among all peoples with such tremendous histories as the British, although its classical illustration is in the parable of David and Goliath (I Samuel ch. xvii); here the experts, the warriors of Israel, faced with an adversary unknown in their experience (an armoured giant), could do nothing. They could only imagine what they had been taught: a bigger and stronger Israelite was needed to crush Goliath. Since no such man existed they were facing disaster. But the little child, David, proved himself the greatest among them; he was a child who had no experience of armour and could see that the search for the bigger and stronger Israelite was misconceived, so that Goliath had to be dealt with in some other fashion. The way was therefore open for him to pose the key question: 'Given that there is no man to throw at Goliath, how else do we kill him?' It is a fair statement of Action Learning to paraphrase this question as: 'Now all of us can see – even the experts, too – that our ideas simply do not work, what we need is to look for something that is quite new'. No question was ever more important to the denizens of this Sceptred Isle; somebody should launch a campaign to change its patron saint to David from Saint George.

We must not give the impression that it is only traditionalists such as the soldiers who have trouble in changing their conceptions; on the contrary, many of the greatest inventions are the products of conflict, for then we are obliged to think to save our skins. Nor must we imagine that our (supposed) intellectual leaders will necessarily come up with the new ideas; for example, an extrapolation of the current unemployment figures recently made by some professor suggests that 90 per cent of the population will be out of work by the year 2000 – although he does not say how many of these will be professors. What can be done to deflect the course of history, so as to avert this terrible calamity with but one person out of ten in work? The academic seer, exactly like the Israelites, finds the answer in his own past experience: more education. At the very moment in which the country needs as many Davids as possible, to help the rest of us become again as little children and to enter the kingdoms of heaven of our choice, we are to be exposed still more mercilessly to the dialectic of scholars and the sophistry of books.

So far Action Learning has been presented merely as another interpretation of well-known historical events and biblical quotations. It is as old as humanity, illustrated in the Old Testament, justified in the New and implicit in classical philosophy. What, then, is original about it? Only, perhaps, its method. But, before we dismiss this as incidental, let us recall that every branch of achievement advances only as fast as its methods: without telescopes there could be no astronomy, without computers no space missions, without quarries and mines no walls, no houses, no tools and therefore not much else.

This relation of what can be done to the richness of the means of doing it is, of course, another statement of Action Learning itself; its specifically useful method for the 1980s is not only in making clear the need for more Davids, but in setting out to develop them. It may, in essence, be no more than learning by doing, but it is learning by posing fresh questions rather than copying what others have already shown to be useful – perhaps in conditions that are unlikely to recur. Most education, and practically all training, is concerned in passing on the secrets and the theories of yesterday; before anything can be taught, or before anybody can be instructed, a syllabus must be prepared out of what is already known and codifed. But if today is significantly different from yesterday, and tomorrow is likely to be very different from today, how shall we know what to teach? Does not the parable of David and Goliath justify this question? Action Learning is not opposed to teaching the syllabus of yesterday, nor of last year, nor even of antiquity; Action Learning merely asks that, in addition to programmed instruction, the development of our new Davids will include the exploration of their own ignorance and the search for fresh questions leading out of it. Action Learning is a method of building on the academic tradition, not (as some seem to fear) a simplistic challenge to that tradition. As another authority has it:

> Think not that I am come to destroy the law, or the prophets: I am not come to destroy, but to fulfil (Matthew Ch v, v. 17)

The search for innovation began at the nationalization of the British coal industry, when it emerged that much less was known about how to run a pit than the experts would admit to – particularly when they were overwhelmed by the political hurricane that had struck their ancient culture. The colliery managers themselves were soon able to recognise that their new problems were beyond their individual capabilities and, in those early days they had little confidence in the administrative hierarchies established as their new masters. Thus, the suggestion made to the colliery managers' professional organization by its former president, Sir Andrew Bryan, that the managers themselves should work together, despite their self-confessed shortcomings, upon the here-and-now troubles of their own mines, was discussed with a cautious curiosity and accepted with a confident determination.

For three years a representative sample of twenty-two managers, drawn from pits all over England and Wales, worked together to identify and to treat their own problems; they were helped by a small team under the technical leadership of a seconded manager (who returned to run his own pit again) and by a dozen graduate mining trainees. Together with the staffs of the twenty-two pits themselves, the team worked through the symptoms of trouble indicated by the managers themselves, who met regularly at each other's mines to review not only the evidence that had been collected, but also the use made of it to improve the underground performances of the systems to which that evidence referred. Learning by doing took on both a structure and a discipline: identifying the problem by following up the symptoms, obliging those who owned the emergent problem to explain to their colleagues how they imagined it to have arisen, inviting proposals about early action to deal with it, reporting back to those same colleagues the outcome of such proposals for evaluation, and reviewing progress and prospects. The managers met regularly in stable sets of four or five; they were constrained by the nature of their operations and by the discipline of observation not only to examine with their own underground officials what might be going on around them, but also to disclose to their learner-colleagues why they might have held the many misconceptions uncovered by these practical exercises.

One manager agreed to study in depth the system by which he maintained his underground machinery, he encouraged interested parties from other pits to share his results, not so that they may instruct him on how to do a better job but because they want to understand more clearly some troubles of their own. In this way he is launching a community of self-development whose credentials are the ultimate values of the managers themselves. There are many forms, no doubt, of education and training that enable the well-informed to make a point or two for the benefit of others, but invariably it is not clear that the points so made are also for the benefit of the here-and-now conditions in which those others may work. Facts that are incontrovertible in discussion may be ambiguous in application, and those unskilled in application may, simply by instructing others, nevertheless deceive themselves. There can be no place for this in Action Learning: all statements, whether of fact or of belief, whether of observation or of policy, whether about one's problems or about oneself, are all subject to the impartial responses of nature and to the sceptical judgements of relentless colleagues. Only those who have suffered the comradeship in adversity of an Action Learning set, each manager anxious to do something effective about something imperative, can appreciate the clarifying influences of compulsory self-revelation. This alone can help the individual to employ better his existing talents and internal resources, revealing why he says the things he says, does the things he does, and values the things he values. As one of the fellows in an early Belgian programme remarked at its final review: 'An honest man, did you suggest? What is an honest man? And what ought I to do to become one?' It is the participants themselves, each wrestling with his own conditions of ignorance, risk and confusion, who drag such questions from the newly-explored doubts of their macerated souls: they have no need for case leaders nor for programmed instruction (save on such technical details as they themselves can spot), since their growth is symbiotic, with and from each other, out of their own adversities, by their own resources and for their own rewards.

The reference to how Action Learning (as a specific social process) began in the collieries offers the chance of its further description. First, we notice that it was intended, not as an educational instrument, but as an approach to the resolution of management difficulties; the principal motivation to Action Learning was not a desire to teach anybody, nor even the hope that somebody else might learn: it was to do something about the tasks that the colliery managers were under contract to master. The argument was simple: the primary duty of the National Coal Board is to ensure that coal is drawn up the shafts of its pits at a reasonable price and in adequate amount; the training of colliery managers to help the Board fulfil this duty is quite incidental. Action Learning maintains the proper priorities by suggesting that the managers continue with their contractual obligations of drawing coal, which they now do in such fashion that they succeed in doing it better tomorrow by reporting to their colleagues how well they are doing it today. The managerial task itself is both the syllabus and the lesson.

Secondly, the learning of the managers, manifested by the improvement in productivity, consists mainly in their new perceptions of what they are doing and in their changed interpretations of their past experiences; it is not any fresh programme of factual data, of which they were previously ignorant but which they now have at their command, that enables them to surge with supplementary vigour through the managerial jungles. Perhaps for the first time in their professional lives they are able to relate their managerial styles (how to select objectives, evaluate resources and appraise difficulties) to their own values, their own talents and their own infirmities. If, as will at times occur, any particular member of an Action Learning set recognizes that he has need of technical instruction or programmed knowledge, he may make such arrangements as he can to acquire it. But his quest need no longer be seen as cardinal to Action Learning, even if his further success in treating his problems must depend upon the accuracy of his newly-to-be-acquired techniques; Action Learning will soon make clear the value of his latest lessons, and may even encourage him to be more discriminating in any future choice of technical adviser.

Thirdly, we see from this distinction between the reinterpretation of what is already known on the one hand, and on the other, the acquisition of knowledge formerly unfamiliar, another characteristic of Action Learning: it is to attack *problems* (or opportunities) and not *puzzles*, between which there is a deep distinction, yet one frequently overlooked. The puzzle is an embarrassment to which a solution already exists, although it may be hard to find even for the most accomplished of experts. Common examples are the crossword puzzle, the end game at chess, and the A-level examination question demanding a geometrical proof. Many technical troubles of industrial management are largely puzzles, such as how to speed work flow, measure costs, reduce stock levels, simplify delivery systems, optimise maintenance procedures and so forth; industrial engineering and operational research are systematic attacks upon manufacturing puzzles more often than not. The problem, on the other hand, has no existing solution, and even after it has been long and deliberately treated by different persons, all skilled and reasonable, it may still suggest to each of them some different course of subsequent action. This will vary from one to another, in accordance with the differences between their past experiences, their current values and their future hopes.

In the treatment of problems, therefore, as distinct from puzzles, the subjectivities of those who carry out that treatment are cardinal. All who treat the same puzzle should arrive at much the same conclusion, consonant with some observable outcome. But, in the treatment of a problem, none can be declared right or wrong; whether any particular upshot is acceptable or not, and to whom, depends (and must depend) upon the characteristics of the individual to whom that upshot is made known. While it may be a substantial *puzzle* to measure how many unemployed persons there will be in Britain next New Year's Eve, those who set out to do the measurement should be in significant agreement. But the managerial (political, governmental) *problem* as to what, if anything, to do about it will scarcely be an object of agreement. Such proposals for action will be strongly coloured by all manner of personal beliefs and interests, ranging from bank balances to international sentiments, and from the estimate of oneself being out of work to the (possibly subconscious) appreciation of what a power of good this experience would do to those who write so eloquently about its reinvigorating effects.

However, Action Learning makes no claim to develop the skills for solving puzzles: this is the role of programmed instruction in the appropriate profession, trade or technology; the mission of our method is to clarify the problems that face managers, by helping them to identify, through the enticing distortions and deceitful recollections of their own past triumphs and rebuffs, what possible courses of action are open to them. It is when these are then surveyed in detail that the puzzle solving expertise is called for. Our experience of many Action Learning programmes then suggests that this expertise is generally at hand in the very organization tormented by the problem to be resolved; if it is not, then there is almost invariably another organization represented in the Action Learning programme that will be most happy to supply it.

All may learn with and from each other, not just the participants alone but on a larger scale the concept of a *learning community*, that emerged from the Inter-University Programme of Belgium, is perhaps the highest expression of the social implications of Action Learning that we can find. The ease with which such a community may be formed out of the organizations that choose to work together in an Action Learning programme is evidently a measure of the readiness with which they communicate both within and between themselves. It has long been known that high morale and good performance are marked by speedy and effective systems of communication, and it is these which enable their managements to learn. When tasks are carried out in settings that soon make clear the consequences of those tasks, then life becomes not only intelligible, but is in itself a learning process and an avenue to self-respect and confidence.

So far this chapter has concentrated on the advantages of working in the set of manager-colleagues, each of whom is endeavouring to understand and treat some problem allocated to him. It may be (as it was with the participants in the pioneering programme among the mining engineers) a series of troubles arising in his own command, so that, if the manager is to carry on with his own job, he is able to work only part-time on his assignment; on the other hand, the manager (as in the first top level exchange programme in Belgium) may be working full-time in some other enterprise and upon a problem in some functional field remote from his own. There are many different options available to the designer of Action Learning programmes, but all must be characterized by two criteria: the set, in which real managers tackling real problems in real time are able freely to criticise, advise and support their fellows, helped as the participants feel appropriate by external specialists; and the field of action, wherein the real problem exists to be treated by other real persons in the same real time. In other words, Action Learning demands not only self-disclosure of personal perception and objective, but the translation of belief and opinion into practice; all that goes on in the set must have its counterpart in the field of action, and the progress of this counterpart activity is constantly reviewed within the set.

Thus, action learning not only makes explicit to the participant managers their own inner processes of decision, it makes them equally attentive to the means by which those processes effect changes in the world around them. After twenty years observing what the set members have to say to each other about success and failure in the field of action, it is possible to suggest that what might reasonably be called the 'micropolitical' skills needed by managers to judge what is relevant to building into a decision, on the one hand, and to secure what is essential to implementing that decision, on the other, can be significantly developed by Action Learning. In other words, those who participate in successful sets can also learn to penetrate the mists of field diagnosis more clearly and to bring a surer touch to their field achievements.

This is not the place to enter into a detailed discussion of what these micropolitical skills may be, but an understanding of them seems cardinal to any general theory of human action. For the present, it is sufficient to summarize the successful diagnosis in the three questions: 'What are we trying to do? What is stopping us from doing it? What might we be able to do about it?' (and it is interesting to write down what David might have answered to them all); and to perceive effective therapy as a campaign of allies who answer to the specification: 'Who knows about this problem? Who cares about it? Who can do anything about it?' It is the quality of the successful fellow to identify these allies and to recruit them throughout his project into an action team (known in Belgium as the *structure d'accueil*) to serve whoever may own the problem on which the fellow is to exercise and develop his managerial skills.

The literature of project design and negotiation must be consulted by those who wish to take Action Learning beyond the report writing stages that many see as its conclusion, for the complexities of taking action (which demand commitment and anxiety) go far beyond those of suggesting what action might be taken by others (which call only for intelligence and loquacity); all that must be observed now is that exercises that call only for (supposed) analysis of field problems, and are completed without the (supposed) analysis being put in action, are simply not Action Learning as it is defined in this chapter. This, of course, is no reason whatsoever for regarding them unfavourably; as with the case study, in which the participants neither collect the evidence from the field before discussing it nor, after their discussion, do anything to implement their conclusions, much may still be gained – in particular, dialectical skill in knocking the arguments of others to bits. For many of life's occasions such skill may be a most useful asset. It is, all the same, a mistake to imagine that the facts of nature in all her raw relentlessness are quite as readily disposed of as are the arguments of one's more vulnerable opponents in the classroom. It is not enough for managers to know what is good, nor even to convince other managers that they know what is good: they must also be able to do it in the real world. In this life it is generally a mistake to confuse *talking about* action with action itself.

The other contributions to this book will give some indication of the present condition of our subject; the central thesis – that responsible action is our greatest disciplinarian as well as our most sympathetic helper – will appear in every light, in every setting and in every culture. It will do so, not because Action Learning has any claim to greatness nor to originality, but because it is in the very nature of organic evolution. Nevertheless, so numerous are the possible variations upon the themes that run through this book that Action Learning may seem to be all things to all men. Certainly, I for one am often confused by reading of some development that is what I would have called pure Action Learning, but that is described by some other name, such as 'activity learning', or 'action teaching', or 'participative management', or 'management action teamwork', or any of a score of other titles; it is only when I refer to the date of publication of such accounts (usually in the past couple of years) that I can be assured that my writings of the 1950s are not unconscious plagiarism. I am also mystified, from time to time, to read confident reports of successful achievements in the field of management education that are listed as Action Learning, but later perusals still confirm my inability to detect in them what I have set forth in this chapter as characteristic (for me) of Action Learning. But of what importance is my failure? If we give our attention to the main process by which mankind has dragged itself up from the abyss to which some of its representatives seem so anxious to return, we must not be surprised if there is disagreement as to the nature of that process. For all that, however, I cannot put out of my mind two references, whenever the nature of Action Learning is compared with what, during my spell as President of the European Association of Management Training Centres, was for a generation regarded as management education. The first is from Plutarch's *Lives* (Agesilaus p. 726):

> Agesilaus being invited once to hear a man who admirably imitated the nightingale, he declined, saying he had heard the nightingale itself

The origin of the second I can no longer recall, except as a threat by my mother when I was inclined to stray beyond the garden wall; it was that I might be stolen by the gipsies and then so disfigured that even she would be unable to recognize me were I offered back to her on sale. It is astonishing to discover, so late in life, how vividly I remember her words on reading yet one more article on what is new in Action Learning.

2 A biography of Action Learning*

Ronnie Lessem

*Each person must take the risk of creating a life of his own. . . .
When you think about it, you are the thread that holds the events
of your life together*[1]

Introduction

Dedicated athlete, follower of the Bible, scientific analyst.
Action, feeling, thought. Reg Revans has taken the risk, over
seventy-five years, of creating his own life. In the course of
doing so, and in the face of continuous scepticism and hostility –
particularly in his own country – Revans has woven together a
rare fabric. The fabric is made up of the physical, emotional and
intellectual strands that constitute his own self. Bringing this
three-fold self to bear upon the task, Revans has woven together,
in a masterful and evolving synthesis, the basic polarities that
are a feature of our social fabric (see Figure 2.1). In trying to
resolve the conflicts, dualities and paradoxes of his own personality, Revans has attempted to heal the schisms within his society.
In describing the way Action Learning has evolved, I hope to
convey the intricacy, harmony and significance of Revans's synthesizing activity.

*This chapter originally appeared in *The Origins and Growth of Action
Learning*, edited by R. W. Revans, Chartwell-Bratt, 1982.

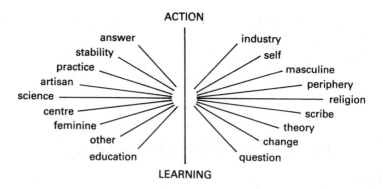

Figure 2.1 The field of polarity

Scribe and artisan: mind and body

In his early years Revans gave parallel attention to the development of body and mind. He became an Olympic long-jumper
and a Cambridge physicist. This particular duality was never to
leave him. After this career as both athlete and physicist, he
joined the Essex education authority, on the outskirts of London,
soon to find himself trying to bridge the gap between body and
mind, first within the health service. In 1938, while looking into
'The entry of girls into the nursing profession' he became pre-
occupied with the divisions between consultants and administrators on high ('scribes') and nurses on the shopfloor ('artisans').
It was this duality between matter (physical achievement) and
spirit (conceptual attainment) that attracted Revans to a training
and development role in the coalmining industry.

Education and industry: ivory tower and colliery shaft

The mind-body split revealed itself, not only in the divisions
between scribe and artisan, but also in the conflict between
education and industry at large. In fact, the remoteness of the
ivory tower from muck and brass has been very apparent in
Great Britain, if not in the world as a whole. The recent call for
the regeneration of British industry, accompanied by the urge to
make education more relevant, is symptomatic of this split.
Times have not changed since Revans was writing about 'A staff

college for the mining industry' in 1945 – or even much earlier, 'The overture to 1945'.

Revans's starting point at the time was the need he perceived, in the wake of increased mechanisation, for people to be trained to understand both the limitations of machines and how best to use and take care of them. He was quick to point out, however, that.

> . . . technical progress is made only by the cutting edge of the weapon of general understanding. If the temper of that body of general knowledge is poor then no amount of sharpening will make it hold an edge.[2]

Here we get a first tangible token of Revans's relentless synthesizing activity. For example, he does not advocate the teaching of English as a language to miners, as something worthwhile in itself. Rather, he claims, that only the man who commands his language can use it to describe what he sees in front of him: his powers of description grow with the knowledge of his own tongue. If by improved command of his words he can send in a more lucid telephone report of some accident or breakdown, he may save valuable time in arranging for it to be dealt with.

Revans, by implication, is bridging the gulf between the 'two cultures', rather than merely setting them up side by side. He is weaving one culture into the other to create a whole that is greater than the sum of the parts. So many attempts at so-called interdisciplinary education or multinational enterprise have failed because there has been no genuine synthesis. Separate 'apartheid' regimes have been manipulated into mutual opposition rather than developed in a mutually reinforcing way:

> It is simplifying the problem too much to say that the education authorities will deal with the theory and industry with the practice. That, in theory, might be an administrative formula, but, in fact, each side of the programme is woven into the other[3]

So, the interweaving of education and industry is accompanied by the integration of theory and practice. Revans had sown the seeds, in the 1940s, of 'The Theory of Practice in Management', which was to appear in the mid–1960s. But something else was going on in his mind and body, still concerned with the connection between the two. For the conflict between education and industry was paralleled by the man-technology duality. Revans argued that the boy who drives heavy nails near the end of a hardwood board and is angry when it splits is the boy who will later hit a conveyor bearing with a hammer after, through neglect, it has been allowed to seize up. Furthermore, ignorance breeds hostility to innovation: men may refuse to adopt new machines simply because they do not know how they work. It is for such reasons that education and industry, training and tools, people and technology, need to be united. The coming together of the ivory tower and the colliery shaft starts with a nut and a bolt. Or does it?

Self and other: miners as teachers

The split between body and mind, head and limb, is one thing; the division between thoughts and feelings, head and heart, is another. In looking into the recruitment and training of young boys as miners, Revans's heart reached out to the new recruits. He emphasized that the persons with whom the boys came in contact should treat them as personal friends. But there were further implications:

> . . . it is evident that, in an industry as human as mining, there are the men to be found who are genuinely interested in the boys, who can remember, sometimes painfully, perhaps, their own introduction to the pits, and who have a little insight into the adolescent mind . . . [4]

The miners themselves, then, should 'carry the educational can', particularly when able to combine the technical know-how with an interpersonal sensitivity. In fact, Revans marked these out as the essential qualities which the manager of any large undertaking should also possess. In so doing, he became a forerunner of the whole 'sociotechnical' school of management which was to blossom in the 1960s. But there was more to follow. . . . For Revans went a step beyond friendship and interpersonal awareness to propose that miners and managers should also learn with and from each other. He suggested that a Staff College be formed, through which people with common problems would be brought together:

> . . . in relating their difficulties or successes to their colleagues, those who come into contact with these questions have much both to learn and to give . . . [5]

For people engaged with similar work tend to encounter similar difficulties, and can often suggest practical solutions to each other. Learning is thus enhanced by the coming together of people in the same boat to work on live problems of common concern.

Centre and periphery: industrial morale and size of unit

In what context then are people able to work on (and to learn from) live problems of mutual concern? This question led Revans to consider the effect of size of unit on morale. For he had noticed, in the collieries, that management that was psychologically or physically remote inclined the miners to see their own employment as an insult to their self-respect. Throughout the 1950s he undertook extensive researches in the pits, in industry and in hospitals, to discover that there was a significant correlation between the size of the work unit, on the one hand, and, on the other, the level of absenteeism, accidents and disputes. He was led to conclude that

> ... it is the big organisation that suffers, for it is in the big organisation that the centre of decision and the periphery of action face the greatest risk of mutual misunderstanding[6]

Revans's major contribution has not been to make out that small is beautiful, although it is revealing to learn that he was writing about it long before Schumacher, his colleague at the Coal Board. What does make Revans unique is the way he has linked together industrial relations (artisan and scribe), human relations (self and others), technological change (education and industry), and the whole question of scale (centre and periphery) with information processing, problem solving and learning.

In the early 1960s, when Revans was achieving this synthesis, management education was already in full swing, both in Europe and America. While Business Schools were offering separate programmes in production, financial and personnel management, attempts were also being made to integrate these functions under one overall umbrella. A central or core programme (usually the so-called 'business policy') was supposed to help the student hang the separate business functions together. The predominant educational form was the case study, with the university courses tending to be peripheral to industry and commerce themselves. Business policy was taught in an impersonal way, remote from the actual student of management, so that no attempt could be made to bring together learner and learning. This also prevailed in the so called 'management sciences', where only what was quantifiable was also permissible.

Revans, meanwhile, placed at the centre of things the 'springs of human action'. It is one's perception of the problem, he said, one's evaluation of what is to be gained by solving it, and one's estimate of the resources at hand to solve it, that supply these action springs. Since these judgements, moreover, are largely based on one's relations to others, and since current rates of technological change the problems to be solved one day to the next, it follows that

> . . . everybody in the organisation, from those who frame the policies to those who manipulate the ultimate details of technique, *must be endowed to the greatest possible extent with the means of learning* . . . [7] [The stressing in this quotation, as in all the others in my paper, is my own: R. L.]

Such learning must demand not only information about the latest shift of policy; it must also demand the power to get the knowledge needed to see one's part in what is going on, and, in particular, to know the effect of one's behaviour upon those with whom one works. So problem solving, human relations, information, learning, change and proximity all come together under the springs of human action.

Science and religion: thought and action

A lot of modern management theory considers human action in terms of either tasks or relationships. Back in the 1940s Revans was talking about technical knowledge and interpersonal sensitivity as the two prime managerial attributes. However, by 1957, he maintained that any division between industrial 'processes' and 'people' was an illusion. In his 'Analysis of Industrial Behaviour' he showed that human relations in the factory were strongly influenced by the extent to which men perceived themselves to be economically and effectively organized. Or, to put it another way, whereas the overcontrolled factory impairs freedom of thought and local decision, that which is too often haphazard fritters away men's valuable time. . . . .the one thing that can never be recalled. So, in essence, tasks and relationships are inextricably interwined, as are personal consciousness and management technique, religious faith and organizational science.

In the mid–1960s Revans published his first book *Science and the Manager*. He had carried his scientific past along with him and had never let it go. He particularly ensured that it was never cut off from the 'feeling life' nor from personal consciousness. The following illustrates the point:

> There are four forces bearing upon management today that encourage a new approach to its primary task of making decisions. The first is the need for *economy of managerial time and effort* . . . the

age of science is one of economy, of prudent thought, precise design, exact calculation . . . The second . . . is the entry into management of the *analytical approach*, familiar for over three centuries to the scientist: while intuition, or the unremembered urges of the past, must always be the first weapon of the manager, he must also be able to grasp the underlying structures of the situations that challenge him. Thirdly, the *study of variability* through the language of statistics has brought to the manager a language to describe the unexpected, the capricious and the random elements of these tasks. Fourthly, the *social sciences* have thrown a little light on the human forces that, in the final analysis, determine whether or not any enterprise will succeed.[8]

Revans's language flows in and out of the subject and object like a stream of dual consciousness. At the same time, moreover, as he was writing about *Science and the Manager*, he was also dealing with *The Bible as Appointed to be read by Industry*.

The idea that there can be no comfort in external solutions to one's own intimate problems of security, Revans claims, comes from the earliest annals of our race. Taking this belief a step further, he maintains that the 'Kingdom of God' is to be found within a nation's own shores and within the wills of its own people. In other words, on the one hand, the salvation of Britain is not to be found by observers scanning the world in the hope of turning up some miracle; and, on the other hand, the educational task of the West, in relation to the developing nations, is not to instruct them in the records of its own achievements. It is rather to help them, the developing nations, to tackle their own problems as they perceive them, to strive after the goals they have set for themselves, and to offer such help as is appropriate to the points that they have reached and to the ends for which they seek. Thus a lesson drawn from the Bible has alike personal, national and international implications.

The Theory of Practice in Management, published in 1966, is a true synthesis of thought and action. In this book, Revans explains that the scientific method is merely a model built out of thought, just as thoughts themselves are models built from consciousness. In his next book, *Developing Effective Managers*, which came out in 1971, Revans turned this general statement into a specific method of achieving managerial objectives. The model, which he calls System Beta, involves five distinct steps:

- survey, a stage of observation
- hypothesis, a stage of theory, of conjecture
- experiment, in which practical tests are carried out
- audit, during which actual and desired results are compared

- review, relating the particular result to the whole context.

These stages in fact constitute a learning cycle popularized by David Kolb from M.I.T., and published two years after Revans's visit there with a consortium of twenty managers, described in *Developing Effective Managers*.

Contrasted against System Beta is System Gamma, based on the individual manager's subjective consciousness, or 'predisposing mental set' as this bears upon a particular problem in a particular setting. In between the subjective and the objective is System Alpha, which moves from personal values to external circumstances and internal resources:

- by what values am I guided?
- what is blocking their fulfilment?
- what can I do against such blockage?

Whereas System Alpha is concerned with the manager's use of information in designing objectives (strategies), System Beta is oriented to achieving them (negotiation), and System Gamma monitors the outcomes for adapting to experience and change (learning).[9] While all three circumscribe the processes of management, another six elements constitute what Revans calls the 'media of management analysis'. These serve to highlight once again the interactions between thought and action, intellect and faith, scientific method and personal conviction.

> A real *decision*, firstly, is always that of a particular person, with his own ends not to be neglected, his own fears to amplify his problems, his own hopes a mirage to magnify his own resources, and with his own prejudices, often called experience, to colour the data with which he works. A choice of *goals*, secondly, so much bound up with decision theory, is yet distinct from it, in that the ends for which one strives, deliberately or unconsciously, as an individual or with others, are but partly determined by the calculations of economic strategy: behind them jostle the egocentric drives of the individual as the person he is. Thirdly, the relevance of *information*, that product of which the raw material is data and the creative process the personal sensitivities of the manager himself. Fourthly, the theory of *systems* describes the web in which the world-line of that particular manager is entangled. The assessment of *probability* is, fifthly, that farrago of mathematical statistics and simple guesswork, by which we attempt to assess our forgotten experiences, our present wishfulness, and our future hopes. And, sixthly, the *learning process*. . . . .integrating everything that one has so far become, and one's sole hope for future improvement.[10]

Action and learning: changing system and self

Back in the 1950s Revans had stated that the study of industrial behaviour was still awaiting its Faraday or its Chadwick. He confessed the metaphor might oversimplify the problem because, whereas Chadwick called up one single entity and Faraday no more than three, industrial behaviour must take into account scores of independent factors. But this, in itself, he said, should not prevent the discovery of simple laws. Whether or not Revans has discovered even one such, he has certainly evolved a method that is, in one sense, inordinately simple and, in another, extraordinarily complex. But first let me retrace steps, before elaborating further.

In the 1940s, Revans had worked on the dualities between artisan and scribe, education and industry, self and other, with particular reference to the coalmining industry. In the 1950s he was principally concerned with questions of scale and their implications for communications and learning, in both the mines and the hospital service. The 1960s saw him establish management education programmes, most particularly in Belgium, while evolving both a management science and a managerial consciousness. In the 1970s the action learning concept was hardened out and applied, for the first time with discipline and design, in British industry.

Action learning, at its simplest, is an approach to management education. At its most profound it is a form of personal therapy, a means of social and economic transformation, and even a way of life. Let me try to reconstruct Revans's argument, step by step.

We start with the symbolic amalgamation of 'artisan' and 'scribe'. Knowledge, for Revans, can be only the outcome of action. By wrestling (as artisan) with live problems, and subsequently reflecting (as scribe) upon the results of his achievements, the learner acquires knowledge. Revans continues with the symbolic intermingling of 'education' and 'industry'. For the knowledge acquired is not so much the facts or techniques imparted by an educator, but, more appropriately, the reinterpretation of the practitioner's own existing knowledge. This reinterpretation is best achieved through the meeting of 'self' and 'other', that is of 'comrades in adversity'. It is not a question of the blind leading the blind, but that . . . the blindfold shall help the blindfold to strip away the veils and bandages of custom and practice.[11] Action Learning employs the social process by which a 'set' of four or five learners, by the apparent incongruity of their exchanges, frequently cause each other to examine afresh both 'project' design and its implementation.

Action Learning is also a personal activity which combines objective analysis ('science') and subjective commitment ('religion'). Its logical foundation is the structural identity of the scientific method, of rational decision making, of the exchange of sound advice and fair criticism, and of the learning of new behaviour.[12] Yet, while talking and argument call only for intelligence or quickness of wit, doing and action call for commitment or true belief. For, in taking action, Revans claims, especially after one has clearly exposed one's motives to close and critical colleagues, one is obliged to explore that inner self otherwise so often taken for granted. In seeking answers to difficult work-related questions, especially in conditions of risk and confusion, miners, nurses and managers begin to learn who they themselves may be: to answer their 'work-questions' they must, at the same time, explore their 'self-questions'. The fundamental law of industrial behaviour, that Revans was seeking in the 1950s, may well have been discovered by him in the 1970s: '. . . knowledge is the consequence of action, and to know is the same as to do,'[13] or, to elaborate: '. . . the underlying structures of successful achievement, of learning, of intelligent counselling, and of what we call the scientific method, are logically identical'.[14]

Stability and change: today and tomorrow

Revans has developed another law, which can be associated with that already cited. Learning, he says, for the individual or for society at large, must be greater than the rate of change. To put it another way, you cannot change the 'system' unless you also change your 'self'. In other words, external impact and internal development go hand in hand. He has called this 'the principle of insufficient mandate'.[15]

In an article on 'Management, Productivity and Risk', published in 1981, Revans has described the relationship between learning and change, at individual and societal levels. When the world does not change, the son may follow in his father's footsteps, by repeating what is already in the books. But, on the precipice of change, taking the climber into a new world at every rising of the sun, the primary need for learning is no longer programmed knowledge, but an ability to pose the questions proper to the microcosm of uncertainty now to be entered:

Our ability to adapt to change with such readiness that we are
seen to change may be defined as learning.[16]

Those able to do tomorrow what there is no need to do today
will have learned, just as have those who can do today what was
unknown yesterday.

The signs of our times: masculine and feminine

In epochs of convulsion, Revans maintains, such as the present,
there is nothing more necessary than that we should understand
the conditions of our own learning:

> . . . *programmed knowledge* can be acquired through the published
> syllabus of the teaching institution, while *questioning insight* comes
> only from a recognition within oneself that one's perception of
> what is going on in the here-and-now falls short of one's responsi-
> bility for doing something about it. Programmed knowledge is the
> product of technical instruction; questioning insight is to be sought
> through Action Learning. If we call the first 'P' and the second
> 'Q', we might write the general learning equation: L is f(P, Q).[17]

Learning, and the fundamental law that Revans has developed
out of it, involves a programmed push and a questioning pull.
Erich Jantsch, in his revealing work on *Design and Evolution*,
has identified 'planning' and 'love' as the two essential complementary aspects of 'human design':

> Where planning, the MASCULINE element, aims at stabilisation
> which in turn makes it possible to act out power or focussed energy,
> love, the FEMININE element, introduces the instabilities which
> elevate the plane of human action to ever new dynamic regimes,
> thereby ensuring the continuously renewed conditions for human
> creativity, for the life of human systems[18]

It is, surely, no accident that Revans has done most of his work
with nurses and in the National Health Service, on the one hand,
and with managers in industry, on the other. Anima and animus:
together constituting the whole person or society. In searching
relentlessly for the *Gestalt*, Revans has brought together masculine and feminine, and this, perhaps, becomes most apparent in
his work on human and industrial relations.

In the early 1970s Revans, having first run the international
project for The Organization for Economic Cooperation and
Development (OECD) on *The Emerging Attitudes and Motivations of Workers*,[19] then edited its proceedings. Already at that
stage he chose to comment on one Japanese example of work

relations. He referred particularly to its establishment of small work groups, not only with a high degree of autonomy, but organized in such a way as to endow their members with a continuous opportunity to learn and to develop. The groups were constituted, in other words, not only for effective PRO-DUCTION, but also for continuous LEARNING. Production and learning, which can be associated with animus and anima, can also be related to Alan Watts's description of masculine and feminine traits:

> ... all philosophical dispute can be reduced to an argument between those who are tough-minded, rigorous and precise and like to stress differences and divisions between things (PRO-DUCTIVITY), and those tender-minded romanticists who like wide generalisations and round syntheses, and stress the underlying unities (LEARNING).[20] [Bracketed insertions by R. L.]

In a subsequent article, *'Worker Participation as Action Learning'*, Revans refers to the great changes that top managers will need to face in the 1970s:

> The qualities to be called for. . . . .will be temperamental and emotive rather than intellectual and cognitive; they must be involving rather than detached, questioning the self no less than quantifying the situation.[21]

He goes on to proclaim, on the one hand, that autonomy is the central theme in participation and, on the other, that the vitality of participation is its local relevance. In other words, the individual must be able to relate his autonomous part to the accessible and integral whole. Thus, participation is linked not only with the impact of scale, but also with the immediacy of task:

> The talisman that will release the enthusiasm of those who do the work is the specific difficulty of that work in the here-and-now.[22]

That work must be neither too difficult and challenging, nor too easy and unchallenging. Risk and innovation need to be balanced by support and accommodation. We need both to confront and to accommodate change; to hunt for solutions and to bring home the answers to share.

The desirability of harmonizing technological and innovative assertiveness (masculine) with a social and nurturing receptivity (feminine) was stressed by Revans already in the early 1960s. In his research paper, 'Industry and Technical Education', he lamented the shallowness of the roots of technical education in the British soil. On the one hand, he contrasted the twentieth century with those earlier times, when the master craftsman

'. . . was enjoined by his guild to treat the apprentices as members of his own family . . .'[23] and, on the other, he asks why technical education should have been so neglected in an industrial nation like Britain? Whereas success itself has detracted from introspection, more importantly:

> We have overlooked the price, in social disintegration, of that final triumph of Eighteenth Century rationalism, the Division of Labour.[24]

The social and economic disintegration already apparent when those lines were written has become much more apparent now.

Action Learning has, indeed, come into its time. As educational method, form of personal therapy, and vehicle for social transformation, its time is ripe. For as our society stands on the watershed between breakdown and breakthrough, so action learning has evolved to accommodate both. Revans, in synthesizing his own thoughts, feelings and actions has brought a holistic approach to bear upon our society's physical, social and economic problems. Action Learning, in addressing itself to artisan and scribe, education and industry, I and thou, centre and periphery, science and religion, stability and change, and to male and female consciousness, serves both a multitude and a singleness of purpose.

Two things, finally, stick out in my mind when recalling my own conversations with Revans. The first was his saying that Action Learning and Buddhism were one and the same thing. The second was his thanking me for sparing half an hour of my time to listen to him. The philosophy is the man. . . .

References

1 Viscott, D. (1977), *Risking*, p. 131, Pocket Books.
2 Revans R. W. (1945) *Plans for Recruitment, Education and Training for the Coalmining Industry*, Mining Association of Great Britain, October p. 5.
3 Revans, R. W. op. cit., p. 8.
4 Revans, R. W. op. cit., p. 5.
5 Revans, R. W. op. cit., pp. 111, 112.
6 Revans, R. W. (1964), 'Bigness and Change' New Society, 2 January.
7 Revans, R. W. op cit.
8 Revans, R. W. (1965), *Science and the Manager*, Macdonald pp. 55, 56.
9 Revans, R. W. (1969), 'The Managerial Alphabet' in 'Approaches to the Study of Organisational Behaviour' Tavistock Publications.

10 Revans, R. W. 'A Vocabulary of Managerial Debate', unpublished memorandum used in The Inter-University Programme of Belgium.
11 Revans, R. W. (1981), 'The Psychology of the Deliberated Random,' unpublished paper, p. 1.
12 Revans, R. W. (1971), *Action, Creativity and Learning*, Prakseologia, Polish Academy of Sciences.
13 Revans, R. W. See 11 above.
14 Revans, R. W. (1981), 'The Nature of Action Learning' Omega, International Journal of Management Science, **9** (1) p. 22.
15 Revans, R. W. op cit. p. 16.
16 Revans, R. W. (1981), 'Management, Productivity and Risk', Omega, International Journal of Management Science, **9** (2) p. 136.
17 Revans, R. W. op. cit., p. 137.
18 Jantsch, E. (1975), *Design and Evolution*, Brazillier.
19 Revans, R. W. (1972), *The Emerging Attitudes and Motivations of Workers*, Directorate of Manpower and Social Affairs: OECD, Paris.
20 Watts, A. (1972), *Book on the Taboo Against Knowing Who You Are*, Random.
21 Revans, R. W. (1971), 'Seminars for Top Management', unpublished memorandum Fondation Industrie-Université, Brussels.
22 Revans, R. W. (1975), 'Worker Participation as Action Learning, Part III'; unpublished paper.
23 Revans, R. W. (1962), *Industry and Technical Education*, University of Leeds, Institute of Education October p. 1.
24 Revans, R. W. op. cit., p. 2.

3 Management development as moral art

Mike Pedler

Introduction

In this chapter I focus upon the moral philosophy of Action Learning and trace some of the implications for the practice of management development. Management development by Action Learning is put forward as a moral art: moral because managerial action influences both the world in which it takes place and the responsible actor; and art because managing goes beyond exercising individual skills and competences to creative collaboration in organizing. Significant learning, which changes both the person and the world, is always concerned with moral values. Following Snell, 'moral' is taken to refer to any position adopted with regard to 'right' or 'wrong' purposes, actions, ways of living and so on.[1]

The first section of the chapter addresses the relationship of management and morality. As a result of recent events, including those affecting the environment, the behaviour of some financiers and trading relationships between rich and poor countries, there is a rising interest in this issue. 'Right' managerial action seems to involve a wider accountability than that of the narrow 'bottom line', but how may this happen? Assuming that they wish to, how can managers (and other responsible people) learn to exercise better moral judgement, set themselves higher standards and set others a better example?

The middle section examines the workings of Action Learning particularly with regard to the interaction of person and problem. It is argued that Action Learning, with its emphasis upon manager development taking place within the context of managerial action (and vice versa), provides the appropriate conditions for developing the capacity for making moral judgements.

The final section of the chapter extends the argument beyond the individual to the organization. Does the extent to which individual managers can make moral choices depend upon the 'ethical climate' of the organization? Does 'ethical' management development lead to ethically sound organizations?

Managing and morality

In our increasingly interconnected world the costs of bad managing become ever more serious. From the polluting and alienating businesses of the northern hemisphere to the poverty and famine of the south there is a need to bring new ideas to this crucial social role.

In the north the burgeoning business of management development has plenty of advice, elixirs and 'new' ideas on offer. Such recent wisdom as 'a bias for action', 'staying close to the customer' and 'sticking to the knitting' has been much appreciated.[2] For the manager, seeking succour in a world described as 'hyper-competitive' and 'turbulent', characterized by 'uncertainty', beset by 'megatrends' and so on, there is much temptation to purchase. This persuasive packaging of the often already well known is part of a current cultural ethos.

That Action Learning should have grown to maturity in such times is somewhat ironic. In so many ways the Action Learning idea stands against consumerist values. Where we are exhorted to buy the latest package, Action Learning sharply questions its validity, suggesting instead, in David Casey's words, that each manager needs to re-invent the wheel of their own managerial practice. In Action Learning there is less trust in short cuts and quick fixes, more emphasis on the courageous struggle to act and understand. Yet 'Action Learning sets', 'management action groups' or 'learning sets' are now almost an essential part of any well-designed management development programme. While it can often be asked, 'Is this really Action Learning?', the small, self-managed group which meets members' needs for peer support and advice as well as having the 'bias to action' is proving increasingly popular.

Becoming a better manager in the energetic West often seem to start and finish with achieving action. Revans warns against the compulsive drive to act exhibited by many managers with his customary vivid imagery:

> Most managers, tormented by the ticking of the office clock and the fall of the days from the factory calendar, will respond sooner to the urgencies of the moment, however inconsequential, than to the suggestion that they ought to clear the decks and heed the long-term warnings; this is Gresham's law of management: 'Short-term issues drive out the long'. Thus one observes the managerial chefs singing as they peel the managerial spuds or roll up their sleeves to scour out the administrative pans.[3]

In managing, weighing long-term consequences against short-term advantage can create moral dilemmas. MacLagan provides some evidence of increasing interest in moral and ethical issues in business management.[4] Three strands are identified. First are the moves towards the 'professionalization' of management called for by recent reports in the UK, including the need for better management education. While there are doubts as to whether management can be a profession, given the diversity of roles and tasks undertaken, the debate about professionalism and accountability means that greater consideration is being given to questions of ethics. Ethical conduct is a concern for all professions and guidelines are usually enshrined in codes, policed by committees and so on. These alone, of course, do not guarantee high standards of behaviour, and indeed, codes of ethical practice by apparently tackling the issue may even take genuine ethical questions off the agenda.

The recent enthusiasm for management competences in some quarters, and the formation in the UK of the Management Charter Initiative to enhance national managerial competence, also poses ethical questions. Boyatsis, for example, is vague on the link between competence and ethical conduct but allows that competences 'could be associated with higher stages of moral and cognitive reasoning'.[5] Burgoyne has accused the current competences debate of overemphasizing the technical and understating the ethical issues involved.[6] MacLagan maintains that competence, individual maturity and moral development go together and that 'maturational processes hold the key to moral development'.[7]

A third strand is represented by the movement towards greater discussion of business ethics in many parts of the world including the USA, Europe, Japan and UK. The idea that managers have no choice but to behave in accordance with loyalty to the 'bottom line', or the maximization of profit, is being challenged. While historical challenges have come from trade unionists or public health authorities, currently they come from environmentalists. 'Bottom line-ism' is revealed as an ideology, rather than as a statement of the obvious, as many apparently ingenuous souls would hitherto have had us believe.

Learning to be better managers

If ethical and moral development in individuals and organizations is of increasing concern, then the next question is – how may this take place? MacLagan quotes Kohlberg on the three stages of moral development whereby people may pass from the *pre-conventional* where 'right' action is determined by rewards/-punishments by authorities, through the *conventional* (conforming to social norms/being 'well behaved') to the *post-conventional* or *autonomous* stage where the individual attempts independent, reasoned judgement. Pedler and Boydell have adapted and extended these ideas for managers.[8] Moving towards autonomy with the associated higher levels of moral development is necessary not just for doing good business in the commercial sense but also in the wider arenas of citizenship. Bettelheim, for example, links the achievement of autonomy in individuals with avoiding the re-emergence of Fascism and authoritarianism.[9]

Movement between stages is not, however, automatic and many researchers suggest that some 'crisis' or 'perturbation' is necessary to cause us to question our current mode of operation and trigger a learning process. Although this idea is more usually applied to individual learning, it is also central to thinking about organizational learning. Argyris & Schon make it clear that for organizations to engage in 'double loop learning' the current operating norms and assumptions must be challenged and transformed.[10] This notion is central to Revans's idea of Action Learning: '. . . there can be no learning without action, and no (sober and deliberate) action without learning'.[11] This statement makes it clear that we are not to escape from the responsibility for our acts, and that it is from these acts that we learn. While the simple imperative to act may well lead to leisurely repentance, defining what constitutes 'action' in managerial settings is problematic. For managers, action can often take the form of words.

If words constitute action then why not thoughts? As Braddick and Casey note, what managers often need to do is to 're-frame', to re-order their thoughts.[12] Right thinking is an inseparable part of right action.

Learning, as something that changes us and our relationships with others and the world, is part of what shapes our actions – past, present and future. If what we learn over the years is part of what forms us and goes to make us what we are, then it follows that management development is concerned both with right managerial action and with the continuing development of the manager as person. Both these aspects, the outer action in the world and the inner becoming of the person, are matters which are finally judged against moral and ethical criteria. In Revans' writings, issues of value – of right and wrong – are always at the heart:

> The criterion by which such behaviour should be judged is not intellectual ability but personal values. The opposition to novelty is not due to pure obtuseness, to an incapacity in following the cycle of the scientific method as it unrolls the truth. It is that the truth contradicts existing values, if these are known; or that it demands facing unpleasant risks if one is to work out the consequences of embracing some different notion. Thus it was that the single idea discovered by the top managers in the First Inter-University Programme of Belgium to be of the greatest interest to them was that of a *value system*. What were the standards of integrity against which all final judgements were made by those with whom they worked – including themselves? It was a notion bound to arise out of the set discussions in which the fellows stripped each other naked, an experience that led them to define the most valuable question they had learned as: 'What is an honest man, and what need I do to become one?'[13]

Here is an acid test: you can tell whether this is Action Learning or not by whether people are exercising moral imagination, by how often they question their own and each other's actions and by how much they strive towards integrity for themselves and their colleagues.

This leads us to the process or method of Action Learning; the formulation of 'outer' (actions) and 'inner' (learnings) is one in which questions of value interact with the practical matters of managing. If there are many pale imitations of Action Learning to be had, it is because this is a rocky road beset with difficulties – out there and in here.

Fat Alice

> Alice was the very fat mother of a fat family. She was grossly
> overweight. Her doctor had advised her to diet on many occasions.
> He had tried everything he could think of. Finally Alice submitted
> to the most drastic treatment – she had her jaws wired together
> and could only take liquids. A month later and she had not lost a
> pound. On being cross-examined Alice admitted that she had
> learned to melt chocolate and suck it through a straw.

Action Learning has much in common with Weightwatchers and
other DIY support systems. It shares the basic assumptions that
we can act to change ourselves, and that our will to change
is immeasurably strengthened by the encouraging presence of
'comrades in adversity'. Moreover, Action Learning makes no
distinction between therapy and development. The cessation of
suffering and the path to living a more fulfilling personal and
social life are one and the same. The sad tale of Fat Alice
illustrates dramatically that intervention from outside will not
change anything unless the person inside wants it. And more
shocking still, even when we want it, what a capacity we have
for sabotaging ourselves. Alice isn't so unusual. Much of her
energy was going into subverting the oppressive expertise of the
doctor rather than dealing with herself. For 'doctor', read any
authority. There are plenty of us in organizations who will sabotage 'better' ways of managing:

> . . . but there are those who *soberly and deliberately refuse to
> learn*, because the new knowledge, whilst consonant with the scien-
> tific method, is inconvenient for other reasons. . . . New ideas
> suggesting new behaviours may be soberly and deliberately sup-
> pressed because they contradict established values and accepted
> traditions.[14]

Managing the visible and the invisible

Management development has commonly concerned itself with
outer knowledge, of marketing and production, of planning and
organizing, of motivating and so on. The inner processes of the
manager – thinking, feeling and willing – are not visible, and
can only be inferred. Yet moral choices about right actions are
made within. In seeking to make good decisions these invisible
aspects of us are most important:

> We can all see another person's body directly. We see the lips
> moving, the eyes opening and shutting, the lines of the mouth and

the face changing, and the body as a whole expressing itself in action. The person himself is invisible. . . . All our thoughts, emotions, feelings, imaginations, reveries, dreams, fantasies are invisible. All that belongs to our scheming, planning, secrets, ambitions, all our hopes, fears, doubts, perplexities, all our affections, speculations, ponderings, vacuities, uncertainties, all our desires, longings, appetites, sensations, our likes, dislikes, aversions, attractions, loves and hates – are themselves invisible. They constitute 'oneself'.[15]

Our recent traditions of empiricism and positivism have encouraged us in the belief that 'knowledge' is defined by what can be perceived via our physical sense organs and the 'five senses'. As this view developed and powered advances in the natural and then the social 'sciences' we have learned to direct our attention to observing and discriminating outwardly in the physical world. We have defined 'knowing' as that relationship between an object identified and an external observer. We have come to know the world, as it were, from the outside; as if we ourselves were not part of it. If we are not part of it then we are not responsible, except perhaps for keeping a proper distance. Out of this tradition, managing is something done to others. In popular terms we have defined a manager as someone who is responsible for the work of others and who achieves results through others.

The soul goes out and returns . . .

But, as Henry Mintzberg pointed out in 1973, echoing a line of researchers who looked closely at managerial work, this does not even tell us what managers actually do. When we look at what they do, the skills and abilities they require and their need to develop new capabilities, we are turned inexorably inwards. We find that managerial work is inseparable from the person who does it. Matters of personality, style, experience and preferences come to the fore. To illustrate the interaction of the invisible inner processes and the visible outer actions, consider the case of Gordon, a 34-year-old quarry manager, member of an Action Learning set, whose problem was to increase profitability and reduce waste:

JOHN:
If these piles of waste have been here longer than you, why hasn't anything been done about them before?
GORDON:
Well, it's obvious that when you quarry you get waste . . . depending on the product, you can get up to 90 per cent . . . I started in

this quarry 12 years ago as a graduate trainee and in that time I should think I've worked every job here – boy and man you might say! (*laughs*)

FIONA:

How big are those piles?

GORDON:

Very big! (*laughs again*)

FIONA:

I mean, how many tons? How much is added each day . . . each week?

GORDON:

Blimey. I've no idea. How should I know . . . they were here before my time remember.

FIONA:

But they're getting bigger every day . . .

GORDON:

Of course they are!

DAVE:

Don't you think that the manager of a quarry ought to know how much waste is being created each week!?

Here is a good example of that everyday occurrence which Revans has called 'the idolization of past experience,'[16] where what we already know blocks us from new knowledge. Here the acquisition of managerial skill requires an inner transformation before a changed outer performance is possible.

To learn something new, Gordon has to accept that the mountains of waste are worth his attention. To do this he has to overcome a lot within him. Those piles of waste have been there for ever. They are outside his office window, outside of him, yet they are mirrored by something inside him that accommodates them. He has an inner block to match the tipping zone of the quarry.

Is he really blind or is he turning a blind eye? For Gordon to be able to act he first has to come clean with himself. This coming clean involves a willingness to explore oneself, one's motives, the unforeseen consequences of one's actions and inactions. It also involves being able to bear the truths of others. The revelation of blind spots come as a shock, but the concealments, deliberate evasions and especially the old lies about ourselves are perhaps the hardest to open up. As Roger Harrison (1962) has said, to a large extent we *are* our defences – we've lived with them for years, they are part of us, and they enable us to be comfortable with ourselves.[17] We are not always happy about these barriers; and this is suffering we all carry. Where it can be released, this is only done with courage, help from trusted friends and some tears; but it is usually easier to walk by on the other side, turn a blind eye or engage in a bit of sabotage.

Action Learning stresses the interaction of inner and outer as a primary motif. This accords with what Snell calls 'holistic ethical education' in which people 'examine managerial decision making as they engage in it daily in the conduct of their lives' and which he recommends as the best way forward for management education.[18] In Action Learning, development of problem and person proceeds via a continuous passing from outer actions to inner processes to outer actions and back. This is a modern managerial application of old wisdom. Writing in 1916 on the necessary unity of Eastern and Western approaches to knowledge, Edward Carpenter put it rather well:

> The Indian methods and attitude cause an ingathering and quiescence of the mind, accompanied often by great illumination; but if carried to excess, they result in over-quiescence, and even torpor. The Western habits tend towards an over-activity and external distraction of mind, which may result in disintegration. The true line is not in mediocrity, but in a bold and sane acceptance of both sides, so as to make them offset and balance each other, and indeed so that each shall make the extension of the other more and more possible. Growth is the method and the solution. The soul goes out and returns, goes out and returns; and this is its daily, almost hourly, action. . . . [19]

The epistemology of Action Learning holds that person and problem are defined and redefined in continuous interaction. Neither inner self nor outer world is sovereign; they are, in a sense, co-creations. One of Revans's key teachings is that no problem can exist independently of some human being who knows, cares or can do something about it. The designation 'problem', part of which is out there, part in here, signifies my ability to do one or more of these three things. Equally it is our ability to engage with problems which shapes us and ultimately confers on us our personhood. From the Action Learning perspective the end is not the solution of this or that problem (only puzzles get solved in any case) nor the specific learning of the actor. These are usually hoped for and desirable consequences of Action Learning, but they are not what is ultimately signified. Our reward for transforming a problem and ourselves is that we are thus enabled to go on to our next step.

If Gordon agrees to pit himself against the piles of limestone, in order to help him we have to work with both the limestone and with Gordon. Outside – How much is being wasted? Why is it wasted? What happens to the non-waste? and so on; and inside – How is it that you've done nothing before? What do you want to do now? Who else can help to move these piles?

Progress on the problem can only come if the search passes from inside to outside and back again. Gordon must feel committed to his problem. He must feel able to do something about it. He must feel he is amongst friends. The problem cannot be transformed, however many operations management textbooks are supplied, unless Gordon questions himself and gains new insight. Learning = some P and some Q.

As the search passes to and fro, the thread thus spun creates, out of the former duality of Gordon and the limestone, a new entity which contains the part of Gordon which is to do with the limestone and the part of the limestone which is to do with Gordon. Thus, when we manage to connect, we extend our mind.

At last – some proper action

Passing backwards and forwards, Gordon begins to see things differently. He sees that what goes on inside him – his thoughts, fears, likes, dislikes, prejudices and so on – are intimately connected with the piles of limestone outside the window. Having made this connection the observable action looks simple: in this case he agrees to come back with some figures. Before the meeting breaks he is asked for his estimates. Two weeks later, to his shame and surprise, the weekly additions to waste turn out to be three times his own rough estimates. This new knowledge increases his connection with the 'problem'; he can no longer proceed on the old assumption.

Subsequently Gordon begins to work on ways of reducing the waste. This is mainly done by seeking new products and new markets. He forms a 'think tank' with the marketing manager and a few others to see what can be done. Over a few months various ideas are put into practice, which indeed result in decreased waste and increased profits. Gordon learns that 'we can improve anything we choose to look at'.

This happy tale has everyone winning: profits are up, waste is down, Gordon is accepting his responsibilities. Many of the moral dilemmas faced by managers are not so conveniently resolved. Where managers may increase safety at increased cost, or decrease environmental damage with a lower quality product, there is no such happy coincidence. Yet we can try to be as good as we can afford to be. Whether we will or not depends a lot on whether we are encouraged or expected to by the wider 'ethical climate'.

Good company

A consultant friend came away from a retail company in an angry mood. He had carried out an operational audit and proved, to his and the unit manager's satisfaction, that with a little expenditure and effort a 40 per cent increase in profit could be achieved. At first the manager was excited by the prospect but later cooled on the project. Soundings among his colleagues and his regional manager had discouraged him from attempting such a large increase in performance. 'For a start', he said, 'they'll want to know why I've been so inefficient for so long . . . For another, it will only upset my colleagues, after all I'm already achieving my profit targets.'

Anyone who has worked in large organizations will have a feel for this manager's predicament, even though they may not admire him. He probably does not admire himself very much. Certainly he is not doing much to make the company better, which is what made my friend angry. Action Learning could help to make him and his company better through challenging such backsliding and avoiding. It does, however, take moral courage and imagination.

To extend the example of Gordon and the limestone, we could point to companies, perhaps in the engineering sector, who are wizards at invention and construction but who lack all curiosity for marketing and customer relations. Over the years, as well as building machines, the people in the company have constructed an image of the outside environment which is most unfriendly: cutthroat (other people's machines cost less); unpredictable (new designs appear all the time); and unsympathetic (no one values quality engineering any more). Many of these widely shared beliefs are myths, half-truths at best, but no one challenges them. Not until, that is, the firm goes bankrupt or is bought up by a predator. Why cannot the firm change?

The Principle of Insufficient Mandate – 'Those unable to change themselves cannot change what goes on around them' – is, according to Revans, the prime principle of action learning.[20] In the engineering company, as with Gordon and his quarry waste, people have agreed that things are like such and such, and have then acted for years in a way which sustains that belief rather than challenges it. Over those years we have built up a joint picture, supported and elaborated it in our conversations, gossiping and stories, and now we are stuck – with it. Believing that environment to be unfriendly – cutthroat, unpredictable, unsympathetic – it is a long time since anyone has been out to test the theory. 'We just know it.'

As the patterns of thought in the mind of the individual are part of the problem, so the organization is part of the larger system we call environment. When we say that most of our problems come from 'the environment', perhaps we are saying that there is not much we can do about this. It can be a way of excusing ourselves, of turning a blind eye.

The revival of interest in organizational learning may bring about some much needed developments here. Important as it is to improve the actions and learning of individuals, we also need to develop our understanding and practice of organizational transformation if these individuals are to flourish. Amongst others, Revans has pointed to the need for organizational learning with his 'The enterprise as a learning system' (1969) [included in this volume]. With colleagues I have used the term 'learning company'.[21]

Applying the adjective 'learning' to the collective 'company' creates both philosophical and ethical problems. We must define terms carefully if we are to claim learning (usually seen as a property of individuals) on the part of any collectivity. Moreover, while we may regret that a child has learned to steal or throw tantrums, what are we to make of organizations that 'learn' to engage in corporate misdemeanours?

The 'stakeholder model' of organizations is one way to tackle the issue of corporate responsibility. For Morris, the company which operates to the 'mutual advantage' of all stakeholders – capital, employees, customers, community and so on – is the 'good company'.[22] This approach, which has much in common with the 'total quality movement', offers a way forward for managers who aim at increased professionalism and for companies who aim at developing rather than exploiting their environments.

Talk, however, is cheap. Do we really think such notions will stand up to commercial pressures, to the drive for 'competitive advantage' and so on? The pressures for profit maximization will always be with us. Nevertheless, if the bottom line remains because it is an essential condition of doing business, it is surely an insufficient one for doing good business in this world. If there is a sense in which we are as good as we can afford to be, then there is a countervailing moral imperative that those who know better should set an example.

Questions of moral action cannot just be left to 'individual conscience', so often a convenient form of corporate 'blind eyeism'. Government and international action is necessary to create the climate in which individuals and individual organizations can exercise judgement. However, it is only through individuals exercising this judgement, and choosing 'good' rather than 'bad' actions, that progress towards 'better' business can be maintained. The 'ethical climate' of an organization or a nation constrains or encourages particular actions on the part of individuals. Just as we learn better where there is an enabling learning climate, so we are likely to behave better in a climate which supports a high standard of ethics.

References

1 Snell R S (1990), 'The Development of Ethical Awareness & Personal Morality by Managers Through Work Experiences: An Agenda for Research', *Personnel Review* 19(1), pp. 13–20.
2 Peters, T. J. and Waterman, R. H. (1982), *In Search of Excellence*, New York: Harper & Row.
3 Revans, R. W. (1983), *The ABC of Action Learning*, Bromley, Kent: Chartwell-Bratt.
4 MacLagan, P. (1989), 'Management Development & Moral Development', paper presented at the British Academy of Management Conference, Manchester Business School, UK, 11 September.
5 Ibid
6 Burgoyne, J. G. (1989), 'Creating the Managerial Portfolio: Building on Competency Approaches to Management Development', *Management Education and Development*, **20**(1), pp. 55–61
7 MacLagan, P., op. cit., p. 4
8 Pedler, M. J. and Boydell T. H. (1985), *Managing Yourself*, London: Fontana, and Aldershot: Gower.
9 Bettelheim, B. (1986), *The Informed Heart*, Harmondsworth, UK: Penguin.
10 Argyris, C. and Schon, D. (1978), *Organizational Learning: A Theory in Action Perspective*, Mass. USA: Addison Wesley.
11 Revans, R. W., op. cit., p. 54
12 Braddick, B. and Casey, D. (1981), 'Developing the Forgotten Army – Learning and the Top Manager', *Management Education and Development*, **12**(3), pp. 169–80
13 Revans, R. W., op. cit., p. 55
14 Revans, R. W., op. cit., pp. 54–5
15 Nicoll, M. *Living Time*, quoted by Schumacher, E. F. (1978), *A Guide for the Perplexed*, Abacus, p. 43.
16 Revans, R. W., op. cit., p. 37

17 Harrison, R. (1962), 'Defenses and the Need to Know', *Human Relations Training News*, **6**(4).
18 Snell, R. S., op. cit.
19 Carpenter, E. (1916), *My Days and Dreams*, London: Allen & Unwin, pp. 144–5.
20 Revans, R. W., op. cit., p. 55
21 Pedler, M. J., Boydell, T. H. and Burgoyne, J. G. (1989), 'Towards the Learning Company', *Management Education & Development*, **20**(1) pp. 1–8.
22 Morris, J. (1987), 'Good Company', *Management Education and Development*, **18**(2), pp. 103–115.

4 The power of Action Learning

Bob Garratt

Action Learning is a process for the reform of organizations and the liberation of human vision within organizations. The process is based on taking one or more crucial organizational problems and, in real time, analysing their dynamics; implementing proposed solutions derived from the constructive criticisms of colleagues; monitoring results; and through being held responsible for these actions, learning from the results so that future problem solving and opportunity taking is improved. In theory this is little different from the logical procedure of any rational person attempting to solve organizational problems. But organizations rarely behave rationally. In practice irrationality is generated by misunderstanding the complexities and uncertainties of modern organizations. Such irrationality interferes with achieving the blend of logic and emotionality necessary to transcend organizational difficulties. The Action Learning process attempts to achieve this blend through giving rigour and pace to the cycle of learning and, through using the positive powers of small groups, to sustain this discipline and rhythm. Structural elements of Action Learning are that the authority and responsibility for analysis and implementation are given to those people who have psychological ownership of the problem and must live with their proposed solution. The whole is underpinned by the proven assumption that people learn most effectively with and from colleagues in the same position.

As such it is a very powerful organizational tool for the reform of working systems and the subsequent restating of organizational objectives. Its power derives from releasing and reinterpreting the accumulated experiences of the people who comprise the organization. The combination of this released energy and the act of moving the authority for problem solving to those people who must live with the consequences is a deliberate devolution of organizational power. Such devolution has two major benefits. First, giving responsibility to those who own the problem gains commitment to any proposed solution, offers participants the chance to consciously develop their own learning, and demonstrates to all concerned the benefits of more autonomous group working. Second, the learned autonomy and reintegration of work groups allows the top managers to concentrate on the increasingly necessary roles of monitoring the uncertain environment, and designing the future to ensure the organization's continuity, with the time released from not having to watch constantly day-to-day activities.

Action Learning can be seen as so powerful by perceptive but faint-hearted souls that they will not allow its use in their organizations because of the perceived risks to the organization and their careers. The fear is usually that uncovering the inadequacies of the organization, and the blocks to reform, will unsettle the stability of all concerned. This is part of the process. Action Learning is concerned with risk and uncertainty, but its focus is not on the destructive aspects of negative criticism and buck passing often associated with them. It concentrates on managing risks and uncertainties and on learning from them for the benefit of the stakeholders of the organization. As the recession in the West continues and the uncertainties and risks in just surviving become painfully clear, many people are realizing that there are no risk free remedies for their organizational ills. They are, therefore, looking for processes of organizational learning and adaptation which though incurring risks are creative, motivating, and cost-effective. Action Learning meets these criteria, but it needs some organizational clout to get it started effectively enough to sustain itself as the style of managing and thinking suitable for the turbulent 1980s. One of the few constructive things to come out of the present economic and social recession is that it is creating crises in organizations. As this is the only condition under which truly radical rethinking of the means and ends of an organization can be undertaken, and the results implemented systematically and rapidly, it bodes well for Action Learning, for Action Learning thrives in crises.

Given that Action Learning is a powerful process of organizational reform; that it involves the devolution of powers and the recasting of managerial roles; and that it is often instigated in conditions of crisis; it is essential that the present holders of organizational power understand both logically and emotionally what is likely to happen in their own backyard if they use this process. It has long been an axiom of management that for any significant changes to occur in an organization the top management must be committed to, and informed of, the proposed changes. Action Learning goes a step further and says the top management must be willing to learn from the resulting analyses and implementation in their turn, i.e. that they need become part of the total organizational learning system and must play a continuing part in the development of it.

This is essential for Action Learning as it is based on the synergy of simultaneous development at the personal, organizational, and business levels to achieve its powerful impact. Such synergy is beneficial both to top management who see it as a suitable and socially acceptable return made on their investment in people – the learning resource of their organization – and to the employees of the organization as it allows them to reform their ways of working by removing the sources of frustration whilst also developing themselves as more rounded people. So for any simultaneous development to occur through Action Learning, no matter what the level of entry to the organization, it is essential that top management is prepared for the opportunities and risks they face.

Top management commitment and the consequent change in their behaviour is necessary because its symbolizes that changes in all the stakeholders' attitudes are to be encouraged as the meaning of what is meant by 'work' in their organization is reconsidered. This process will often seem uncomfortable, even alien, to the people concerned. Hence any evidence, however flimsy, that top management is not serious in their commitment will be used to abort the process. It is the role of top management to provide sufficient personal and organizational 'cover' for those people participating in an Action Learning programme to ensure they are not punished under the existing organizational rules whilst they strive to develop new ones. Time is needed for any significant behavioural and attitudinal changes to occur so carefully monitored 'pilot projects' are a useful way of signalling that change is being encouraged from the top and the authority for day-to-day problem solving devolved.

Many people feel that they would like to use Action Learning in their organization but have not sufficient power or rhetoric to make the case. In the next few paragraphs I have outlined the arguments I have found effective in convincing top managements of the benefits of using Action Learning to reform their organizations. It is not 'pure' Action Learning theory because it draws pragmatically on the work of many people where this has been found to make a point effectively, but the structure and logic of the argument is very much Action Learning's own.

Convincing top management

I assume that top managers are interested in the survival and growth of their organizations. In the present age of uncertainty and discontinuity both aspirations are increasingly difficult to attain using current organizational thinking and structures. One is looking, therefore, for a way of thinking and acting which helps cope with these uncertainties and discontinuities. We know from the study of ecology that the essential formula for the continuing survival of an organism is that its rate of learning must be equal to, or greater than, the rate of change in its environment. (See Fig 4.1.) If its rate of learning is less than the rate of change, then it dies. This formula is usually symbolized in the Action Learning writings as $L > C$. It seems to hold good from the simple amoeba to the largest trans-national corporation. Its usefulness is in its focus on learning as the crux of surviving environmental change. In organizations this argues for the development and maintenance of a system of organizational learning to monitor environmental change and take appropriate avoiding action.

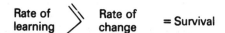

Figure 4.1 The crucial formula for the survival of an organism

The only resource capable of learning within an organization is the people who comprise it. The very diversity of the experience of the people in the organization is a valuable asset, if one can learn to use it. No technology can learn to cope with the managerial problems of organizations because it is designed to cope with the solution of technical 'puzzles' rather than managerial 'problems'. Problems are rooted in the quality and quantity of the organizational learning resource and, therefore, reflect the quality of top management's investment in that area.

Action Learning is most effective when used to confront organizational problems rather than technical puzzles. As learning is at the core of its process it is particularly valuable in developing the structures and dynamics of organizational change. It is, therefore, immediately attractive to top managers as an obvious way out of the present organizational difficulties. But their acceptance is often without sufficient consideration to the unique strengths and weaknesses of their organization. For a system of organizational learning to be developed for effective organizational problem solving, it is essential that top management accept there are no cut-and-dried answers to what are seen as common organizational problems. The different social history, personalities, and organizational culture, will determine the boundaries of resources and values within which any possible solutions will lay. Encouraging the employees to find effective solutions within these boundaries is a task of top management. They have available to them a highly cost-effective set of tools – the talents and experiences of the people they employ. It is vital that they release and tap the springs of self-sufficient learning within their organization, establishing the atmosphere in which reinterpretation and constructive criticism of people's experiences is encouraged on a regular basis which is central to this style of managing, so that failure to meet targets can be discussed openly and more realistic targets be mutually agreed. This will enable employees to rise above the usual interpersonal bickering and subscribe to important common tasks which transcend the petty politics and concentrate on the survival of their organization.

It takes time to change organizational culture, management styles, and organizational structures. Action Learning is significantly faster and more effective in achieving these ends than other forms of organizational change. However, the interim period is always difficult so 'cover' within the business for the first projects is essential. Whether these are called 'pilot programmes', 'management action groups' or other such names is unimportant. What is essential is that the top managers are sufficiently committed intellectually and emotionally to want to become part of the organizational learning system. However, it is often alarming how quickly top managers 'buy' the Action Learning idea intellectually without having bought it emotionally. Then, as information is uncovered that does not fit their stereotypes, they withdraw co-operation or react negatively to the initiative. Questioning their assumptions and work processes is an essential part of the organizational learning process. Once they can be seen to change when faced with authentic information which questions their operating assumptions, then the change in organizational attitudes will disseminate rapidly through the organization.

The organizational learning of which I am talking is not just the acquisition of impersonal and codified knowledge. It is not just a matter of collecting as much data as possible on any problem area. Data, the ocean of facts available in the world, is useless on its own. What are needed for effective managerial decisions are the attitude and skill to select from that sea of data the specific pieces which form the information needed to resolve the problem. So I am looking for a meaning for 'learning' in an organization which integrates attitudes, knowledge, and skills through action on live problems into a process of reflection and reinterpretation that develops higher quality question posing and answering. This I see as the core of the learning organization.

Built into organizational learning in a rapidly changing world is an ever present element of risk taking. This is why developing higher quality questioning is central to managing such risks. We have seen that the application of technical knowledge alone is insufficient to resolve complex organizational problems. Even if it were, the intervention of a single variable, time, is sufficient to ensure that managers are usually unable to have sufficient learning to take risk free decisions. It seems to be an axiom of management that decisions have to be taken always before one has had time to gain the full facts. The consequence is that the difference between the level of learning held by a manager, or an organization, and the level needed theoretically for a totally risk free decision is a measure of the amount of risk being taken. (See Figure 4.2.)

My argument is that it is impossible to avoid risks in the present economic climate so a prime role of top management is to create the organizational climate in which thoughtful risk taking and subsequent learning are encouraged. Top managers face the same risk taking dilemmas as the employees they lead. We all fantasize about the amount and consequences of the risks we face. Recent work has shown that there are three main categories of risks about which people concern themselves – physical; financial; and emotional. In an unsupportive or destructively critical organizational environment fantasies about all three types breed with each other and stifle action. 'Dynamic conservatism', or creative inactivity, are common causes of learning loss

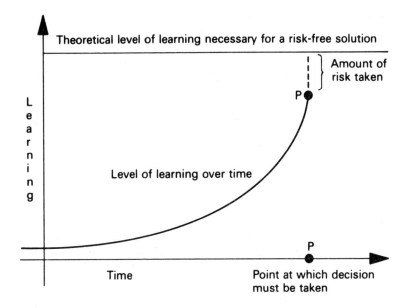

Figure 4.2 Diagram of the typical amount of risk taken by a manager

in organizations. Action Learning counters learning loss by encouraging supportive and constructively critical behaviour within individuals first, and then disseminated it throughout the organization.

An essential foundation of the Action Learning argument is that of ensuring that the authority and responsibility for action and learning is passed to the lowest appropriate part of the organization for the work in hand. This is usually in direct contrast with most behaviour in organizations. The argument for doing this is that a system that encourages people at all levels of their organization to be as self-sufficient as possible is inherently healthy in itself as it will keep up the necessary rate of learning. But more than that it also releases the time and energy of top managers to look upwards and outwards to undertake the strategic aspects of their jobs which are often neglected in times of crisis. It assumes that the daily operational problems are dealt with by the people who must live with them and any proposed solutions; whilst senior managers get on with monitoring the environment and integrating the boundaries between the internal

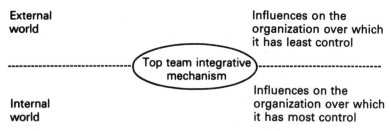

Figure 4.3 The two worlds of the organization and the integration mechanism

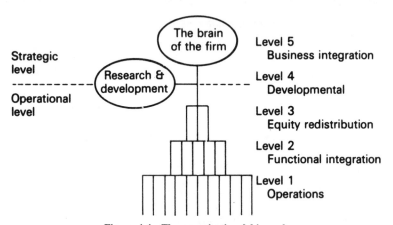

Figure 4.4 The organizational hierarchy

operational world and the external environment. (See Figure 4.3.)

Two models seem to help top managers clarify their thinking in relation to what will be an appropriate launching and development Action Learning strategy for them. The first concerns the organizational structure and roles of their business. It is a highly simplified version of Stafford Beer's excellent 'Brain of the Firm' (see Figure 4.4), where the notions of what should happen at the equity distribution and business integration levels can be usefully debated. Most Action Learning interventions in the UK have happened at level 3 as this is typically the area where externally or internally-generated crises are felt. Action here can usually be disseminated downwards, to where the work is happening, very fast. With the time then released top management can give better thought, and develop better questioning, about the strategic levels, reasonably secure in the knowledge that the operational side is self-regulating within its agreed plans.

This can be represented by a simplified adaptation of Argyris'

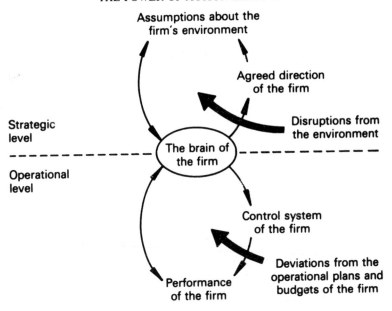

Figure 4.5 Operational and stragetic learning loops

model of 'double loop learning' (see Figure 4.5) i.e. the idea that the internal operational sphere and the external strategic sphere need integration through a learning mechanism. In terms of an intervention strategy for the use of Action Learning by top management this could be seen as:

1 Activation of senior functional managers to tackle key organizational survival projects.

2 Dissemination of the approaches learned by senior managers to the wider employee base, to encourage their reconsideration of present work practices and structures, in preparation for the devolution of authority to become self-learning and self-regulating within the plans agreed with top managers.

3 Activation of the top management to reconsider their thinking and roles following the devolution of most daily operational problems; and their need to concentrate on environmental monitoring and the integration of strategy with operations.

These simple models and arguments have proved sufficient to

convince a range of top managers to launch pilot activities for the reform of their organizations in many parts of the United Kingdom, France, and The Netherlands in the early 1980s.

Making it operational

If such arguments are powerful enough to cause debate amongst the top team and demands for subsequent action, then the focus turns to 'What do we do from here?'

The four key elements of the Action Learning process:

1   a crucial organizational problem

2   people willing to take risks to develop themselves and their organizations

3   authority to take action on the problem

4   a system for learning reflectively

are all that are needed to guarantee success with the pilot programme. The reader should now be able to design his/her own programme subject only to the personalities and history of their organization. The rest of what I have to say is, therefore, more anecdotal and may overshadow the simplicity of the above elements. What follows is a distillation of my experiences over the last ten years. It is not a series of formulae the application of which will guarantee that what you are doing is Action Learning. Only you can decide that through your learning.

One thing I have learned is that there is a need for a 'programme manager'. This is not necessarily a personnel or training department person. Line managers are just as competent to do it. The role is arduous and political – a good training for general managership. It is the link between the logic of top management's Action Learning strategy and the emotional responses, positive or negative, of the employees. It is therefore not an easy job, but any risk taking manager can do it. Perhaps one of the most regular surprises for people taking the programme manager role for the first time is just how fast top managers grasp the idea of getting cost-effective development launched in their business. Within this enthusiasm for the logic of the idea there are a series of traps for the unwary programme manager. There is no direct connection between the acceptance of the logic of an idea and its emotional acceptance. This latter aspect requires an attitude and behavioural change which the former does not. So, rather than just accepting top management's verbal acceptances of the logic, the programme manager must be courageous and keep a firm link with the top team to gain their emotional commitment to the practice of Action Learning within their organization.

Whilst this can appear initially as a daunting prospect to a new programme manager it is a necessary test of the resolve of each side in the process. An honest and humble approach to working alongside the top team to research their views as to what are the crucial problems of the organization can build the credibility of the programme manager rapidly with them. The selection of key problem areas by individual top team members usually generates a varied list which needs debate and comparison by the whole team before they can focus on the structural elements of policy and strategy for their organization. From this debate it is usually easy to identify one or more managerial problems that need resolution within, say, twelve months and would, therefore, make suitable Action Learning projects. Once the top team has selected these projects the programme manager is locked into a line manager role. He or she needs to operate within the time and money budgets agreed with the top team to achieve the stated performances. Any deviations from the required targets will need careful monitoring and reflection by the top team to determine whether their target setting is unrealistic, or whether the failure to achieve lays with their employees. In either case there is a need to develop a system of organizational learning which allows the business to do significantly better next time.

Elements of programme design

Having gained the commitment and operational targets of the top team, the next stage is essentially one of design. Dogmatism can raise its ugly head at this point as to what is the nature of 'real' Action Learning. Rather than become embroiled in a fruitless game of restrictive definition I prefer to take a contingent stance and stress that, if there exist the four key elements mentioned above (pp. 31–2), the appropriate design will depend on the history and resources of the organization, the personalities involved, and the wit and creativity of those charged with the programme design.

Central to an appropriate design is an awareness of the processes by which adults learn. Reg Revans in *The ABC of Action Learning* describes four typical managerial blockages to the problem of deciding honest sources of information in conditions of uncertainty and risk – the four corrigible handicaps:

1   the idolisation of perceived past experiences

2   the charismatic influences of (other) successful managers

3   the impulsion to instant activity

4   the belittlement of subordinates

Within the employee's energy and enthusiasm for actions based on ill-considered learned responses – their action fixation – lays both the blockage and opportunity for true learning. We know that adults learn best from live projects; from the support and constructive criticism of colleagues; from rigorous self-reflection leading to serious reinterpretation of their previous experiences; and from a willingness to test their hypotheses in action.

We need to design, therefore, an organizational learning process that links analysis, prognosis, implementation, and testing, with a group of colleagues facing similar problems who will respect the personal experimentation and reconsideration that lies at the heart of the Action Learning process. This grouping of colleagues is called the 'project set'. It is a group of comrades in adversity who will give, and expect as a reciprocal, personal support and honest, constructive criticism as the rights and duties of each project set member. The set gives the rigour and pace through the regularity of its meetings for each individual to develop the ability to reflect upon both proposed plans of action and the consequences of them. Then it encourages reinterpretation of the realities of that plan and its implementation as they unfold.

The Action-fixated cycle of learning can be characterized as shown in Figure 4.6 and can be contrasted with the Action Learning cycle shown in Figure 4.7. At this point in the design the programme manager can link the projects, as agreed with the top team, with the participants in the project set. We can then characterize the basic logistics as shown in Figure 4.8. The elements I have now added are those of the 'client' and the 'set adviser'. The client is the person who ultimately owns the problem under investigation – the person who will finally be held responsible for the resolution of the project on which the participants work. In pilot programmes the client is typically the top team member with responsibility for the key problem area. The set adviser is usually a person external to the organization who helps with the developmental processes of the individuals and

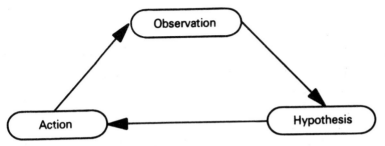

Figure 4.6 Action-fixated cycle of learning

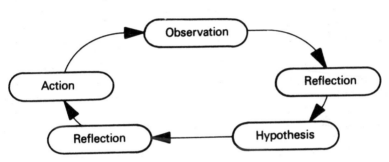

Figure 4.7 Action Learning cycle

the set. Whilst theoretically unnecessary because the experiences already reside within the employees and simply need reinterpretation, they are usually helpful for a first programme both to 'legitimize' the Action Learning process within the organization and to help participants experiment with the changes in learning and management style demanded.

There are characteristics of successful programmes which depend on a combination of project type and situation. The simple matrix which describes these can be shown as in Fig. 4.9. Observation of the effectiveness of each part of this quadrant seems to show that:

1   Own job projects tend to be effective for personal (role) development and the reinterpretation of specific jobs within an organization.

2   Internal exchanges tend to be effective for personal development and establishing better links between specialist functions within an organization.

3   External exchanges tend to be highly effective for personal

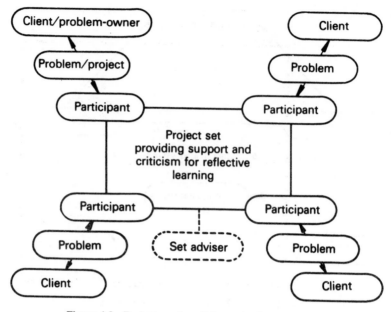

Figure 4.8 Projects and participants in the project set

development and in helping the client organization learn to value different experiences and views.

4 Technical exchanges tend not to be effective for the development of managerial problem solving because of their over-concentration on technical puzzles but are useful for the dissemination of best practice.

The programme designer has a number of permutations of personal and/or organizational development to negotiate with the top team using this quadrant. Many highly successful programmes have been completed over the past twenty years using the individually-orientated approach mentioned above. However, in the present economic conditions, it has been noticeable that top managers have been keen to get fast and cost-effective results throughout their organizations. In these conditions the personally-orientated approaches tend to be seen as too slow and other approaches are needed. Within the last two years there has been a rise in the number of team based programmes. In these small teams – typically four or five participants usually but not exclusively from one organization – work on a crucial problem of the

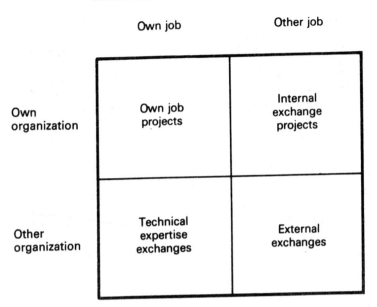

Figure 4.9 The job/organization matrix

business as a single project. As a team they form a much stronger political force for change in the organization than an individual. This increased strength usually guarantees that changes will disseminate fast once the Action Learning process is under way. Team projects are, therefore, a powerful tool for organizational renewal.

This demand for increasing the scale and speed of dissemination of Action Learning within organizations, and its focus away from individual development towards the reform of the total organization, brings into sharp relief the earliest and rather neglected work of Reg Revans in the National Coal Board, the Hospital Service, and West Africa. These emphasized the need to develop a 'learning community' attitude at all levels of the organization. This change of scale does not negate the fundamental idea of using intelligent people, naive to the functional specialism that forms the basis of the project they are confronting, asking basic questions about fundamental organizational problems. The power of 'intelligent naivety' in questioning the working assumptions of an organization is the leading edge of the Action Learning process. The rigour and pace of the project set forms the plane; and the motive force for organizational take-off is the energy released through the devolution of authority to solve problems. With this combination it is possible to truly undertake organizational reform.

The changing roles of trainers and developers

Other chapters in this book will deal with life in project sets, the processes of personal development and organizational change, and the advantages and disadvantages of using advisers for the project sets. What interests me is the significant change in roles 'traditional' trainers or developers need to embrace if they are to become effective practitioners of Action Learning. Systems of organizational learning are much too important to be left to trainers. They are central to the survival and growth of any organization and therefore reside ultimately with the top team. The practice of developing such a learning system is a line management job in its own right and needs, therefore, line management skills. Perhaps the biggest trauma for a trainer or developer to face is that the programme manager need not be a trainer; but any trainer undertaking the running of an Action Learning programme must be a line manager. An entrepreneurial, risk taking, stance is essential if the programme manager is to be successful. I use the word 'entrepreneurial' here both in the sense of selling to top managers the cost-effectiveness of the proposition and, more importantly, in its original French sense of a 'stager of dramas'. The use of the Action Learning process with its resultant release of hitherto untapped energies is most certainly a drama to be staged and managed. This is easily understood by line managers but often proves more difficult for trainers and developers to assimilate, particularly if they have been running courses or programmes which have been hermetically sealed from the real time pressures of their organizations.

In addition to the entrepreneurial role, there is that of programme designer. Here it is not sufficient to be just a technical expert on Action Learning or the processes of the project set because both lock the trainer back into the easy stereotype expected by participants. This will inevitably lead to the rejection of the trainer and the possibility of rejection of the total process. A more appropriate stance for a programme designer seems to be that of the contingent consultant working from the problems as they exist and, through using a wide and flexible range of behavioural, attitudinal, and cognitive inputs, working towards the assimilation of the Action Learning process within the brain of the firm through the demonstration of its effectiveness.

Parallel with the entrepreneurial and design stages, and continuing throughout the programme, is the adviser and counsellor role which helps everyone involved in the process interpret it through their own experiences. This calls for the ability to explain what is proposed and expected in a language appropriate to each part of the organization. An essential part of this role is the ability to demystify the fantasies of the participants as to why 'they' (top management) wish to launch the Action Learning process, and then following through the process by highlighting the individual and group learning as it develops. As the total strategy unfolds, then the programme manager needs to ensure the development of the top team's strategic role and ensure that it links into the operational learning systems as they grow.

In all these new roles it is impossible for the trainers to maintain a safe, off-line, role. Commitment to launching Action Learning processes in an organization is undoubtedly more risky than traditional stances. But the reward is in bringing the trainer directly into the line functions as part of their career development. It seems that the management of an Action Learning programme is a useful test of general management competence. Perhaps in the future we shall see this as a natural move in any manager's career path as the acid test before general managership.

5 Questioning ourselves

Mike Pedler

The idea of action learning comes down to a matter of Ps and Qs. Briefly, individuals and organizations need to learn at a rate that exceeds the rate of changes thrust upon us if we are to survive and prosper. We are hindered from learning chiefly by our idolization of the past and our belief in yesterday's answers. Learning is a combination of selected past knowledge reorganized on the basis of a few discriminating questions. [L = some P + a few Qs]. P is 'programmed knowledge ' – that which we already know, contained in books, libraries, polytechnics – the answers that we have gleaned from solving yesterday's problems. Q is the 'discriminating question' – put in conditions of chaos and uncertainty and in the absence of a definite answer. Such a question may lead us to a course of action rather than an answer.

Universities, schools and so on set out to teach P while Action Learning attempts to produce, capture or discover Q. Learning in educational establishments tends to consist in acquiring 'programmed knowledge'. Action Learning is a product not of teaching but of tackling *problems* to which there is no right answer and is about acquiring the ability to ask good questions of oneself, of others and of situations which leads to an increased ability to tackle problems in the future.

Perhaps the defining characteristic of Action Learning is this learning to question and not the requirement for action. This latter requirement often seems to distinguish Action Learning from conventional management education, but what is 'action'? 'What we don't do everyday as managers', one person once told me. Whenever we attempt to define this imperative of action we fail – one person's 'action' is another's inactivity. We have all noticed in sets that some people *do* lots of things and learn little – activity as a substitute for thought and reflection. Indeed this could perhaps be described as one of the central pathologies of the manager's job. On the other hand some people seem to do very little and actually learn a lot. Casey and Braddick were puzzled because their top managers did not want to take action and tackle work tasks, they wanted to sit and talk about themselves and their lives. They conclude that members were learning by 'reframing' their problems: members are prisoners of their own beliefs and of their past and persisting efforts to change things; past attempts at solutions have failed and made things worse, reinforcing the original problem; change can now only be introduced by first abandoning what has up to now felt like the 'right' approach and then stepping out of this frame of reference to 'reframe' the problem.[1]

Models of adult learning and development support this thesis. Many theories of development suggest that some sort of surprise,[2] crisis[3] or perturbation[4] is necessary for the development process to begin. Some rejection of existing schema and beliefs is necessary before we can see a problem differently. Indeed Revans's System Beta (see Chapter 2) begins with 'an attention-fixing event'[5] and Revans concludes that for the fellows on the Belgian programme 'learning came relatively suddenly' although he suggests that learning may be both sudden and continuous in that the moment of insight is only possible after some patient accumulation.[6]

We might describe this conundrum in common language as learning occurring 'when the penny drops', whilst recognizing that quite a lot of preparation and prior action is required to get the penny into the correct position. We clearly cannot guarantee that learning will happen via our Action Learning design, but one of the critical prerequisites is whether the individual *wants* it to happen for her/him.

Such 'wanting' however, is something more than a simple expression of desire. It is a deeper feeling of need that draws us forward despite the rebellion, the distractions, the easier options and all the thousand and one blocks to learning which we have built from our previous experience. To a great extent we *are* our defences – particularly when we are under threat or pressure as action learners often are. With our backs against the wall we need what is tried and tested, not what is unknown and risky. Against the defensive wall we build around us we also have 'a need to know'[7] which can come to the fore given the right conditions. The simultaneous support and challenge of the 'comrades in adversity' in the Action Learning set meets these requirements from time to time when it truly becomes a 'learning community'.

To try and illustrate these largely invisible learning processes, here are two case studies based on people I have met in Action Learning groups. They give some flavour of what Action Learning is.

Case Study 1

David Docherty is the 29 year old director of a small but rapidly expanding engineering business. In fact, Harborne Engineering now employs 60 men and has been tripling its turnover in every year of its 5 year existence. There are three directors, including the MD, who all helped found the company. David is mainly responsible for site work and equipment whilst his fellow directors handle the manpower and selling aspects. Harborne Engineering does all its work on other people's premises and may be working on 30 or 40 jobs at any one time throughout the British Isles – and even abroad.

David Docherty has an engineering background but no formal management training. He came to an Action Learning group because his boss, Bill Harborne was concerned about two things:

1 The company's rapid rate of growth was putting a strain on existing management and their 'systems' which were very ad hoc and depended very much on David and Graham Anderson chasing men and equipment around personally.

2 David was spending far too much time on the equipment side of his job. It could take 30 or 40 hours out of a week and he was not infrequently spending 12 hours on Sunday checking equipment for safety, loading trucks and generally being at the heart of the action.

David saw himself as a straight talker with an open relationship with Bill Harborne. Bill was almost a peer rather than a boss. David had an inbuilt 'crap detector' and if he thought the group was wasting his time he said so. At an early meeting he said he would not attend unless he got value out of it.

One of the first things he was asked by the group was how many items of equipment the company had. 'About 800' was his estimate as he had been the man directly responsible since the founding of the company. He was pushed, a bit unwillingly, into making an inventory for a future group meeting. Such a thing had not existed before – to the amazement of the big company engineers in the group. His inventory got to over 2000 items before he gave up, admitting that there was other equipment on various sites he had not been able to trace. With items varying between a few pounds for a chock or sledgehammer and several hundreds for a 30 ton chain or block and tackle, there was a lot of money involved.

David then had to go abroad on business for a month and his problem was shelved in his absence. When he returned to the group a number of sessions were devoted to attacking his problem. Numerous suggestions were put forward from the group involving systems to solve his equipment problem. There was no shortage of ideas but it seemed that none fitted the bill. There was always a good reason from the hard-headed David which effectively meant the system would not work. Eventually the group lost patience. After going round in circles for some time and after five hours of tiring discussion, one member said 'You don't really want to solve this problem do you David?' This was said and meant aggressively. David was not ruffled – he was used to violent arguments. He reiterated all the reasons he had for resolving the problem – it was taking up all his time: as the company expanded it would take more time unless a system was instituted; his wife was complaining about him working 60 and 70 hours each week. But the group were not satisfied and he did get ruffled and rather angry and eventually the meeting broke up.

A few weeks later the problem was resolved. A simple form, a simple filing system, a part-time old age pensioner and some meetings with the fitters were the components of it. The details are not important – all of them had been thrown up by the group weeks beforehand. Most of the other participants worked with far more complicated paperwork systems. So, why wasn't the problem resolved in week one?

The answer to this is not simple. When someone begins to tackle a problem in their own company they are often part of it themselves and if they are not personally involved then their boss usually is. Before it can be resolved they may have to look at the problem and themselves from a new angle. This is what takes the time and, in normal day-to-day managerial routine rarely happens. David had to see for himself the paradox of his time pressures on the one hand, and his own need to hang on to what made him feel important and indispensable. He had to admit that a paperwork system – 'an alien thing which only happens in big bureaucracies' – could take over *some* aspects of what he did at present all on his own.

Finally he had to face the consequences of what would happen if he got rid of half his workload – what would he replace it with? If it was selling and meeting clients could he do it as well as Bill Harborne? At the end of the Action Learning group, David was left with some of these questions still unanswered. One problem was resolved, but it had uncovered several more.

Case Study 2

Eric Harper is an area librarian with managerial responsibility for ten branch libraries manned by some 40 staff. In his late 30s, professionally qualified and with some experience of short courses on management techniques he was an initially lukewarm participant in the Action Learning group. He came because the director thought the library service should be more professional managerially and saw Action Learning as a possible way of achieving this.

Eric's problem was to achieve better utilization of staff in his area. Of the staff, a dozen were professionally qualified and members of NALGO. The remainder were either non-professional full-timers or part-timers, and members of NUPE. One odd-man-out, an ex-caretaker, was a member of ASTMS. The professional staff were grouped in 5 of the 10 branches, which meant that the other 5 got no professional service. NALGO had a firm policy that there would be no increase in flexibility or productivity without more pay. Eric had to improve the professional service to the branches without spending any money: indeed, he was encouraged to cut the budget. Additionally the library service is highly stratified with status barriers almost as rigid as the Indian caste system. Promotion opportunities were limited for professionals and virtually non-existent for non-qualified people.

Eric's initial lack of commitment and personal diffidence made for slow progress. For some time he sat back as his impression was that the group was responsible for solving his problem. It gradually became clear that no one but the problem owner can solve the problem – although other people can be very helpful.

Eric's breakthrough finally came after a one-to-one session which he had with one of the other group members when a possible new structure emerged. This gave better utilization of staff, with some increased promotion possibilities and even a potential saving in salaries – although this saving would not occur for two years or so. The breakthrough was achieved with a mechanical engineer who knew little about libraries but who understood planning and control systems.

Working out a possible solution was however, only a start. By the time the Action Learning group came to a close Eric had persuaded his boss that this was a good solution. For Eric this was no small step. For a number of years he had not 'got on' with his boss and found it difficult to talk and impossible to disagree with him. Eric had been sponsored by the director, not his boss, and an added complication was that the sponsor and the boss also had different views about how to resolve the problem. Poor inter-personal relationships between top managers was a major obstacle to overcoming the problem – in fact they contributed to the continued existence of the problem. It was also difficult to avoid the conclusion that Eric had been 'sent' to the group to achieve a breakthrough in this deadlock. It seems that one of the inevitable consequences of trying to take significant managerial action is that the participant comes up against the politics of top management. If a change is to take place as a result of action then the political system – essentially geared up to *resist* change – has to be manipulated to make it possible.

Eric had taken some action, but management action cannot be taken as swiftly in a public authority as it can in a small company. Before the new staffing structure could be operational it had to go from the top management, through the Recreation Committee of the Council and finally to Management Services Department to be negotiated with the unions involved. Eric had seen some personal development, particularly with regard to his management style and his ability to perform the skills associated with problem solving. Whether his solution will finally resolve the problem may take another twelve months or so to find out.

References

1 Braddick, W. and Casey, D. (1981), 'Developing the Forgotten Army: Learning and the Top Manager', *Management Education and Development* **12**(3), pp. 169–80.

2 Charlesworth, W. R. 'The role of surprise in cognitive development', in Elkind, D. & Flavell, J. H. (eds) (1969) *Studies in Cognitive Development*, New York: Oxford University Press, pp. 257–314.
3 Lievegoed, B. C. J. (1979), *Phases – Crisis & Development in the Individual*, London: Pharos.
4 Pedler, M. J. & Boydell, T. H. 'Is all management development self development?' in Beck, J. & Cox, C. (eds) (1980), *Advances in Management Education*, Chichester: Wiley.
5 Revans, R. W. (1971), *Developing Effective Managers*, New York: Praeger, p. 105.
6 Ibid., p. 111–114.
7 Harrison, R. (1962/3), 'Defences and the need to know', *Human Relations Training News* **6**(4) Winter.

6 Minding our Ps and Qs

John Morris

> Whatsoever we pursue, some ways of saying or doing fresh things can be got from others – whether we like it or not. . . . Throughout life one is told by endless authorities what to do next, and one learns to obey. Much so picked up has already long existed, so it is here called *programmed*, and denoted by 'P'. Yet much other learning also comes, neither from command nor example, but from one's own experience. Finding out for oneself may also be very mixed. . . . Knowledge, ideas, attitudes, skills, new perceptions of what goes on are always turning up; what is so discovered, moreover, generally tells one something new about the self. 'Well, I must say! You do live and learn!' is so often said after the shock of finding out from one's own experience that some hallowed belief was long untrue. . . . Learning of this nature comes from *questioning* insight, and is denoted by 'Q'. . . . Simplistically, we may say that fresh learning is the sum of programmed instruction and questioning insight. . . . [1]

You may have recognized the distinctive tones of Reg Revans, the formulator of Action Learning, making one of his many useful distinctions. For Revans, education and training have placed far too much dependence on P, taught by accredited experts, rather than Q, initiated by people questioning their own direct experience. Fresh experience comes from action, rather than habitual repetition, and a major contribution to human understanding has come from Revans's work on Action Learn-

71

ing: the deliberate commitment to learning from one's own engagement in action, and forming Action Learning groups, together with fellow learners who are also committed to learning from their own direct experience.

Action Learning has been accelerating rapidly, after a slow start. It has many advantages, notably its immediate relevance to the challenges and demands of real life in a period of unprecedented change. It is also immensely flexible, and attractive to adult learners because it respects their independence and experience. In particular, the questioning approach[2] adopted by Action Learning is essential in those situations where a ready-made answer is unacceptable, or impracticable. A significant problem of Action Learning is one that is shared with all approaches that take learning seriously (as distinct from indoctrination or other forms of conditioning). It is no respecter of potentates or hierarchies, since it seeks to empower everyone to learn from personal experience, and to find the confidence (and possibly courage) to act in the light of that experience, and the questions that it raises as the living spirit encounters the dead letter. Fearless questioning is at the heart of Action Learning, and those who rule through fear know a threat to their power when they see one.

Having stressed the vital importance of Q, as discriminating questioning, to Action Learning, it is necessary to refer to the indispensability of P as the context of Q. No one faced with a challenging situation, and hard pressed to find a way of coping with it, is likely to ignore P in the form of wise guidelines, useful know-how, and good practice. P may have much that is out of date or downright misleading, but it also contains the wisdom of the past, which we ignore at our peril. P – as the total stock of established knowledge – is also being added to constantly, especially in the fields of science and technology (much less, alas, in morals, politics and even common sense).

So the question arises: how can we gain a deeper understanding of the contributions of P and Q, as two basic approaches to the kind of learning that practitioners need and value? P attracts the busy practitioner, keen to save time and energy, by providing the ready-made answers to many questions, and Q puts into a useful and pertinent form the questions that, as yet, have no such answers. There is no doubt that for Action Learning, with its concern for coping with fresh challenges, Q is the senior partner. The situations that appear to demand action often confront us mysteriously, even in disguise. This is because we are seeing them afresh. They are not readily identifiable, except perhaps as a 'mess' or 'some kind of opportunity, possibly'. And they are most certainly not labelled with the proportions of P and Q appropriate to their effective handling, let alone the sequence or combination in which P and Q are to be deployed.

In such circumstances we have to remain fully alert, giving our whole attention to whatever it is we are trying to understand; that is, we have to keep minding our P's and Q's, taking care to get the best value from these two basic approaches to learning. We must take action in the ever-rolling present. While P always seems to pull us towards the past, with its established answers, Q keeps its options open and looks to the future which its decisions will shape.

This chapter is an attempt to contribute to the task of maintaining an effective balance between the virtues and vices of these two approaches. In the process I have drawn on my experience of working as a consultant and adviser in many different Action Learning activities, most of them concerned with the development of experienced practitioners in management, medicine, higher education, architecture, and technology.

Action Learning provides splendid opportunities for drawing lessons from good and bad practice in both 'action' and 'learning'. Education and training have been inclined to establish their own congenial centres, where they will be undisturbed by the daily flux and urgent demands of work. Action Learning makes a virtue of its constant association with actually learning from making things happen. Its greatest achievement is to be indistinguishable from planned and reflective development work, in the form of projects, assignments, or what is now coming to be called the 'learning organization.[3]

Over many years of such activity I have learned three lessons that seem particularly relevant to the issue of P's and Q's. The lessons have come from seeing, within and beyond the flexible framework of Action Learning, how effective practitioners develop 'good practice', both in doing their work and in learning from it.

First, the most effective practitioners are strongly biased towards using any form of P that seems to work in the challenging situations confronting them. P may take a strikingly condensed form ('Keep it simple, stupid!', 'Keep experts on tap, not on top'), or it may take the form of an elaborate display of 'state of the art' professional competence (such as the latest approach to Intellectual Property Rights, or the relevance of 1992 to one's business). In contrast to P as it appears in the often fixed forms of educational programmes, the P applied by effective practitioners is limited only by their resourcefulness and ingenuity. Metaphors, slogans, myths and legends all play their part, together with solid stuff from science and technology. P is strongly preferred in the form of *knowing how* rather than *knowing about*, and is especially valued when it helps to specify a particular line of action, rather than merely staying on the level of a windy generality.

These practitioners are constantly stirring up P, keeping it lively, as a useful stock of knowledge and skill. For them, P is seldom if ever organized neatly and rather passively into the intellectual disciplines so dear to academics. Rather, it is part of an organic network that relates to personal experience, and to the key events, incidents and episodes that have become, as it were, nodes in that network. Or course there is often room within the network for innumerable lists – check lists for action, price lists, stock lists, lists of do's and don'ts for various situations – which are but part of an active store, merely grist to the mill of a constantly working conversion process of turning each and every occasion to advantage.

Second, effective practitioners are completely committed to a questioning approach: many of them have obviously practised it from their earliest years, so that it has become as natural as breathing. This approach is much more basic than the highly skilled discriminating questioning designated as Q. At the same time, it provides a fruitful mental set which, in turn, can provide a strong support for the later development of Q. A serious problem for many practitioners who are towers of strength in clearly defined operational jobs is that their questioning stays on a level which fails to question its own assumptions and purposes. Action Learning can, and often does, provide an indispensable transition from the operational loop of achieving a planned target to the directive loop of setting and reviewing a strategy, and changing a culture.[4]

Revans has continually reminded us that Q, unlike most of P, does not only enable us to add the sum of knowledge, but provides the spur for *re-organizing* it. This is one reason why Action Learning, unlike the many 'quick fixes' available to the busy practitioner, can provide moments of truth that stick in the memory and may provide a turning point in one's life, not to mention the life of the organizations within (or between) which Action Learning takes place.

Re-organization of one's experience can be painful, and an essential part of Action Learning is that it provides the opportunity of learning in a *fellowship* of co-learners, who can find

out at first hand how to provide one another with the most
fruitful combination of challenge and caring support. Discriminating questions, of the kind that provide a turning point in the
process of working and learning, do not have to be harsh, or
tough, or unfeeling, though it seems to be the current conventional wisdom to believe so.

Third, the most indispensable characteristic of effective practitioners is their capacity to balance the Ps and Qs constantly
arising. It is not only *different* requirements and options that
must be balanced, within and between the various Ps and Qs,
but those that are apparently incompatible and contradictory.
Rosabeth Moss Kanter, in her latest and most brilliant book (of
the rare kind that effective practitioners, however busy, will
happily find time to read and learn from), provides a superbly
well-documented account of the situation:

> The mad rush to improve performance and to pursue excellence
> has multiplied the number of demands on executives and managers.
> These demands come from every part of business and personal
> life, and they increasingly seem incompatible and impossible:
>
> - Think strategically and invest in the future – but keep the
>   numbers up today
>
> - Be entrepreneurial and take risks – but don't cost the business
>   anything by failing
>
> - Continue to do everything you're currently doing even better
>   – and spend more time communicating with employees, serving
>   on teams, and launching new projects
>
> - Know every detail of your business – but delegate more respon-
>   sibility to others
>
> - Become passionately dedicated to 'visions' and fanatically com-
>   mitted to carrying them out – but be flexible, responsive, and
>   able to change direction quickly
>
> . . . Even the best companies and the best people are dropping a
> few balls because they have so many in the air, and they are
> disillusioned with 'superhero' stories – a backlash against legends
> of still one more Superwoman or Supermanager or Supercompany.[5]

As Kanter demonstrates in detail, the task is to achieve a continuing balance between these apparent incompatibles, rather
than to tackle them as though each were the major objective.
And this is a task for everyone, and not only the inflated individuals whose colossal failures are rapidly making 'Super' into a
term of derision.

So I have been encouraged to find that the basic and indispensable unit of Action Learning, the 'set' of about five or six co-learners, becomes a living demonstration of mutual support, drawing on the values of both co-operation and individual achievement. Because the members of the set are all engaged in work that takes them outside the set itself, they are constantly required to consider the nature of their own relationships. The set is obviously too small to sustain a comfortable illusion of independence (unlike many organizations in everyday life, even quite small ones). It must constantly consider its own links with other, and mostly much larger, enterprises. This provides a continual spur to learning, since learning comes from the need for a new initiative or a fresh response.

To return to our opening quotation from Reg Revans. The penetrating and valuable kind of Q called 'questioning insight' is linked with 'finding out for oneself', while much of P comes from 'endless authorities'. Revans has argued, therefore, that P is the domain of experts, and Q is the practice of leaders. However, if effective practitioners are constantly using both P and Q, separately and in fruitful combination, we must recognize the need for a fruitful balance between leaders and experts; or putting the matter slightly differently, a balance between leadership and expertise.

In our rapidly changing and confused Age of Unreason,[6] which often places far more emphasis on hasty and unconsidered action than reflective learning, we are in grave danger of confusing leadership with expertize. Experts, with their dependence on the authority of P, draw their strength from the past, from their demonstrated effectiveness in knowing what to do in situations that either repeat themselves or can be brought under the control of an established technique. Leaders draw their strength from a clear and forceful vision of an achievable future, to which they are dedicated. Experts are inclined to follow a well-trodden path, while leaders make tracks in uncharted territory. Some experts – particularly dangerous – promise to make the present a comfortable extension of the best aspects of the past, a kind of heritage for perpetual tourists. And there are leaders – even more dangerous – whose vision of the future promises perpetual domination for their loyal followers.

In our hunger for security in these difficult times, we demand 'expert leaders', often in a form that is humanly impossible to provide. We want guaranteed (and preferably simple) answers to newly arising and complex questions, and 'charismatic' leadership that is democratically acceptable. This provides a splendid opportunity for poseurs and charlatans who neither provide useful answers nor an inspiring and empowering vision. True leaders evoke responsibility rather than credulity, a sense of adventure rather than the arrogance of certitude. Such a leader engages others in a fellowship, bringing people together through strong personal ties based on shared values, a clear and accessible vision towards which to work, and a recognition of the contribution that each can make in achieving the common cause. The key characteristic of the leader is the provision of a visible example, a living and inspiring demonstration to others, who come to recognize that the outstanding quality of leaders is to empower their fellows to join in taking a lead themselves.

Of all the manifold needs that the different forms of learning must meet, surely the greatest is the need for leadership, rather than the need for acquiring stocks of established knowledge. It is just this need that Action Learning meets, with its combination of discriminating questioning related to the key opportunities and problems facing us, served by relevant information and know-how.

We live in a time when, world wide, there is great impatience with established, but clearly incompetent, authority. Many of the questions asked are ill-considered and confused. But now the nuggets of gold are gleaming among the gravel (to borrow an inspired phrase from a managing director in a recent Action Learning set), and truly discriminating questions are being asked and given wide attention, although they often lack suitable facilities for being worked on and learned from. I have encountered them most frequently in the domain of business enterprise:

- In whose interests are those 'at the top' acting?

- If it is the 'investors', how interested are they in the other stakeholders of the organization that provides their income? (for example, the managers and workers, the suppliers, and the public at large.)

- What place is there in the organization for 'quality'? (Not only quality of service and product, but quality of working life, for example.)

- What value is placed in the conventional form of organization on those who actually do the work of the business?

- What place is there for fairness in the conduct of the business and the allocation of 'rewards'?

- What place for loyalty being given by those at the top to those at the bottom?

We note that the organizations which find sensible and even inspiring responses to these questions are those which are widely seen as effective, not only by single interest-groups such as investors, but by all those 'stakeholders' associated with the business. I call these 'good companies', because they demonstrably provide good company for those who work in them, those who buy from them and those who sell to them, as well as those who place money with them as investors.

Good companies achieve an acceptable and continuing balance between these interests, and are particularly concerned with the interests of those who use the products and services of the company, and those who provide those products and services: the 'customers' and the 'workers'. Unfortunately, these companies, together with other forms of organization that provide 'good company' for those associated with them, are still a relatively tiny minority. Others are too embattled or too unreflective to see the relevance of the knowledge about good all-round performance that is piling up and to be aware of the questions that are being asked of them.

The nature of the modern media of communication, with their incessant hunger for dramatic contrast, makes both the example of the good companies and the dismal performance of the bad increasingly visible. So we can expect the widespread unease to grow and be expressed more vigorously, until the strong purposes of those who are directly interested in the companies are recognized and met.

It is no use trying to answer these challenging questions in the conventional fashion; that is, by chopping them up into recognizable categories and handing them over to groups of experts. In modern Britain, beset with confusions about its role, we have experienced not only the ill-feeling, poor quality and confusion that arise from an over-dependence on narrowly technical expertise, but also the invasion of human qualities and values by such expertise when it goes beyond its proper bounds. Now is the time for a change of focus. By taking responsibility for our own actions, we become 'self-managing' rather than conventional role-players. When we truly take responsibility for ourselves, in action, we can take difficult initiatives – initiatives which engage us in hard work, development work – rather than be constantly seeking ready answers from above.

In taking initiatives we may find that we are seen by others as leaders; but we will not be solitary 'leaders', beset by constantly unsatisfactory followers. We will be taking our share of leading within a learning community, which is based on fellowship, working and learning close to the truth of our own fresh experience, and we will be helping others to do the same. By continually minding our *own* Ps and Qs, in a working partnership with others similarly engaged, we learn to bring these two great approaches to learning into a mutually supporting balance.

Through constant questioning, we see more clearly just who we really are, and what remarkable resources we have access to. We will also see more clearly what is really facing us, and we will become more capable of accepting and responding to change. By looking attentively at the *relevance* of best practice for our own conduct, we may learn to emulate others who have gone beyond us, using our intelligence and ingenuity to the full rather than just copying the shells of their achievements. In giving our single-minded attention to ever-present reality, we can become capable of throwing light on the way forward and of leading through clear vision and simple warmth of heart.

As I contemplate this vision of good company, I see clearly that this is exactly what has been pioneered on a small scale in the initiatives of Action Learning. But Action Learning is an approach that lends itself to many scales of operation, as this collection of studies, among others, makes clear, and the time is ripe for a really rapid expansion of both the degree and extent of Action Learning work throughout the world. For it is now mature enough to take its place as a mainstream development activity, and to make a unique contribution to the development of resourceful and effective practitioners, able to lead and empower others.

I opened this chapter with a quotation from a recent contribution by Reg Revans. Let me close with another from the same piece. In reference to his basic distinction between P and Q, he asserts: 'So brief an outline of learning afresh tempts further terms . . . [but] given range enough within themselves, P and Q are sufficient.'[7] Given that effective practitioners invariably do better with a few basic ideas that touch a powerful nerve than with subtle and complex ideas that do not, I heartily agree. If we mind our Ps and Qs skilfully enough, as we take the necessary initiatives that the current circumstances require, and in the spirit of Action Learning, I think we will have found some really practical guidance for our troubled times.

References

1 Revans, R. W. (1987), 'The Learning Equation: an Introduction' in 'Action Learning', *Journal of Management Development* **6** (2).
2 Lawrence, J. K. (1986), 'Action Learning – a Questioning Approach', in A. Mumford (Ed.), *Handbook of Management Development*, 2nd edn, Gower.
3 Garratt, B. (1988), *The Learning Organization*, Fontana.
4 Garratt, B., op. cit.
5 Kanter, R. M., (1989), *When Giants Learn to Dance*, Simon & Schuster.
6 Handy, C. (1989), *The Age of Unreason*, Hutchinson.
7 Revans, R. W., op. cit.

7 The enterprise as a learning system*

Reg Revans

This paper was written in the last months of the Inter-University Programme of the Fondation Industrie-Université of Belgium. It had been discovered during the course of that momentous experiment how the presence of a visiting manager within an enterprise whose management had become convinced of the need for a lot of those employed there to learn, particularly when supported by a band of allies, could in fact engender an enlightenment previously unsuspected. Our key assumption was that the presence within each enterprise of an outsider undisguised, simply behaving as the intelligent learner about some problem he had never before encountered, soon set off a secondary, but nonetheless powerful, campaign of learning among the subordinates on the spot and with whom he regularly discussed his lines of enquiry.

Since the visitor was not only trying to understand his own approach to conditions of ignorance, risk and confusion, but was also the agent of the home management equally concerned to make sense of what appeared to them an intractable difficulty, a very simple question arose: Was the secondary (autonomous) learning process engendered merely because the majority of subordinates had become aware that the problem existed, and that

*This chapter, originally appeared in *The Origins and Growth of Action Learning*, edited by R. W. Revans, Chartwell-Brett, 1982.

it was seen by their top management to be serious? Or was the visitor more than an agent, in the sense that without him there could not possibly have started any autonomous curiosity among the home subordinates at all?. . . . If there is in most organizations staffed with normally intelligent persons a latent desire to behave sensibly in front of colleagues (as the visiting fellows of the programme seemed to have discovered) could this desire not be identified and turned to constructive use without needing to go through the elaborate ceremonies of exchanging senior managers? If the enterprise was, in fact, already a potential learning system could its capacity for self-development be exploited autonomously by the top management taking the lead? Why, except when the learning of the senior managers was the cardinal objective, do more then get the local staffs and their existing subordinates running their own enquiries?

Alas, the suggestion was grossly premature; it was rejected even by those who had had the courage to open their secrets to the exchanges of the Inter-University Programme. Not until the Japanese menace of the late 1970s introduced the Q-circle to Europe could the issue once more be raised.

The enterprise as a system of systems

Many persons concerned with the business enterprise, whether as director, employee or adviser, will have their own professional reasons for perceiving it as some manner of system: for example, the controller, who needs to ensure that its total revenue exceeds, one year with another, its total expenditure, without the specific costs of such-and-such a department necessarily being met by its own specific income; the manufacturing superintendent, who will expect some overall balance between its flow of goods and materials, not being embarrassed at one moment by a chronic shortage of stock to meet his orders, nor at another by a sharp reminder that too much capital is tied up in a superabundance of raw materials; the personnel director, who hopes that, five years hence, the enterprise will still be able to rely upon eighty per cent of the staff now serving it, each and every one richer by five intervening years of precious experience . . .

All these senior men, to ensure continuity and balanced effectiveness, need to think in terms of inputs, flows and outputs; none must envision the enterprise as a series of isolated and independent jerks of activity, springing at random into local effect and unrelated to any larger and continuous totality. Such

systemic approaches would be readily claimed by most departmental heads: to ensure such organic thinking there exists a vast
range of professional teaching and qualification, embracing such
arts as budgetary control and standard costing; production scheduling and inventory control; manpower planning and staff development, and an inexhaustible army of managerial techniques
marching in acronymic procession across the prospectuses of the
business schools – PERT, CPA, DCF, TWI, MBO, OD, OR,
X or Y, and a score of others.

The individual and the task

Such unifying ideas arouse little contention. They have, indeed,
entered deeply into the planning both of the working organizations themselves, and of many education programmes enticing
managers to think of their firms or departments as 'systems' with
many interacting parts. It would hardly be rash to suggest that
one-third of all published management literature is concerned
with such issues of functional organization, nor that an even
larger proportion of time is devoted to them on management
courses.

But there is now evidence that, however useful, however valid,
may be this functional approach, the concept of the enterprise
as a system has quite other but no less significant interpretations.
The tasks that every person carries out in the course of his daily
employment, whether at first sight concerned with purchasing,
design, manufacture, marketing, transport, accountancy, personnel development or wages payment, contain another systemic
element, the potential power of which is only of late becoming
recognized. As the chief executive of one of Britain's largest
firms recently remarked:

> Our main concern is no longer to ensure that we find, train and
> keep the biggest share of Britain's leading chemists; nor is it solely
> to concentrate on the maximum return on our investment. These
> are necessary ends, but of themselves are insufficient. Our need in
> the 1970s is to see ourselves as a developing system of two hundred
> thousand individuals.

A digression on management techniques

We see there is little new in this expression of need; almost the
same sentiment was declared by Robert Owen a century and a

half ago; similar things are said in Eastern Europe and by Chairman Mao. But we do not here interpret the enterprise as a human system in the light of this nor that political doctrine. Nor are we suggesting the need for some super-system, stored in a gigantic computer, to which the controls of orders, purchases, production, quality, cost and so forth alike report. For, in whatsoever political system, whether in the countries of OECD, in Eastern Europe or in the Third World, we now observe some impatience with – indeed, a revolt against – the systematizing experts who, during the past century, have over-regulated the tasks of men at all levels.

Industrial engineering, work study, incentive payment schemes, task specialization, timetabling and scheduling and, above all, the machine pacing of human work are now held up as a caricature of Charlie Chaplin's *Modern Times*, and all carry within themselves the seeds of their own destruction in proportion to the authority of the experts who exploit them. The latest casualty among these managerial bailiffs is, it seems, productivity bargaining; this rigmarole of wage assessment, exalted three years ago into the very diadem of behavioural science, was recently appraised by some jaundiced personnel expert as a dead duck.

The enterprise as a learning system

We observe that all the expert systems here referred to must now be imposed upon the enterprise from above or from outside. But Action Learning must seek the means of improvement from within, indeed, from the common task. An essential quality of human behaviour is that, although in some degree innate or inherited, it is in great part learned: present conduct is largely our visible response to past experience newly interpreted. It follows, first, that the daily round offers constant learning opportunities and, second, that these opportunities should be of great interest to managers. When, moreover, we discover that the quality of such learning is largely determined by the morale of the organization that offers it, that interest becomes profound. Indeed, we may now assert that the observable differences between organizations otherwise comparable in technical, financial or environmental character, are determined by whether or not their members are likely to develop in and from the course of their daily employment. One enterprise can, in short, behave as a learning system, constantly and fruitfully working out autonomous solutions to its own problems: its neighbour, built to the same technical specifications, engaged in the same tasks and reporting to the same higher authority, may be an organizational sore, running with irresoluble conflict and unendurable frustration. (Many years after the note was first drafted in 1951, we may now see that the great differences in accident and strike rates between geologically identical adjacent collieries, noted in *Group Factors in Mining Accidents*, are the differences between managed systems that either learn or do not learn from their daily crises.) It is thus to the enterprise as a learning system that we need to attend; we must understand how it is that one management continuously act to encourage such an elevation of the spirit, while their colleagues across the way live under the constant threat of rebellion from their own subordinates.

The qualities of autonomous learning systems

Our research evidence to suggest whether or not its management policies are likely to develop an enterprise as an autonomous learning system may still be incomplete. But the conditions for success seem to include the following:

1   that its chief executive places high among his own responsibilities that for developing the enterprise as a learning system; this he will achieve through his personal relations with his immediate subordinates, since the conduct of one level of a system towards any level below it is powerfully influenced by the perception that the higher level has of its own treatment from above; in the consortium of hospitals described in this series (*Action Learning takes a Health Cure*) the correlation between systematic development (attitudinal change, learning) and interest of top management as +0.91; in the secondary modern schools of Lancashire the correlation between the estimates made by the children of their teachers' skills, on the one hand, and their assessment of them as approachable human beings, on the other, was +0.87; both of these add a veneer of quantitative cunning to the immemorial verse: 'As the judge of the people is, so are his officers; and what manner of man the ruler of the city is himself, so are all they that inhabit therein,' (Ecclesiasticus ch 10 v 2);

2   the coalition of power that runs the enterprise has clear ideas about delegation, with the maximum authority for

subordinates to act within the field of its own known policies *that become known by interrogation from below*; systems of delegation, in other words, are constantly worked out as part of the contract between the person, his task and his superior; the success of delegation depends significantly upon the quality of the data/information made available; in one experimental enterprise the correlation among fifty graduate senior managers between the perceived quality of their information system, on the one hand, and their own personal satisfactions as departmental managers, on the other, was +0.78;

3 in consequence, codes of practice, standard rules and procedures, works orders and other such regulations are to be seen as norms around which variations are deliberately encouraged as learning opportunities; they will therefore contribute to the improvement of the data/information flow and may even bring into a common learning experience different members of an organization who, under codes rigorously observed, might rarely, if ever, meet;

4 any reference of what appears an intractable problem to a superior level should be accompanied by *both* an explanation as to why it cannot be treated where it seems to have arisen *and* a proposal to change the system so that similar problems arising in future could be suitably contained and treated;

5 persons at all levels should be encouraged, with their immediate colleagues, to make regular proposals for the study and reorganization of their own systems of work; such proposals should generate discussion between vertical levels and horizontal departments of how the work is currently managed, and of how its outcome is determined, such as by the content, order and distribution of individual tasks, the use and maintenance of equipment and supplies, and the flow of information essential to performing the tasks; above all, in any suggestions about the reorganization of the work, first attention should be given to its group or autonomous aspects (see particularly *Worker Participation as Action Learning* and *Project 'Management Efficiency'*).

Autonomous learning not managerial abdication

A management that interprets the employment of its staff as a continuous opportunity for their self-development does not, by setting aside the mythologies of 'scientific management' about commanding, coordinating and controlling, thereby resign to the understrappars all responsibility for running the enterprise. It merely acknowledges that the enterprise is the setting in which the staff spend most of their active lives, and that the total contract between it and its employees is wider than an agreement about who is to be paid for doing what.

This wider bargain, even if not explicit, has deep implications for personal development and personal autonomy: outstanding persons should be encouraged to develop themselves to the limits of their capacities and ought not to be restricted entirely by ingenious mechanistic programmes devised by quickwitted experts trained not to ask questions outside their own fields. Indeed, the present relation between those who perform and those who plan calls often to be stood upon its head; it is for the individual worker, as a member of a wealth-creating group, to suggest his optimum conditions of work and to set his personal standards of achievement, and for the expert to solve (with the help of the group) whatever problems the worker may introduce.

Such new approaches to work organization will offer managements their own opportunities to learn; they are certainly no invitation to their subordinates to take over and run the whole show. (Some senior managers may, of course, offer to take over, or even to buy out from the main shareholders, their section of the total enterprise; this will be a measure of the present need for the enterprise to learn.) The most precious asset of any organization is the one most readily overlooked: its capacity to build upon its lived experience, to learn from its challenges and to turn in a better performance by inviting all and sundry to work out for themselves what that performance ought to be.

Limited first applications

Although the general arguments of this paper, and the experimental evidence on which they are based, apply not only to senior management, but also to supervision and the shop floor, it would be prudent to confine any discussion aimed at developing an enterprise as an autonomous system, *in the first instance*, to managers not below works level or its equivalent. Any attempt, however reasonable its factual illustration and however secure its logic, to influence managerial opinion in this totally new sense is bound to be met with all manner of unforeseeable objections. These will differ greatly from one senior management to the next; their collisions will be highly instructive to all parties, but should be kept, to begin with, from the subordinates. It should, however, be possible to employ the ideas of *Para.* 5 above to heighten the learning processes of the seniors called upon to discuss this paper for the first time.

PART II

APPLICATIONS

8 A range of applications

David Sutton

It was easy to write this chapter for the first edition. Even as late as 1983 there were only a small number of Action Learning practitioners and the range of programmes, outside the well-documented and well-known programmes directly associated with Reg Revans, was limited. The few that were 'different' were known to those at the centre of the still embryonic Action Learning movement and most of the significant variations were included in the half-dozen quoted examples. The change in six short years is amazing. Whether they agree with the ideas or not, few practitioners in human resource development can be unaware of Action Learning principles. The numbers who actively follow the Action Learning banner can now be numbered in their cohorts and platoons rather than as individuals. Selection for this edition is therefore that much more difficult. The uniqueness of Action Learning lies in its facility to generate a wide range of seemingly different applications, each suited to its own purpose whilst retaining the basic elements.

The principles of action learning

Action Learning has been described as 'a problem-centred approach to personal and organization development which both intensifies the learning and improves the quality of the problem solution'. The essential criteria for an Action Learning programme are:

1 The vehicle must be a problem not a puzzle – that is, a difficult question to which a correct answer exists which can be discovered provided the right techniques are used. A problem is a difficult question to which there is a range of possible answers, the selection of the most appropriate being the result of value judgements.

2 The problem must be real, in urgent need of solution and capable of both intellectually stretching the problem solver (or problem solving team) and putting them at some risk in exposing their ideas and ideals.

3 The participant(s) must not only research, diagnose and offer a solution to the problem; they must also take action to implement the solution(s) they have proposed.

4 The participants must meet regularly to discuss progress, setbacks and proposals for tackling their problems, and to consider their own development, attitudes and actions. In particular they try to recognize and learn from the changes which they see taking place in themselves, their colleagues and the organizations in which they are working.

Whilst it is conceptually wrong to see problem solving and personal development as separate activities, these objectives have often been evaluated separately. As well as the participants and set advisers, there are two other roles critical to the success of an Action Learning programme:

1 The client: the person who 'owns' the problem, who put it forward for solution and who has a deep-seated desire for action which will at least move the problem towards a solution, if not actually solve it.

2 The sponsor; who has nominated a participant with a view to helping in his development and producing a more effective manager.

The practice

Perhaps the 'purest' Action Learning programme was that undertaken between June 1969 and September 1972 for the mentally handicapped living in the community. A team led by Reg Revans, Ali Baquer, Janet Craig and Diana Cortazzi ran the project and it was written up by Ali Baquer and Reg Revans[1,2]. A characteristic of this work, which has no rival for its comprehensive nature in the field of Action Learning, lies in every element being in the hands of the participants.

The foundation question was 'What needs to be done to improve the care of the mentally handicapped living in the community?' The team was drawn from seven local authorities and many different levels of bureaucracy, from front line workers to senior administrators. They belonged to nearly all of the professions involved in the care and treatment of the mentally handicapped, and they worked through the following stages:

- deciding on a target sample;

- deciding what information was needed;

- designing a questionnaire;

- administering the questionnaire to completion;

- analyzing the questionnaire;

- defining from the questionnaire analysis what were the most pressing problems;

- forming teams to tackle these problems in a manner consistent with what we now consider to be good Action Learning practice.

Later programmes have usually had a more general, less research-based orientation, and the programme designers have intervened by choosing the programme's objectives (improved productivity, individual management development, implementation of change, and so on), selecting the participants and frequently choosing the projects.

The range

From these beginnings, running alongside the highly successful Belgian Industrie-Université programme,[3] Action Learning developed a range of applications to meet the aims of programme designers who have seen the value of the concept. Many are variations on the numerous themes composed by Reg Revans but an increasing number explore new ground. Revans's great advantage has been the originality of his ideas backed by a powerful intellect and an impressive personality. He has, therefore, been able to attract funds and engage the attention of top industrialists in a manner which has made his range of activities unique.

Following the leader

Some Action Learning programmes have been developed by following directly on the management development work in which Revans led the way. The most influential of these was initiated by Reg himself although the detailed design and the implementation were in other hands. This was the first GEC programme, which differed from the Brussels programmes by being confined within one organization and using a reduced academic input. Reg Revans and Mike Bett of GEC set the programme under way and agreed the choice of fellows, but the design and operation of the programme rested with David Casey (Action Learning Projects International) and David Pearce (GEC)[4].

One of ALPI's conditions for taking on the programme was that they would not take on a second programme: if it was successful GEC themselves should take over. True to their word ALPI passed the reins to GEC after the first programme and the work has been carried on by Dunchurch Staff College.

The nearest approach in prestige terms to the Brussels programmes were those run by Jean Lawrence for ALPI under the title 'The Rolling Programme'. For each programme a group of companies nominated senior executives to work on projects in each other's firms over a six-month period. This programme was supported by several 'blue chip' firms including Courage, Cable & Wireless, Foster Wheeler and Southern Gas. The programme only ended when ALPI was transformed into the Action Learning Trust and discontinued direct training work.

Management Development programmes, using variations of the now generally accepted 'four elements matrix' of familiar/unfamiliar locations and familiar/unfamiliar project, have been run many times: sometimes using outside agents to design, set up and set-advise on the programmes, frequently designed and run by internal training Just how many are currently operating it is impossible to tell and many of them depart, to some extent, from the original principles of Action Learning. The most common deviation is for the programme to deteriorate into a project-type programme ending with conclusions and recommendations and not moving on to the action phase. Nevertheless, many firms world-wide are using Action Learning as an important part of their management development strategy.

The Revans continiuum

Reg Revans has never relaxed his attempts to spread the word about Action Learning and to encourage its adoption; both by exhortation and by designing and running programmes. His recent new programmes have concentrated largely on communications (often in deprived communities) and on social issues. His work among the black community in Hulme Manchester and the unemployed in Wolverhampton has built on his concepts of 'comrades in adversity' working on problems of importance to themselves, for which they design and implement solutions, while at the same time pursuing their individual development and that of their community.

Innovative academic programmes

So many organizations, training agencies, consultants and educational institutions have adopted Action Learning as the whole or part of their work, that it is impossible to keep track of the many variations. Some have been the result of programme designers wanting to produce a distinctive flavour. Others have been at the behest of programme users who have asked for 'personalized Action Learning'. Providing always that such programmes have observed the basic precepts of Action Learning, and that the designers have had faith in the ability of people to learn with and from each other and not by sitting at the feet of the expert, such programme have been successful. To quote David Newton of the Manchester Polytechnic MSc programme, 'The users are not concerned with the how and the why of Action Learning. They see that it works and are satisfied.'

The Manchester Polytechnic programme (more details of which can be found elsewhere in this book) is part of one of the two main streams of development which have followed the earlier work. Apart from the research programme and an MA incorporating Action Learning at Lancaster University, the universities have made little use of Action Learning. The Polytechnics have, however, initiated several academic qualification programmes using Action Learning. Depending upon the approaches of individual tutors, Action Learning has been used to lesser or greater degree in project work for a wide range of programmes at Certificate and Diploma level. Bachelor's degrees by Action Learning have been seen as a contradiction in terms, in that a BA or BSc is knowledge – based. A Master's degree by Action Learning has, however, been adopted by several institutions.

An action learning blanket

An interesting development has been the organized wide use of Action Learning to waken people to the scope and potential of their jobs, and the contribution which they as individuals and their associated management team can contribute to their enterprise. This has been done in a selective way by several groups – Jean Lawrence with the NW Water Authority, David Casey with the Local Government Training Board and the IMC in-company programmes with Allied Irish Banks, Ernst Whinney & Co., and others.

The most comprehensive programmes were at opposite ends of the world. In Australia, as early as 1977 Roy Gilbert was using Action Learning in the Victorian Public Service to enhance commitment and collaboration in the Public Service Board. At Senior Manager, Department or even office level Action Learning sets were tackling real problems and, in the process, learning more about each other and themselves. As Roy Gilbert points out[5] the problem is to get people to think about how they do their job.

In the United Kingdom, Alec Lewis, Wyndham Marsh and Ed Moorby headed an equally all-embracing project in the Prudential Insurance Company – an approach which has subsequently been matched by other organizations[6]. Their aim is to change the culture of the organization by developing a new approach in field managers. This has been done by involving as many staff as possible in Action Learning exercises to solve important outstanding problems. In the process, individual, team and organizational standards and efficiency have been enhanced.

The consultant/teacher/facilitator role

An interesting feature of the spread of Action Learning has been the way in which powerful trainers have responded to the influence of Revans's preaching by adding their own flavour and have influenced the approach of institutions in which they regularly work. Programmes which might still have existed under their present name if there had been no Action Learning movement are operating in a way which would not have been considered ten years ago. The result has been that large areas of work in major prestigious institutions and in large and small training consultancies are, often without using the words Action Learning, reflecting the Revans approach in the work they do.

Most of this work can be associated with the earliest UK practitioners, such as David Casey, David Pearce and Bob Garrett (Ashridge), Ian Cunningham (Roffey Park), Mike Pedler (Sheffield Polytechnic), and David Newton (Manchester Polytechnic). The result has been an Action Learning approach, operating through these powerful and influential management development institutions, which is now a major strategy in the development of British managers.

Much of the Action Learning in UK is still dependent on the work of individuals: some in-company trainers, some working with training bodies, some in consultancy firms, and some as lone consultants. Through this body of practitioners a wide variety of programmes is operating, although there is a tendency to concentrate on in-company, own-discipline projects. The reason is simple. A seminar paper written for the Action Learning Trust in 1980 pointed to the cost of marketing Action Learning: the number of marketing unpaid days in relation to the number of working (paid) days being greater than in other types of training consultancy. The result has been that, not only has the in-company, own-discipline project begun to dominate, but also there is a tendency towards team projects – partly to increase numbers on programmes, partly to even out the variations in ability between participants, and partly in an attempt to combine Action Learning with team building.

Despite this narrowing down there is a wide variety of work being done and, in addition to the 'traditional', the 'academic/training institutions' and the 'company-wide'approaches, there have been:

- Programmes for chief executives, meeting to discuss life at the top and its problems.

- Programmes for specialist managers (marketing managers, quality controllers,training managers) from different firms.

- In-company team programmes in which two or more teams have the same problem.

- In-company team programmes in which the sets meet regularly with each other to discuss progress on both problem solving and individual learning.

- Programmes incorporating a vertical slice of the organization working either on individual projects each tailored to the needs and ability of the individual or on team projects.

- Team programmes aimed at tackling one particular aspect

of the organization's activities. The best known of these is the 'Quality Circle' which shares much with Action Learning. Denning's 'Total Quality Management' originates from a similar philosophy.

- Working groups, following the work of Drs Coghill and Stewart at the Middlesex Hospital, where the topics for investigation and action are those currently concerning the working group.

One of the special features of many of the Action Learning programmes has been the way in which groups inside organizations have continued to function after the programme has finished. Inevitably, transfers, promotions and resignations eventually break the teams down but, while it may be a subjective judgement, it does appear as though an Action Learning programme cements long-term relationships.

To sum up

This chapter must end where it began, by admitting defeat. The cause of Action Learning has so taken over the work of all forward thinkers in the fields of human resource development that the only way to write this chapter for the third edition will be to copy Beachcomber's famous cab drivers of Huntingdonshire and say, 'Exponents of Action Learning include Aaron C, Aaron G, Abade J, Abba C A, Abbas Dr G . . .'[8] and 3 000 words will be quite inadequate.

References

1 Baquer, A. and Revans, R. W. (1973), *But surely that is their job?*, ALPI.
2 Revans R. W. and Baquer, A. (1972), *I thought they were supposed to be doing that*, King's Fund Centre.
3 Revans, R. W. (1982), *The Origins and Growth of Action Learning*, Ch. 27, Chartwell-Bratt.
4 Casey, M. D. and Pearce, D. J. (eds) (1977), *More than Management Development*, Gower.
5 Gilbert, R. V. (1973),'Action Learning: Public Services', IFAL Newsletter.
6 Lewis, A. and Marsh, W. (1987), 'Action Learning: the development of field managers in the Prudential Assurance Company', *J. Management Development*, **16**(2).

7 Sutton, D. F. (1982), 'Action Learning in Management Consultancy' ALT seminar.
8 Preston Telephone Directory (1989).

9   The mixed set

Martin Hughes

When I began to write this chapter for the first edition I thought maybe I could find a clue on how to approach it from the title of this book *Action Learning in Practice*. When I looked up practice in the dictionary it said (among other things) 'action, performance: actual doing: repeated performance as a means of acquiring skill'. In that last sense perhaps we are still practising Action Learning. Certainly my own involvement in part-time groups of mixed composition over the last ten years has left me with some ideas about the subject which are derived from that experience. Equally though, I am aware of some of the things I do not know – to which I will return later. If and when I begin to lose that and become expert, thinking 'I'm getting competent/-good/slick at this Action Learning set advising business' then I think it will be time for me to stop, for certainly my own learning will have stopped then. For some reason this position does not seem too fashionable for an independent consultant, because people seem to want experts, so sometimes I have to pretend to be one, or at least keep quiet about my doubts and talk instead about previous work.

My initial plan was to offer a biographical account of one set with which I had worked. However, I found that when I started considering the sets I had been involved with over the last ten years it was not easy to pick one as appropriate. The anecdotal gems, worst problems, best outcomes and relevant aspects were spread over them all. Hence I want to try to present a distillation of that experience whilst also giving some details of constants.

Getting started

Following my involvement in an Action Learning set for people trying to initiate sets with Mike Pedler in 1979[1] my intention was to form a set from within my own company. However, whilst I was keen some of my colleagues were less so, and that was not practical and thus a mixed group involving two people from my own organization and a further four others resulted. This was undoubtedly a piece of what I recently heard referred to as 'applied serendipity', for I quickly recognized some of the advantages of this situation of a mixed group, composed of people from totally diverse backgrounds, organizations and disciplines.

Working with strangers, individuals are more open and will self-disclose, or criticize their own organization, more freely than in a more familiar group. Because each member is ignorant about others' organizations he is better able to ask penetrating questions, unhampered by beliefs about the insolubility or inevitability of others' circumstances. Hence, participants feel stretched and find that understanding different organizations aids this. The comments made by participants later in this chapter illustrate these points, and because they have been thus confirmed I have continued to work with this type of group.

Whilst these are good reasons for working with mixed groups, this choice does not eliminate any difficulties, undoubtedly the greatest of which is establishing such groups. I have worked with group sizes from four to nine and consider six to be the ideal number. The idea of assembling a group of six people from different organizations would not appear to be difficult, however, it has always taken much longer than planned – in some cases as much as nine months of visiting people, talking, sending out notes, letters, and explanatory articles, lots of telephoning and protracted discussions, before the group is finally assembled.

Sometimes, after a long period of discussion and encouragement with an initial contact the whole process has to be repeated with prospective participants. Generally, however, they seem to react positively to the idea of learning by taking direct action on real issues. Because of the different starting points, and different rates of 'conversion' it has not been uncommon to have some of the participants' organizations ready and willing to proceed, whilst others are still getting to that point. This has necessitated a 'plate spinning' operation to sustain interest until the quorum of participants is ready to move ahead together.

Typically, a barrier to progress, even once the organization or sponsor is committed, has been the selection of a suitable problem upon which to work. I have always been concerned about the negative connotations of there having to be 'a problem' but there seems to be no other convenient shorthand for what could for me equally acceptably be an issue, an opportunity, a topic or a project. (Project is included only with the proviso that no one should view the objective of the activity as being the production of a project report, since it is too easy for this to be substituted for exposure to the risks of taking action.) I do recognize the importance of perturbation or discontinuity in personal development but do not quite share the conviction that this has to involve pain. Such a self-flagellatory position certainly leaves little place for fun, laughter, or even the unknown. Some examples of 'problems' which have been worked on by participants in mixed groups with which I have worked are given in Figure 9.1.

Thinking about participants' projects, and their self-development, four different developmental effects can be described as follows:

1 Stretching   – a project to extend work skills

2 Rounding   – to develop internal skills, attitudes, or personal growth

3 Broadening   – or exploring new ground

4 Strengthening – to consolidate the foundations upon which existing work skills are based, or perhaps fill gaps.

Managers could perhaps discuss with participants what type of development would be appropriate to them as individuals.

In all the mixed groups the same design has applied. Following a prolonged period of negotiation to secure participation and commitment a two day starter residential session is held. In this, the main aims are to develop familiarity and understanding of others' backgrounds and approaches, to develop group cohesion and commitment, to define or explore the problems or issues upon which individuals will work, to explore individuals learning styles, personal objectives and initial actions, to define relationships, with sponsors, with myself as set adviser, and with each other. Almost, universally, this event has been not only enjoyed

Reducing labour turnover among computer staff in a competitive labour market

Marketing strategy following reorganization by a market leader

Improving information systems and reducing paperwork

Implementing changing computer technology in a major bank

Changing from functional to matrix management

How to offer more services using less money in a small branch library

How to take initiatives in community relations when your 'boss' is a committee with 63 members

Managing four shift supervisors of a continuous process operation, to accommodate considerable differences in their performance

Reducing costs by a predetermined amount

Working on individual self-development projects

Development of communications and trust between a personnel department and other areas of the business

The implications of robotics for the training of maintenance engineering staff at a national level

How to adapt one's style when suddenly promoted to a position of authority over previous peers who are resentful

Establishing an information resource within a training board to meet the needs of all new businesses in a region and industry

Managing a neurotic boss

Coping with vandalism in a training workshop for unemployed, disadvantaged young people

Motivational or supervisory relationships in a number of settings

Trying to encourage national labour mobility

Figure 9.1 Some problems or topics which have been worked on by individuals in part-time Action Learning groups

but recognized as important in building the set for subsequently working together.

After the starter session the groups met at three to four weekly intervals for half day, or sometimes whole day sessions. In these the reflection, discussion and planning of action stages of the learning cycle occur. It is really in the life and fabric of group meetings that for many participants Action Learning comes alive.

Particularly when the group spends time considering its own processes participants seem to take 'quantum steps' in their own development. An example from a meeting of a recent set was 'We are all tending to bring questions and ask for and give answers, rather than stating our own position and using the group to reflect on this'. Inevitably the initially defined problem changes shape and sometimes alters completely during the life of the group. I have tried to illustrate how this happens in Figure 9.2.

I do not know of any ideal length of time groups to go on meeting. It will be influenced by the depth of the problems undertaken, the extent of commitment by participants, sponsors and organizations, and perhaps by money. I do feel that there comes a point in the life of most groups when a law of diminishing returns starts to occur, in terms of individuals learning, and they are of course best qualified to judge this. Groups with which I have worked have met for between five and nine months.

Outcomes

Trying to illustrate or quantify the benefits which participants have found in their groups seems wellnigh impossible. The changes or development of those concerned is, and must be, their own. Thus I propose to try to illustrate this with a series of quotations, of varying lengths, and styles but all direct from participants, in one or two cases slightly paraphrased.

Some participants find difficulty in defining the outcome, but nevertheless feel something:

> I feel I've got something out of it.

> . . . as I had no previous knowledge of AL I was somewhat apprehensive. As it happened I found the experience interesting and useful and without doubt derived benefit from it.

Others feel that they can be more specific and identify learning about themselves:

> I have become more courageous in confronting people . . . and

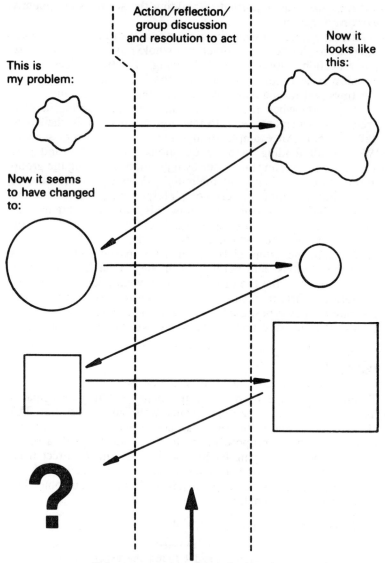

Figure 9.2 The redefinition of the topic at successive stages

aware of some of my resistance to action and me responding to events.

I have seen my problem is me.

. . . increase in expansive thinking and greater confidence.

. . . some knowledge of my effective areas of influence and the importance of working from where you are.

For some it is their learning about organizations and management which is important:

. . . about other people's working environments.

we tend to over-estimate what we can achieve in a political environment – identifying the power points is important.

Conflict relationships can be improved through self disclosure.

Greater awareness of problems of time management.

On the whole I found that Action Learning did enable me to clarify my own management problems and to use the set as a forum for discovering solutions to these problems.

. . . the assumption (which I tended to make) that no one from 'outside' your own organization can really grasp the nature of your problems is false. They can to a surprising degree.

Finally, many participants learn about how they learn, and about aspects of Action Learning:

doing is more important than talking or theory.

. . . some of the problems initially were manufactured rather than real and felt.

That the expectations of the group are a driving force for ensuring that action is taken – and act as an encouragement to stick your neck out a bit.

That some examination or reflection on the group process helps to create an atmosphere of openness and trust which is helpful to the group's achievement, but that there is a need for delicate balance in doing that to ensure that the group is not diverted from its main purpose of problem analysis and action.

AL did not provide the solution to my own task but taking part in the set helped to provide the momentum which took me part way.

The group has helped me to indicate and overcome deficiencies and to clarify my position in the company. Loyalty to the group is important. About my problem I've learnt that it was initially too

wide and not defined clearly enough. Now others are aware of it
and it's not just my problem.

The process of taking action has given me learning.

Undoubtedly there have been those who have not benefited
at all. I can think of two cases where this was something of a
self-fulfilling prophecy of people who were press-ganged into
participation and stated openly at the outset that they had doubts
as to its value but would nevertheless stick with it. They did, to
the bitter end! In another case of little or no learning it was
noted and fed back to the individual concerned that he never
actually did very much. Even though he talked a great deal and
planned various actions these were rarely carried out. I feel that
he knew why he did not get more out of it.

What I do not know about Action Learning

How best to sell it

I find myself saying to prospective participants 'Come with me
and others on an uncharted journey – your destination unknown.
I can't say what you will see, hear or learn on this trip – only
that you will experience it, and that experience may not always
be pleasant'.

To his sponsor or employer I might say 'Give time, money,
encouragement and licence to this person to work with something
which matters considerably to you both. If you encumber him/her
with a trivial item then the benefits to you both will be commensurate with that. There is a risk of failure if you define success
as the solution of that problem, which is as yet unsolved.'

To both sponsor and participant I could say 'You can't really
appreciate what Action Learning is like except by doing it. In
that sense it's like drinking wine, riding a bicycle, or sex. One
can't explain in advance what these will be like, and there are
risks involved – but you'll never know what you're missing until
you try it!'

There seems to be a paradox – that neither will want to do it
unless they can see the potential benefits and that they cannot
see the benefits unless they experience the method first hand.
Involving one or two staff in external groups is a way in which
they can try a 'low risk sample'. In many cases this has been the
seed from which more extensive groups develop later.

Should anyone be trying to encourage its diffusion?

When we do this, it seems to be often through advocacy. I contributed, with others, in 1980 to a publication entitled 'The Diffusion of Action Learning' which largely related experiences of initiation in South Yorkshire and Teeside.[2] In that, Rick Rowell, a fellow member of the initiators group, gave a very powerful trio of descriptions of Action Learning. These were that it can be viewed as a technique, or an item within a management developer's kitbag.[3] Secondly, it can be seen as a theory or explanation of the processes of management. Thirdly and perhaps most significantly, it can be seen as a paradigm, or a way of being in the world. If we accept this last view, then why on earth do we want to 'run' part-time groups or sets? Through doing so we perhaps cement others' visions of Action Learning as only that of a technique, structured or contrived experience – maybe we should instead just allow it to happen.

Now I begin to see a glint of delight in the eyes of many readers. 'Aha!' they say 'I always knew it was only really about just letting people learn by doing! We've been doing that for years only we call it . . .' (insert MBO, project groups, team management, multi-disciplinary project groups, action centred leadership, and so on, according to taste). But I am afraid that will not do for me, because of the reasons which I have already stated for why I find this approach and mixed groups in particular, relevant.

It is nice to envisage a kind of extended set or learning community[4] in which the reality of all experience is the basis for all individual learning and growth. However, how this can be linked to the richness which I feel only external groups can create is a problem to which as yet I do not know the answer. The suggestion is made by Hodgson[5] that advances in information technology could provide this link within an organization. It seems then only a small technical step to link such internal networks to provide mixed sets. Certainly this is intellectually and technologically feasible, but I am not sure that the level of intimacy, trust, or self-disclosure which is beneficial is going to be readily achieved by a relationship conducted via a VDU! (Perhaps that depends on how you feel about your VDU?)

I hope that there are ways in which this kind of cross cultural learning community or Action Learning set could be established without the encumbrance of the technology of structure, dates, times, meetings, etc. whilst also maintaining the discipline of action, reflection, discussion, resolution to act which provides momentum. I do not as yet know exactly how to do this. If anyone does please do not tell me.

These then are some of the things which I do not know about Action Learning in mixed sets. They are my known ignorance. My unknown ignorance is for me a reason for continuing to strive through all the considerable difficulties of establishing and working with these types of group.

I started by asking the question, Why write this? I now think that the reason I have is that I have learned something about Action Learning by doing so. There seems to be a moral in that, about the value of reflection and actual doing. But learning and Action Learning in particular is a social process and I owe a debt of gratitude to all the people with whom I have worked in Action Learning groups. They are now almost too numerous to mention and they are scattered throughout this country, and also the world, but they know who they are, and they have my thanks.

References

1 See Pedler, Mike, (1981) 'The Diffusion of Action Learning', Sheffield City Polytechnic Department of Management Studies, *Occasional Paper*, No. 2, March
2 *ibid*
3 There is a suggestion in the title of one of Reg Revan's recent books that he too holds this view, hence Revans, R. W., (1980) '*Action Learning – New Techniques for Management*' Blond & Briggs
4 See Pedler, Mike, (1981) 'Developing the learning community' in *Management Self Development – concepts and practices*, edited by Tom Boydell and Mike Pedler, Gower, Aldershot
5 Hodgson, T., (1981) 'Stimulating Self-Development, in Boydell and Pedler, ibid.

10   An in-company programme

Alec Lewis

This chapter deals with the initiation, running and evaluation of an in-company Action Learning programme. It reports the stages of building the group and the people involved in the preliminary discussions, and then goes on to describe the meetings of the group. This includes reference to the problem solving activity of the group members, to the way in which individual members contributed to the task and to the emergence of a team approach to the problem. The final two sections of the chapter deal with the assessment of the whole programme, and a consideration by myself of the role I played as set adviser during the life of the group.

Initiation of group

The company from whose staff the Action Learning group was formed is in the textile industry, and the factory in which they work is in South Wales. The company is a large textile group with a wide representation of businesses in the industry. The South Wales factory was one of two factories still organized and managed as a relatively autonomous branch of the group operation. The second factory was in Wiltshire. The sponsor of the Action Learning group was the personnel and training manager of the group company, who had been introduced to the concept and practice of Action Learning at a seminar led by Professor Revans and organized by the South West Regional Management Centre in Bristol. The sponsor became convinced of the potential value of Action Learning and invited me to go to the Wiltshire and South Wales factories to familiarize myself with their operations and to discuss the possibility of establishing an Action Learning group within the business. These discussions further convinced him of the potential of Action Learning to his management and he then identified the client for the group as the production director, who after some questioning and discussion with myself and the sponsor agreed to get a team of people from *one* of the factories to look at a current problem. The identification of a problem presented no difficulty, it was basically one of survival in the highly competitive textile market of today. This was highlighted by the agreement of the client to proceed on the basis of four group meetings only with a review by him of progress at that time before deciding on any further meetings.

The selection staff to form the Action Learning group was carried out by the sponsor and client in consultation with me and a team of eight participants emerged. They were all at a similar level of managerial reponsibility with the exception of the production manager who had been in his post for eighteen months and was senior in rank to the other members. He was directly responsible to the production director – the 'client' of the Action Learning group.

The rest of the members of the group included three forewomen each of whom had responsibility for managing individual production lines and were directly accountable to the production manager. They each had supervisors in their lines. Two managers representing the cutting room were in the group, and a progress manager and warehouse and despatch manageress completed the team.

Apart from the production manager and one of the cutting room managers, all group members had many years of experience with the company and had in fact worked in that factory under different ownership up to some eight years ago. This group therefore represented a cross-section of the production side of the business.

The problem

Although the single word 'survival' would sum up the company's problem at the briefing meeting addressed by the production director, the problem which the group was to devote its attention to was described as:

> We need to improve overall performance. The order book is not healthy at the moment, we have to become more effective in order to keep our prices competitive. We are fine on quality but falling down on deliveries; our production flow is erratic. You are the people who can improve the productivity. How are you going to do it?

He then went on to introduce the concept of Action Learning and the set adviser who in turn explained his role as that of the 'external catalyst' and not the consultant with the magic formula to solve the company's problem.

At this stage there was very much the look of *déja-vu* on the faces of the prospective participants, and an impression of 'acceptance of the inevitable' was prevalent in the rather stilted discussion that followed the briefing. However, all participants finished this session with the commitment to 'give it a go'.

The first four meetings were scheduled as half-day meetings at fortnightly intervals to be held at the factory.

Reflections on the initiation of the group

In this case, which is little different from my other Action Learning initiation experiences, it had taken over six months to get the group started, and this was with an enthusiastic sponsor! Without his enthusiasm the task would have been impossible. His keenness and interest in Action Learning had originated through contacts he had in two different Industrial Training Boards. They had attended various meetings at the South West Regional Management Centre one of which had specifically been organized to discuss the concept and practice of Action Learning. The sponsor met me on two occasions to discuss the concept and how it might be applied to his company, then attended a seminar addressed by Professor Revans in Bristol. This finally convinced him that he should 'have a go'. Five visits later, including two with the client present, and several internal company meetings later the decision to try it on the basis of four meetings then a review was taken.

Looking back it is hard to see how any short cuts could have been taken. The sponsor had to identify the client, the client needed convincing that one of his problems might be capable of being treated in this rather different way, and both had to discuss at some length the composition of the group, In fact this preparatory work is almost as important as the actual group work. There is a lot of anxiety about at this stage and removing at least some from the sponsor and client is an important role for the set adviser. Some fundamental factors which helped to overcome the anxieties of the sponsor in this project were that (a) *he* retained 'control' of the process and (b) he had in fact an important part to play in the exercise. However, it may be more important to help them to 'live with their anxieties' because building false hopes of possible outcomes would be to totally defeat the objectives of the exercise.

The first four meetings

Meeting No. 1

The first meeting started with a restatement of the principles of Action Learning; that this was an opportunity for these people to develop themselves in the context of the problem solving exercise on which they were about to embark. There was obvious anxiety around the table because of the novelty of the situation, and the breadth of the task which was facing them.

Each member of the group was invited to describe their own personal view of the problem and to indicate whether or not they agreed that the difficulties outlined by the client in his brief were the major issues needing solution. In view of the fact that this was fairly obviously the first such opportunity to make such a statement any member of the group had experienced and furthermore were now being invited to express this view in public, it was surprising how honest and open the responses were. A sample of some of the actual statements used may serve to illustrate the nature of these responses and the attitudes held by the participants at this early stage of the exercise.

Forewoman (1): There is nothing more frustrating than running out of trimmings, it's happening all the time.
Forewoman (2): If we waited till all materials and trimmings were here we would never start.

Warehouse manager:	We are always short of a few garments at the end of an order.
Progress manager:	Other manufacturers let us down.
Cutting Room manager:	This is the wrong sort of work for this factory.
Forewoman (3):	Things aren't explained to us – orders are moved from our lines half way through.
Forewoman (1):	We've got all the worst work. (cf. other company factory in Wiltshire).
Forewoman (1):	There's a feeling out there that we cannot survive.
Production manager:	The current financial instability cannot go on.
Forewoman (2):	We get told this every week.
Forewoman (1) (about the Production Manager):	He's so little I can never find him when I want him.

These selected statements from the set advisers scribbled *aide-mémoire* summarise in fairly clear terms the frustrations of the participants all of whom with the exception of the production manager, and one of the cutting room managers, had worked in the factory in the 'good years' when very large orders were the norm, facilitating long and therefore smooth production runs.

However, by the end of the first meeting it was recognized that small orders were a fact of life, and although all the evidence from this meeting suggested to the adviser that no one in the group admitted ownership of the problem, there was some agreement with the suggestions from the production manager at the end of the meeting that:

1   He would discuss with him individually their job descriptions. (Some lack of understanding of them had been revealed in the discussion).

2   This might lead to a change in the current system which meant that seventeen people reported direct to the production manager.

3   An investigation into work flow in the cutting room – and the resources of that room.

He concluded his summary by asking members to think about how they might capitalize on the spirit engendered at this meeting.

Meetings 2, 3 and 4

Although the second meeting started by picking up the specific points from the first which had required action, the discussion soon developed into a repeat of the first meeting with every individual providing anecdotal evidence of the inefficiences of those parts of the system for which he/she was not responsible. This prompted an intervention by the set adviser to look at the work that had been done on job descriptions since the last meeting. This did focus the attention of all participants who agreed that they needed to understand the responsibilities of each function, even if the recognition of the need was revealed through fairly basic observations, for example, the chiding remark from one of the forewomen to the cutting room manager who was supporting the case for a clear job description and for people to know the extent of their responsibilities. She said, 'Let's be fair, R . . . , I've seen you pulling a truck!' This summed up the difficulties in the factory with every member of the group going well outside the range of those activities which were central to their function in order to keep their function 'ticking over'.

By the start of the third meeting each participant had prepared a concise statement of their key roles in the organization and these were discussed in some depth. Inevitably perhaps, the next topic to appear on their agenda was the external factors to their system which could and did upset the smooth running of the factory. The question 'Who makes these promises?' in relation to delivery dates, highlighted the frustrations being felt on the factory floor where so many 'hiccups' were being experienced. One outcome of this discussion however was a recognition by the group that they each had individual responsibilities which were closely linked and even though external factors could sometimes be blamed for loss of production, there were several internal problems with which they should be concerned. This 'consensus' appeared during the debate on the job descriptions for the three forewomen members. Although they described several instances of activities 'we do automatically' – which on reflection could be handled by the supervisors they were in broad agreement on the sections' objectives, namely,

1 To produce agreed quantity to agreed quality

2 To remain within cost limits

3 To meet delivery dates.

These objectives were used as the basis for a discussion on their individual job descriptions. No attempt was made to write them, but again, broad agreement was reached on the scope of their activities from discipline and wage queries to utilization of machinery, identification of problem, of make-up, and liaison with other functions, particularly cutting room, quality control and work study.

The last of the first four sessions was in some ways the most 'intensive' partly because the sponsor was due to meet the group at the end of the meeting to hear the progress reports, but partly because the group was beginning to function, working on current issues which were causing problems in the factory.

Thus, the first hour was devoted to the 'recent problem'. The cutting room came in for some sharp criticism from the forewomen because of an increase in the number of re-cuts and an apparent lack of urgency being given to this task in the cutting room. Interestingly, although the comments were critical and direct, they were accompanied by suggested solutions from the forewomen, for example, take all re-cuts back to original cutter rather than have all re-cuts done by one person. This, it was suggested, may have a psychological impact on the cutter and may help to improve his efforts. This led to a fairly heated discussion of the current general problems in the cutting area of the factory including resources, systems of bundling, checking delivery to production lines. The progress manager made an important contribution here as a dispassionate, neutral observer. The cutting room manager promised to change the current re-cut procedure, and to ensure that his team followed the agreed bundling and checking procedure.

The second part of the meeting was devoted to a debate on the latest production report with the latest financial report on the factory's performance in the previous month. This appeared to be a relatively new opportunity for some group members to comment on the figues. Inevitably, the question of relatively small batch productions was raised as an excuse for the poor overall performance. Two members of the group suggested representatives of the marketing function should be invited to the meetings.

Group review meeting with sponsor and client

At the end of the fourth meeting the sponsor and client joined the group to review its activities and to decide if a further four meetings should take place.

The set adviser had invited the group to consider the following questions to report on to the production director.

1 Identify any changes in individual behaviour or practice with the group discussions had set in motion.

2 Identify any changes in behaviour or practice which may still be needed but which requires further investigation and/or other people's authority.

3 Identify what this group might continue to do without the presence of an external set adviser.

The spontaneous remarks made by group members to the production director encouraged him to believe that the exercise was perhaps *beginning* to show some benefits in that: members were talking *positively* about actions that were starting as a result of the discussions – the *recut problem* was being resolved; changes in systems of bundling and recording at intermediate stages of production were under way, and the progress manager was involved in reintroducing a modified system of production control which had once seemed to be helpful to group members.

The group reported that having an 'outsider' as group adviser was important, because they felt that they could be more honest and critical, and because they felt 'different' from when they were in their normal production meetings. A further four half-day meetings were sanctioned.

Summary of the remainder of the meetings

In fact, after the second group of four meetings a further three were held to complete the programme, which finished on the instructions of a newly-appointed finance director who decided to temporarily cut back on all 'non-essential' expenditure.

The second part of the proceedings of the group followed three phases: 1 frustration, 2 consolidation of the first four meetings, and 3 action.

The frustration phase is in part a description I give to the dominant attitude of some of the group members, but perhaps is also a reflection of the feelings I had as set adviser at this stage of the proceedings. Several factors were contributing to my dissatisfaction with progress. As reported above, it was only at the seventh meeting that the contributions of members moved significantly away from the anecdotal towards the more constructive comments. Although the client had responded very favourably to their report at the end of the fourth meeting, the fifth and sixth sessions were characterized more by a resumption of individuals criticizing the rest of the organization rather than attempting to view the problem as one common to them all. Part of the reason may have been the presentation of another set of disappointing profitability figures at the fifth meeting.

My notes at the end of the sixth meeting may serve to illustrate my own impressions at that time, and also to explain what the group was doing which reflected its own frustration. I made these notes while travelling home from the meeting in order to clarify my own thoughts on what was happening. The heading for these notes was 'Impressions of the group after 6 sessions'.

A Limited success

1   Some learning – in the form of getting to know the whole system and beginning to know the whole system and beginning to admit that 'others have problems'.

2   Another positive sign – showing signs of willingness to admit to own problems and to allow critical examination of reasons for these by other group members.

3   Another positive feature – some problems were actually being tackled – particularly the recent problem. Several group members suggesting practical ways of resolving this one.

B Difficulties – 'failures'

1   Still more willing to talk than 'do'.

2   Some evidence of two individuals not feeling able or willing to contribute.

3   Still too prone to get sidetracked.

4   Feeling growing of fatal inevitability that 'the problems are beyond us'.

These summary notes reflect my anxieties and these are not peculiar to this Action Learning group. The set adviser is prone to get impatient, and to want to see action before a group is ready to move.

These feelings prompted me to talk over the progress of the group with the sponsor and together we decided that we should wait for the seventh meeting of the group where I would intervene on two counts. First, I should ask what specific progress had been made on a job description exercise, and second, I should direct some questions particularly at the two group members who had 'under-performed' in meetings five and six.

In fact the seventh meeting was much more encouraging. Following my introductory questions, all members of the group made positive contributions and within half an hour of the start all members of the group were initiating points of argument and discussion. Even the production manager who had sometimes in earlier meetings lapsed into a chairman's role, was willing and able to accept no more than a fair share of the discussion time. By the time of the eighth and ninth meetings the contributions were less anecdotal and more positively directed towards constructive criticism or suggestions as to how current systems needed amendment. One of the more positive results from this phase was the identification of the need to allow 'supervisors to supervise'.

The three forewomen in the group were taking definite steps to improve their supervisors' knowledge of what was going on, and to delegate to them certain tasks which they had tended to 'hold on to' during the current difficulties. One reported that 'they (the supervisors) are thinking better for themselves now'.

The 'action' phase began between the ninth and tenth meetings. Two significant events changed the course of the group, one external to the group and one intimately connected with it. The first was the successful bid by the company for a large contract to supply uniforms to a large public undertaking. This provided a very positive motivation to the whole group, who had in part blamed the absence of such large orders for the current poor productivity of the factory.

The second event was the resignation of the cutting floor manager who had been a member of the group, and who had been recruited only eight months earlier. Although this decision cannot be directly attributed to the work of the group, the examination of problems and bottlenecks in the factory had repeatedly focused on the cutting room. Group members had proffered several suggestions as to ways the cutting room might overcome some of its problems and the decision of the manager to resign may have indicated his unwillingness or inability to change procedures. The outcome was the appointment of an existing member of staff to the role of cutting floor manager and the ensuing meetings concentrated on accommodating the newly-won business within the changing systems which the group were initiating during this phase.

Assessment of problem solving activity and personal/team development

The diary of meetings summarized above may have indicated little that could be considered to have been problem solving activity. Certainly at the end of the first four meetings the set adviser's summary of progress which I prepared for my own purposes indicated that little real action was occurring between the fortnightly meetings. However, with hindsight, it was apparent that what was happening during this introductory phase was that the group was building itself into a team, albeit very gradually. The eventual acceptance by the group that the problem was one for which they had some responsibility, and for which they should be able to contribute at least a partial solution, was something of a breakthrough. Certainly by the end of the tenth meeting individuals in the group were displaying a willingness to contribute ideas, and practical suggestions for solving minor 'system' problems. They were also trying these out between meetings and reporting back on their progress. The tendency to use the meetings to provide more anecdotal evidence of where the system was failing did die hard. The production of a set of disappointing performance figures in the fifth meeting was all that was needed to push the group members back to their defensive positions, as was reported above. However, in their verbal report to the client, individual members attempted to describe the benefits of working in this group. They chose to do this by contrasting the Action Learning group meetings with their routine Monday production meetings.

The main difference appeared to be that at the latter most of them felt they were there to listen, whereas in the Action Learning group they had *eventually* believed that the production manager was listening to them. Certainly, improved communication between group members and particularly between individuals and the production manager was the major improvement recorded.

The second main difference was that eventually group members were accepting responsibility for action on matters they discussed during the Action Learning meetings, whereas at the regular Monday meetings they felt they were there to receive instructions. They were obviously more committed to taking action on those ideas which were their own or which they had accepted as a result of group meetings, than they were to accept instructions which did not always appear to them to be logical.

One of the benefits which individuals agreed on was that as a result of the lengthy discussions in group meetings on the theme of their individual responsibilities to the team was that they were much clearer on who the 'decision takers' were. There was scope they felt for widening this discussion to include managers who had not been in the group.

The role of the set adviser

Planning and briefing One of the most important parts the set adviser has to play on in-company projects of this sort, is in the planning stages. Constant close contact with the sponsor and then with the client is vital in order to ensure that a complete understanding of the Action Learning process has been achieved among senior management. Then the advice which is needed on problem selection and on who should form the group is an essential contribution from the set adviser. Briefing group members is a vital pre-requisite to an effective group, both by the client, to ensure that the scope of the problem is understood, and by the set adviser to clarify his role and the Action Learning method.

Group meetings The role of set adviser appears to change quite significantly between different groups, and also between different meetings of the same group. In the case of the group described in this chapter, I operated sometimes as chairman, sometimes as catalyst and sometimes simply as observer.

Chairman In the early stages of the group I felt the need to 'set the agenda', using notes I had jotted down from the previous meetings. I also made efforts to include those who tended to be 'low contributors'. Another feature of this 'Chairman's' role was that had I not taken it, it would have naturally fallen on the shoulders of the production manager.

Catalyst Intervention under this heading tended to be more prevalent in the early stages, and was particularly aimed at moving people out of the anecdotal into the analytical mode of behaviour. Thus, regular questions of a factual nature I found were needed to get the group into the position where they could stand back from the daily routine problems and look at the overall situation.

Observer This is the important passive role of the adviser, where one concentrates on the group process as well as what is being said. It is from these observations that one decides whether or not to intervene as a 'chairman' 'catalyst' or some other role which may be appropriate.

Reflections on this group and my role as set adviser

This neat subdivision of the role between chairman, catalyst and observer does suggest a fairly clear definition of the task of a set adviser. However, looking back at this group I can see that there were times when for example I adopted the role of chairman when it might have been of greater benefit for the group to find its own way. One fundamental question which I had in my mind at the end of the project was, 'Did I get the members of the Group to adequately reflect on their own learning?' My efforts in this connection were largely devoted to getting them each to describe how the group meetings varied from the other in-company meetings they attended. Their responses to this indicated a general awareness of a difference in attitude which they felt they brought to the group meetings. They believed that they could be open and critical with each other, and that their views were being seriously considered by the production manager (and sponsor). My informal contacts with the client in the ensuing twelve months suggested that one of the results of the project was to create a more participative and open style of management in the company, as far as this group of managers was concerned. As set adviser I should perhaps have attempted to arrange a follow-up meeting of the group some six months after it had stopped its formal meetings. This would have enabled the group to reflect on its own learning by critically examining any changes in style which may have occurred, with particular emphasis on whether any such change had had any impact on effectiveness.

This raises another question for a set adviser to an 'in-company' group. The follow-up should perhaps include discussions with the sponsor and client on how the organization as a whole might assimilate the learning of the Action Learning group. In the group described in this chapter this was made virtually impossible because all the group members were closely related to the production function. There were special reasons for this, but the learning for the 'organization as a whole' was limited considerably by this design.

In summary, as set adviser to this group, I have confirmed to myself that the role is multi-faceted; that it requires a large degree of adaptability, that it provides a significant level of frustration, but that overall, the evidence of individual managers becoming more confident in their own capacity to manage, makes it a role that can be very rewarding.

11 Supervisory development

David Boddy

Editor's note
Strictly defined, action learning must involve some implementation
of action on problems by participants, and the programme
described here does not fulfil this requirement. However, it is
included as a useful example of the application of action learning
to supervisory development – a level of management who often
have responsibility without the commensurate power to act.

The chapter outlines the use of Action Learning to assist the
development of supervisors. The programme took place in a
rapidly growing semi-conductor plant, and over 70 staff have
now taken part in the activity. Using Action Learning for, in
effect, the first level of management is in itself a relatively
unusual application, and the programme is interesting for this
reason alone. More generally the experience of this event provides some insight into questions which are relevant in the design
of any Action Learning programme such as:

1 What were the effects of the programme and how did these
  relate to its purposes?

2 What kinds of support can senior management give to a
  programme of this nature, and how does this affect the
  results?

3   What criteria should be borne in mind when selecting pro-
    jects appropriate to a group taking into account their par-
    ticular environment?

4   How should set advisers balance the need for good project
    results and for effective learning, if these should sometimes
    appear to be in conflict?

The origins of the programme and its main features are
described, followed by an examination of each of these questions.

The origins and design of the programme

The company manufactured semi-conductor devices and their
output and employment had grown rapidly. The number of foremen and forewomen had grown correspondingly but very few
had been given any formal company training for their supervisory
posts. Some, mainly the forewomen, had started in the plant as
operators and had worked up through the ranks to their present
jobs: thus they had no training in supervision but were well
aware of the mechanics of the present systems and of the people
in the company. The others, mainly foremen, had been recruited
from other companies. Some had previous supervisory experience but were not familiar with this company's ways of doing
things and its expectations of them.

Having recognized that some form of supervisory development
programme was required, the company decided on an Action
Learning approach. There were two main reasons for this
decision. The project based learning was expected to appeal
more to the practical outlook of the supervisors than a traditional
course would have done. More fundamentally Action Learning
is usually seen as a means of developing people's ability to deal
effectively with change and uncertainty – both of which are
among the dominant characteristics of the semi-conductor
industry.

Within that framework the present activity began with a
briefing meeting attended by the managing director and by senior
and middle managers. The proposed form of the development
programme was outlined, the managing director gave his public
support, and the ideas presented were clarified and discussed
with those present. The managers were then asked to nominate
supervisors to take part in the programme and also to provide
suitable projects upon which the participants could work in the
Action Learning phase.

On account of the large number of potential participants, the total activity was conducted in a series of distinct programmes, each to the same design. About 14 supervisors took part in each programme, working as two distinct groups during the Action Learning phase. Each such programme was in two parts. The first was a four day off-site course, designed to introduce the participants to a number of basic ideas relevant to the supervisory role – communication, motivation, group dynamics and so on. The approach was highly participative, using a variety of experiential methods. This exposed the supervisors to a number of relevant ideas about the managerial aspects of their work. It also helped to create an atmosphere of trust and a willingness to work together which was helpful in initiating and sustaining the second part of the programme.

This second part was the Action Learning phase. On the last day of the off-site course, participants were introduced to the basic ideas of Action Learning, and the way in which these ideas would be used in the rest of the programme. (A third phase was introduced in some programmes consisting of short courses in particular skills, such as appraisal interviewing. These are not however discussed further here.)

The projects

Action Learning has normally been based on a series of individual projects with each participant working independently, except when meeting with other members of their group to review progress. Here since many supervisors were to be taking part within the company individual projects were impractical. It was therefore decided to operate group projects: participants were divided into groups of about seven members and each group worked on a single project.

Care was taken in forming groups to mix membership in terms of areas and functional responsibilities. Similarly in defining projects efforts were made to ensure that each group received a project with whose subject members were relatively unfamiliar. The topics all related to current issues facing the organization. For example:

1 Examine and define the existing general stores system and recommend improvements.

2 What do company managers see as the current development needs of their supervisors?

3 Examine the various communications techniques currently used in the plant and recommend changes.
How to promote quality consciousness in the plant.

Time

The participants were expected to carry out the projects on a part-time basis over a period of three to four months. In the earlier programmes senior managers had agreed to release staff from their normal work for at least six half days during the Action Learning phase of the programme. Obviously more time would be required – but this was left to be negotiated between the supervisors and their managers or to be created outside of normal working hours. In later programmes however no specific time commitment was given – all work had to be interspersed with normal duties or completed after hours.

Advisers

Each group of supervisors had allocated to it one of the senior managers in the company who was to act as an adviser to the group. It was made clear that they would not be expected to provide direct help on the project itself but would focus on the way the group was going about the task, helping them to reflect on their own work and activities, and to draw relevant lessons from the experience. It was recognized at the beginning of the programme that it would be desirable to avoid any adviser being a boss of one of the members of the group. As the programmes continued and extended throughout the company it became more difficult to maintain this principle and there were some situations where a senior manager acting as an adviser had a subordinate in the group.

After being briefed on these points the groups began organizing their work on the project which culminated in presentations about four months later.

Phases of the programme

Clearly a detailed account of events cannot be given, but a number of observations which seem significant to the writer can be made. Action Learning can be visualized as a cyclical activity involving three main phases: diagnosis, action and review in order to learn. What stands out about the groups' activities under these headings?

Diagnosis

The diagnostic phase essentially began with an initial client meeting, with the 'client' (i.e. the senior manager who had given the project). At this meeting participants began to clarify the problem and the client's expectations. This invariably gave new insights into the project, as well as defining it more narrowly; both of which enabled the groups to begin planning more precisely the kind of thing which they would need to investigate.

A notable feature was the considerable effort which participants put into gathering and analysing information relating to the project. The process of designing and conducting interviews and questionnaires not only helped the groups in specific task terms, but was also a source of learning. In particular it showed up some points about communication, and about getting the commitment of others, both of which were among the underlying objectives of the programme as a whole.

Action

The essence of this approach of learning is that some concrete action is taken on the problem under review as a basis for greater understanding. The project groups here clearly engaged in much diagnostic action and in the preparation of their recommendations. But the programme was designed to conclude with recommendations to senior management for further action. In several cases a significant proportion of these recommendations were subsequently accepted by management and put into effect. This is however a different process from that in which participants not only make recommendations, but also take on the messy process of implementation and evaluation.

Review

The purpose of the review phase in the Action Learning cycle is to allow reflection to take place: to examine what has happened and to draw out any insights or lessons from those events. As such, it is not an activity restricted to the end of the project, but is something which can usefully occur at relevant points throughout the project work. One of the functions of the group meetings is to provide the occasion for this kind of exploration.

In this case the groups found difficulty in setting aside specific blocks of time for this reflective process. The emphasis was heavily on the discussion of the project itself; and as soon as that had been satisfactorily dealt with, the attention of members clearly turned to the many work activities which required urgent attention. As the group meetings were held on-site, these activities were also physically close, making it all the more difficult to engage in deliberate review and reflection. Nevertheless, it was clear that new ideas were being picked up and in some cases consciously acted upon by the group members. In other words, the reflection phase was being interspersed with those of diagnosis and action, presumably an entirely natural learning process.

Some issues raised by the programme

Having described the broad structure of the programme, we now return to the four questions we posed at the beginning.

1 What were the effects of the programme?

Since the projects were the focus of the programme activities it is worth trying to assess the extent to which these resulted in specific changes being introduced. The principal recommendations from six project teams were analysed to assess how many of their recommendations had been put into action. Of the eighteen main recommendations no action had been taken on six, while the remaining twelve had resulted in some specific action. These ranged from relatively simple ideas like improving the induction training of new employees, to more complex proposals regarding the redesign of some company systems. However, the participants themselves expressed some disappointment about the degree to which their recommendations had been accepted and implemented by senior management, so there is some doubt about the extent to which significant project changes occurred.

Most participants were interviewed to establish the kinds of benefits which they felt they had achieved from the programme. These included such things as:

1 gaining an insight into working with other people;

2 becoming more conscious of other people's points of view;

3 establishing working contacts with people in other parts of the factory;

4 becoming more skilful in working as a member of a group;

5 becoming more confident in dealing with others.

All of these are valuable areas of personal development and there was sufficient corroborative evidence to support the view expressed by participants that they had changed to some extent the way in which they performed their duties.

What is less certain is whether they had learned, and retained, significant new ideas and practices about dealing with change. This theme is often cited as one of the benefits of Action Learning and one which seemed to be consistent with the needs of this particular business. However, the development of skill in this area may have been inhibited in this programme by two factors. The first is one which we have already mentioned and relates to the fact that the main implementation of recommendations was left to be dealt with by management, rather than as an integral part of the project team's work. A second point is that many participants expressed the view that some of the enthusiasm generated during the course was dissipated when they found that their normal jobs had not changed in the period covered by the programme, and that there appeared to be no particular enhancement to their promotion prospects. In other words they had received little practice during the programme in bringing about change, and their existing jobs had not been expanded sufficiently to provide more opportunities for practising such skills.

2 What support should senior managers give to a programme?

It is commonplace to say that senior management needs to demonstrate its support for activities of this kind, but from the experience of this programme it is possible to suggest some more specific ways in which this support can be expressed. The first requirement seems to be that sufficient time must be allocated for the participants to make significant progress on their project during working hours. If, as in the later versions of this programme, management does not allocate a noticeable amount of working time to the activity, and by implication expects it to be done in addition to participants' normal work or in their spare time, this will be seen by participants as indicating a low level of commitment.

A second requirement is that the projects are significant business problems. There was some evidence that participants believed that projects had been put forward as something to do, rather than as reflecting a critical problem. There is clearly a difficulty where managers are expected to allow the use of critical issues for training purposes; but the alternative risk is that the projects are seen as trivial by participants and their commitment declines. A further point is that managers need to be prepared to take the comments of the project groups seriously even if they are moving into risky or controversial areas. There was at least one example in this project where a project team's recommendations were blocked at one stage when it appeared that the sensibilities of managers in a particular department were being offended.

Finally some participants indicated that their bosses had not expressed much interest in their progress on the course, or in what they were learning. Moreover, participants also felt that their jobs had not changed in proportion to the developments they believed had taken place in their own skills. Unrealistic expectations may be involved here, but this only serves to emphasize the things a trainee's manager needs to do to create an appropriate environment for the training activity.

3 What makes a good project?

Several of the projects carried out in the programme served to highlight the advantages of carefully considering criteria for selecting projects. A checklist of questions for project selection could cover such questions as 'Will it involve the participant in bringing about change?' 'How highly committed is the client to the success of the project?' 'Is implementation within the authority of the plant?'

The most successful projects in this programme corresponded closely to these criteria, while others seem to have had serious difficulties. We have already discussed the problems of implementation, and the successful projects tended, for example, to be ones in which participants were able to introduce some changes in the course of their work as well as producing recommendations for others.

The main difficulty, and one which seems highly relevant to other circumstances, concerns the authority of managers in a plant to introduce or even to decide upon any changes that may be recommended.

Where, as in this case, a factory is part of an international organization, there are many areas of company policy which cannot be changed by local management. Projects which are likely to involve participants in making recommendations which push against the limits of local autonomy are probably unsuitable. The benefits of learning about wider power constraints need to be weighed against the perceived waste of effort in making unusable proposals.

4 How should advisers balance the task and learning aspects of their role?

A distinctive feature of this programme was the use of senior managers as set advisers to the project groups. There are financial advantages in using internal advisers in a programme of this sort and also more scope for integrating learning with the normal activities of the business. However, the comments of the participants during an evaluation suggest that two issues need careful attention if the benefits of internal advisers are to be fully realized.

The first is to ensure that they are properly briefed about the nature of their role, and ideally they will have themselves worked as a participant in an Action Learning or similar kind of programme. The second point is that they must be able to distinguish between producing an effective task or project result and helping to bring about effective learning by the participant. Several comments were made which implied that set advisers had tended to emphasize the former without perhaps being fully aware of its implications for the latter. For example set advisers who are seeking a good task result may unconsciously suggest courses of action to participants to help them overcome difficulties in the shortest possible time, whereas effective learning may come about if the participants get into difficulties and find their own solutions.

Clearly there is a danger when using internal advisers that they will come to 'own' the projects, particularly when they know that the final presentations will be made in the presence of other senior managers. It is understandable that they will feel that on such an occasion they will be as much a subject of evaluation as the project or the project team, and that task results will be more visible than learning results. It seems clear that the role of the adviser needs careful consideration and briefing if its potential is to be realized.

Conclusions

The programme outlined in this chapter has clearly indicated the possibilities of using Action Learning for in-plant supervisory development. The benefits are almost certainly greater and longer lasting than we would expect from comparable effort being put into conventional training courses.

To the extent that it has had its limitations, these seem to be related to factors like the amount of time available, the willingness or otherwise to move from recommendations to action, and the advisers perceived emphasis on task performance rather than on learning and exploration. Perhaps these issues reflect the practical, or political, realities of balancing a potentially open and risky learning process with a fundamental desire of senior management to keep things running smoothly and predictably.

12 Improving management morale and efficiency

Norman Brown

The first John Tann Security Ltd Action Learning experiment was based on its Billericay Works. A management action group consisting of four executive managers met part-time over the period Autumn, 1977 to Spring, 1978. The group took as its problem the need to increase output at the plant by 15 per cent without increasing labour or investment.

The utilization of direct labour during the first three months of 1978 compared with both the first quarter and the average for the whole of 1977 showed an increase of 11 per cent. It is felt that the management action group contributed significantly to this result although it is recognized that there were other influences at work.

The works director who sponsored the project, the four participants and the set adviser all agree that there were significant changes in team attitudes and considerable development of the four participants' management skills.

In March 1982 a review of the set was carried out with the works director and the four participants who were all still in the same jobs. This offered an unusual opportunity to look back over four years and to put the work of the set in perspective. Productivity figures continued to rise over the intervening years although it was also less and less possible to ascribe this to Action Learning as more intervening factors were involved. The clearest and most obvious effects standing the test of time were in terms of the development of the individuals as managers, with considerable improvements in team work and also union-management relationships.

The company

The Company makes bank safes, vaults, fire safes and enclosures for the new self-service banking systems. Customers are the High Street Banks, The Bank of England and The Royal Mint, and John Tann supplies almost 50 per cent of the UK market. 40 per cent of company turnover is derived from export markets.

The company employs over 1,000 people on two major sites and is strongly unionized. The technology is heavy metal fabrication and the present group consists of companies some of which were founded in the last century. Current turnover is well above £10 million pounds.

Tann's challenge

There were a number of particular problems facing the directors of John Tann Security:

1 *Fashions of the market place*: Even the world of financial security has its fashions! The most favoured locks and exterior styling in the UK are not *de rigueur* in North America or the Middle East.

2 *Varying mix*: There are a number of different standard products. One range of standard products alone can be in as many as 5 or 6 sizes each with a multiplicity of security features.

3 *Small batches*: The two factors mentioned above militate against economies of scale. There are too many production lines producing too few units.

4 *Fluctuating pound and payment difficulties*: The export turnover of 40 per cent produced its own problems. The fluctuating pound made quoting long term very difficult and altered the competitive position of the company in an arbitrary manner. Additionally, some foreign economies were beset by balance of payment problems resulting in slow transfer of funds.

All the above problems added up to increased pressure on Tann's trading margins and they were actively investigating areas for improvement.

Tann's needs

One primary need was to increase both output and efficiency at the production unit located at Billericay. The board also wished to develop the management potential available at the site. Labour and management had no reputation for successfully pulling together.

The directors' management philosophy

The board had been successful for some years in developing participative management techniques with the unions and in providing a generous industrial relations package.

It was also felt that often good ideas in a company do not originate at board level but are the brain children of senior management. The directors were hoping to establish an environment from which Crown Princes would emerge and ideas would flow upwards through the company structure.

Decision

Norman Wilson, the recently appointed works director of the Billericay Unit, felt that the increased efficiency would result primarily from the development of his team of line managers. He was inclined towards Action Learning concepts and in October, 1977, he decided with main board approval to initiate a management action group at Billericay, choosing as the participants the line managers on whom production most directly depended.

The Tann management action group

The four line managers chosen to form the group were; the production control manager, the production engineering manager, the technical manager and the workshop superintendent. It is important to note that the technical manager who controlled a drawing office at Billericay, was the main liaison with customers' special requirements and had a 'dotted line' responsibility back to the technical director at Borehamwood where the Head Office and most other company functions were located.

The problem was 'How best to increase output and efficiency?' and at its second meeting the group asked for a quantified target and this was set by the sponsoring director at 15 per cent.

The management group adviser, who attended all meetings, was Norman Brown, South Eastern Co-ordinator for the Institution of Works Managers.

Tann management action group format

The group made its own rules and we decided at the beginning to meet for about four hours on the same afternoon each week. This day was made as inviolate as humanly possible and diaries were marked for six months ahead. The first meeting was held on 25 October, 1977, and the twenty third meeting which saw the departure of the group adviser was held on 18 April, 1978. Holidays had postponed several meetings and spread the time scale a little.

The group met in Billericay at the works and although interruptions were minimal, they occasionally obtruded and the participants arrived straight from the trenches with immediate problems in mind. A short journey would have been a psychological advantage as well as providing a communications barrier!

Initial attitudes

Morale among the participants had been low for some considerable time. They had little faith in any improvement and even less in their ability to influence their own or their company's fortunes. They were four individuals with no team identity and scant loyalty to each other, whose relationships were rooted in insecurity.

The attitude to the company was tinged with suspicion although at heart they were still John Tann men. Their director was new to them and an unknown quantity while the Billericay Works had always seemed isolated from the seat of power. The four line managers were unanimous however on one point – their frank scepticism regarding the management action group and its likely efficiency! The group adviser was at first regarded by at least one participant as an irrelevant academic.

The development of the Action Learning group

Four major phases are discernible as we look back on the changing behaviour of the management action group and all five of us, participants and adviser, accept this analysis.

Phase one: first 3/4 meetings

Much of the discussion consisted of post mortems on two-year-old crises, and past failures and confrontations with the union. A great deal of time was spent on comparative trivia and the needle jumped back into familiar grooves at the slightest cue. The gloom was at times gothic and even the cactus in the ladies rest room (where we met) took on a menacing aspect! This apparent waste of time was probably inevitable as the resentments emerged, and the hobby horses ran themselves into the ground.

Phase two: weeks 5-9

New relationships began to form between four familiar colleagues who were meeting regularly in a fresh environment. There were no representatives of those twin millstones, the board and the union. The group adviser, no longer regarded as a creature of the board, began to blend with the wallpaper. The morale improved strongly when the group identified major bottle-necks in the production process. There was a noticeable tendency to enjoy the luxury of going over last week's successes and rediscovering a solution for the second time: it was a pleasant change.

A team loyalty emerged and was a shade self-conscious in the early days. Honest and constructive criticism of colleagues was sometimes muted in case new relationships were destroyed. The set adviser realized that the participants were beginning to look forward to the weekly action group meetings.

Phase three: weeks 10-14

The team began to grow into an effective unit. There was much less defensive reaction and their own self-discipline kept meetings on the rails for most of the time. The participants now accepted criticism and felt secure enough as a unit to criticise each other. Motivation was strengthened by the successes of curing some of the production problems and there was a slow upward trend in output. The improvements were by no means even and some weeks we seemed to go backwards.

Phase four: weeks 15-23

The positive trends continued with behavioural patterns reinforced. The output improvement was now firm. The participants decided to invite their works director to join in from meeting 20 onwards. The confusion between the strategic aims of the management action group and the regular weekly production meetings was finally resolved. Continuation was assured and is discussed later in this chapter.

Effectiveness and motivation

John Tann Security had suffered for some years with a costly problem. It concerned quality and availability of a crucial item purchased. No solution had been found. This problem involved a number of functions and sites and therefore had cross company ramifications. It affected output at the Billericay Works and was tackled by the management action group (MAG) and provides an interesting example of what was achieved.

The matter was first raised during weeks five and six of the MAGs existence and there was a strong feeling that as several previous attempts had been made within the company to improve the situation, Billericay Works might as well accept its lot. Discussion tended to be both repetitive and defeatist.

The action group spent considerable time during its meeting in week nine in picking up the threads from their previous analysis and in recognizing the solution. This solution required joint action by both the Billericay Works and another function within John Tann Security. It was apparent that the plan would get nowhere without the backing of the board and the managing director. At this time morale was still insufficient for the four managers to believe that they would influence the centres of power. The matter was raised again and taken up in writing with their own works director and during weeks eleven and twelve at board level. Morale and expectations at Billericay MAG fluctuated during this period as their plan ran into the anticipated mixed reception.

Finally, in week fourteen, a team from Billericay and head office visited the American supplier to carry out the recommendations of the group. There has been a marked improvement and the complete solution is in sight.

The team had proved to themselves that they could win through if their attitudes changed radically and they learnt by previous mistakes. If there was one identifiable watershed in the development of the MAG, this was it.

The aim for the future

The formal framework of the management action group was some twenty four meetings with the group adviser present, spread over a six month period. We can usefully consider weeks fifteen

to twenty as the consolidation phase of activity. The four participants decided that the weekly team meeting was too positive a
feature to drop. They elected to meet weekly, to rotate the
chairmanship between themselves and to invite their works director to attend. This new format took effect from meeting twenty
and the group adviser attended the next two meetings and has
been back once since. The works director welcomed the invitation and is sympathetic to the goals and methods but his arrival
upset the general communications for two to three meetings!

*What did the participants say about their management action
group?*

'We have achieved a marked improvement in our confidence and
in our ability to solve problems, to manage our factory and to
motivate ourselves and our staff. Both the sponsoring director
and their group adviser agree while recognizing that all the
improvement is not due solely to Action Leaning: it helped!
Everyone knows that there is some way still to go, both in
strengthening the management team at Billericay and in improving efficiency.

The role of the set adviser

There has been considerable discussion within the Action Learning Trust on the way an adviser or counsellor should work and
indeed if one is required at all. Strongly held beliefs range from
'No Play without Hamlet' to 'Where two or three managers are
gathered together in my name, the spirit (or the innate wisdom
and rational behaviour of management) will suffice'. It may be
of interest to record my own aims and experience during this
particular management action group activity.

I began with the conviction that the adviser should be as
unobtrusive as possible, the antithesis of the charismatic lecturer
or consultant. I still believe this is true and that the adviser will
enjoy an ego trip at the expense of the group's learning experience. There is also a danger that he or she may become too
engrossed in the behavioural mechanisms. Nevertheless, there
were times when the collective morale flagged or the group
became engrossed in circular discussions on past crisis, reliving
emotions rather than learning from the patterns. It was then I
caught their eye and asked questions and if a management action
group is to produce a practical result this guidance may well be
necessary. My advice to the would-be set adviser is work yourself

out of a job as soon as possible but do not walk away until you know the group is over the initial ups and downs and is basically self sufficient. This would be irresponsible because self-knowledge can be a shattering experience for some people and a sinking group will leave a wash behind it – for both individuals and companies.

My personal targets as group adviser were to assist the group (a) to develop as individual managers, (b) to learn as a team, and (c) to resolve the problem (production + 15 per cent) and to function as a catalyst, but with half an eye on the calendar.

A review of the experience: March 1982

After the group stopped meeting I wrote a paper and made a number of presentations which aroused considerable interest; mainly I suspect, because the problem presented to the set by the John Tann board was a measurable target. This then was not just another sensitivity experience.

The opportunity to appraise the results of the project retrospectively was both attractive and a shade daunting; had 1978 been a false summer, a prolonged Hawthorne Effect? Norman Wilson, who had originally backed the project was still works director at Billericay for John Tann Security Ltd. He welcomed the idea of a re-appraisal and so did the 'Four Just Men' who had formed the Action Learning set. It was fortunate that they also engaged in the same functions and together still ran the Billericay Works.

Norman Wilson and I met in January 1982 and he subsequently produced a précis of the retrospective judgements made by him and the set participants. This précis formed the basis for a lunch-time discussion meeting held on site in March 1982 involving myself and the John Tann personnel:

	Norman Wilson, works director
the set	John Bird, production control manager
	Les Bye, production manager
	Peter Lovett, technical manager
	Colin Wilson, production engineering manager

It is useful to consider the longer term effects of the project under four headings:

1 the problem; to increase productivity by 15 per cent;

2 the development of the managers as individuals;

3   team building;

4   any spread of Action Learning (AL) techniques within Billericay Works.

Increasing productivity by 15 per cent: the problem

The set met during the period Autumn 1977 to Spring 1978. Productivity is defined in this context as standard work units produced per direct man hour. During the period under review there had been a steady decline in the number of indirect staff employed. 'Waiting time' was not measured before the project began so no comparison is possible.

There was some change to the method of work measurement during 1977 and for this reason 1978 is taken as the basis for percentage productivity figures. It was estimated, however, that productivity in 1978 was about 11 per cent above the figure for 1977 so the figures in the table are that much more impressive.

1978: Datum
1979: +11% (Corrected figure omitting period of dispute*)
1980: +19%
1981 Jan-July: +17%
1981 Aug-Dec: +13%**
* The union took unilateral action in implementing a 35 hour week combined with a work to rule. (This dispute is covered in more detail below.)
** The company suffered a fall in orders and in July announced redundancies to take effect in August. The number involved at Billericay was small but the effect on morale and motivation was considerable.

No one claims that the improvement in the utilization of labour was solely due to the AL project but it is considered to be the major factor.

The development of individuals as managers

All four participants believe that the AL project 'was the most significant factor' in establishing:

1   Confide in their director based on the belief that he wanted them to manage and would allow them to do so. (Not always the same thing!)

2   Better decision making

3   Less defensive attitudes and improved ability to take criticism

4   More delegation

5   Improved self confidence and leadership

6   Proper application of disciplinary procedures

It is interesting to compare the industrial relations in 1977 with what they are today. Previously the four line managers were not confident in either their own judgement or in the company's willingness to back them up. They now deal firmly with problems and the successful handling of the 1979 'reduced hours and go slow dispute' reflects this. (A small number of dismissals have occurred and when taken to tribunal all have been judged 'fair'.) The union unilaterally declared a 35 hour week and all 40 hour staff arrive one hour late each day. The company suspended all weekly staff without pay on the grounds of 'broken contract of employment' and each employee was sent a direct communication. The union viewed the three days as a strike but all employees returned to normal working one day after receiving the company's letter. Long term union-management relations have been much improved and the confidence of management re-inforced.

Team building

Prior to the arrival of the present works director the four line managers all felt insecure. They were suspicious of each other and lacked confidence and group loyalty. They now recall how in 1977 they spent considerable time and energy in blaming each other and the union.

   The four participants are sure that the AL experience welded them into a team and this is borne out by their director. They are now loyal to each other and no longer fall into the trap of allowing themselves to be set against each other.

Continuing use of AL techniques at Billericay

The four participants had in 1978 formed an AL set for their own deputies. The four initiators rotated the role of adviser between them so that they could liven and pass on the techniques they had developed within their own set which had just finished.

   This subsidiary set met several times but petered out. The 'Four Just Men' and Norman Wilson all felt that this was because of the absence of an independent adviser and because each of them was in the company hierarchy, one of the basic tenets of Action Learning was ignored.

One of the participants of the original set wishes they still met, regularly but not too frequently, in a fairly disciplined way to consider general problems which concern the site. They would not wish to have their works director present although the relationships are obviously excellent!

Conclusion

Four years on, the nominating director/problem owner and the participants are agreed that the project was very worth while.

A personal note: has the catalyst changed?

In chemistry a catalyst does not change, but it would be a pity if the experience did not contribute to the learning and the broadening of a set adviser. I hope and believe that in my case it has.

I came to AL five years ago and learnt by making mistakes and listening to advice. The common sense of Reg Revans's approach appealed to me. I do not like to count the number of one-day seminars I have attended, run by a gentleman who was selling one small truth as the universal panacea for all management ills. Here for once was an experience based upon real life situations aimed at developing existing skills. I had been a manager for much of my industrial life and was not a professional trainer.

All my AL experience has been with part-time sets, both mixed company and 'incestuous', where only one organization is involved. I have just read again the comments I made in 1978 concerning the role of the set adviser. My attitude has not changed except that I seemed then to be a shade apologetic for remaining in the set! Reg Revans has long taught that whereas initiators are very necessary, set advisers should be put in a bucket of salt water after the second set Meeting. I must confess to being even more of a heretic now than in 1978!

The sets I have initiated and counselled have been part-time and formed from managers still subjected to the tugs and stresses of their day-to-day jobs. It is a very different world from that of the high flyer from a large organization seconded full-time to a year's AL project.

I am even more convinced now that the set adviser's presence is also required in the role of a subtle but sometimes firm project manager. The on-line pressures take over, morale may flag and we cannot really afford to treat the set as a purely intellectual exercise. It seems to me that there are two reasons for the set adviser's continued presence. Basically, the chap who signed the cheque (and it was necessary) has a right to expect to see some result, some part of Phase III implementation actually under way. If not, he may be forgiven for doubting that any management development has taken place or (and this is the icing on his cake) that he will see a costly problem resolved.

Even more important though. I think there is a potential risk for the participant. The modern manager is made increasingly aware of the difficulty of his task, new techniques and awful warnings abound. Management integrity is only as good as the individual's confidence and I am convinced that one great by-product of an Action Learning set is confidence gained from a difficult project well done. That is the problem if the set loses momentum for long enough then the participants may return to their organizations demotivated and with a sense of failure.

I underestimated at first the importance of the initiator's job. I now know that it is vitally important that great care is taken when:

1   selecting participants; have they been chosen for valid reasons?

2   obtaining the chief executive's commitment for the life of the project

3   helping the sponsoring companies choose tough but soluble problems.

I am still enjoying it!

Acknowledgement

I am grateful to the Institution of Industrial Managers (then the Institution of Works Managers), the Manpower Services Commission and the Board of John Tann Security Ltd, for providing the opportunity. My thanks go to Norman Wilson, works director at Billericay for his faith and encouragement and particularly to my four friends, Colin, John, Les and Pete, who are busy putting some fun back into work at Billericay.

13 Doctors as managers

Tony Winkless

Introduction

In 1984 the National Health Service (NHS) received news of what was for many 'yet another reorganization'. This time (previous significant changes having taken place in 1974 and 1982) the government had commissioned a prominent businessman, Roy Griffiths, to lead a team charged with the job of proposing the changes in its role and structure. Central to the recommendations of the 'Griffiths Report' was the notion of accountable management. Griffiths pointed to the lack of a clearly defined general management function throughout the NHS: 'At no level is the general management role clearly being performed by an identifiable individual. In short if Florence Nightingale were carrying her lamp through the corridors of the NHS today she would almost certainly be searching for the people in charge.'[1]

Thus the old style of what was known as 'consensus management' was to go, with line managers now appointed to replace the old-style administrators who once loyally oiled the system in their quasi-secretarial capacity to the professional parties (primarily the doctors and the nurses) who in turn, largely shared the responsibilities of channelling the complex activities of hospital life. Clearly acknowledging the role of these professionals, the doctors in particular were singled out by Griffiths as needing to be fully participating members of the new-style management:

'Closer involvement of doctors is so critical to effective management . . .'

In the wake of Griffiths there have followed many macro- and micro-initiatives designed for reform, targeted by a variety of actors in the organizational hierarchy from central government through region to unit (that is, roughly, hospital) level. However, unlike the earlier 'reorganizations', there appears to be only one constant: continuous change, not only in organization structure, but also in systems, job content, use of resources and, inevitably, change for the doctors. This is an account of two of the micro-initiatives which have been directed at the doctors to invite them to explore the managerial issues increasingly affecting their previously, largely untouched, sovereign territory.

Doctors and change in the NHS

In the Yorkshire region of the NHS there had been a significant history of interest from some doctors in exploring the nature and implications of 'management' since the early days of 'Griffiths'. The region's training department had mounted a series of courses for senior registrars and consultants, largely based on the traditional format of lecture, discussion and management exercises. These had been attended by around 300 doctors. Arising from these programmes numbers of doctors expressed a wish for further opportunities to examine the managerial changes taking place, and they also talked to colleagues with similar interests and encouraged them to sample what was on offer.

It is important to bear in mind that, due to the nature of this evolution of interest, these doctors involved here were very likely to have been (and maybe still are) atypical of the majority of their colleagues in wishing to attend a management programme. And, although there was undoubtedly some degree of peer pressure, doctors of consultant status in particular had the freedom to choose whether to attend or not – unlike their managerial colleagues who were much more subject to senior management directives. Finally, it should also be appreciated that some of the doctors who attended the programmes were doing so in the face of criticism, and sometimes scorn, from their colleagues, who were suspicious of the motives of the organizers during this early time of reform in the NHS.

Why then the interest at a time of such doubts? Participants were asked this question at the beginning of the programmes.

One response from a senior consultant, provides a good summary (it was subsequently labelled as 'The Manifesto' in the group):

- The NHS is promoting (Management) training – the doctors are not.

- Doctors are probably the best people to manage clinical services.

- If doctors don't change, there will be increasing tension.

- Doctors are not an entirely happy group (the major discussion topic is retirement).

- To maintain the status of the profession.

- To help doctors in their fear of change.

- An opportunity to improve staff relationships, for example, nurses.

- No administrators now, therefore, no scapegoats left?

Action Learning for doctors

Two case studies are included here. The first is concerned with a group of newly-appointed consultants. It is important to realise that for hospital doctors, 'getting a job' means securing a consultant appointment. This is achieved at the average age of 37, and until this time doctors are considered to be in training. Only very exceptionally do consultants then move to other posts or to other hospitals. The second case concerns a group of established consultants.

Action Learning seemed to be an ideal approach to meet the needs of these doctors. An approach that would provide the flexibility needed to allow the participants to explore and experiment in a changing and undefined world of diversity and uncertainty. Revans had in fact pointed this way forward over 25 years before, and it is worth noting his observations which bear an uncanny similarity to many of the current reflections of the NHS:

> How to run a hospital – indeed, how to run the National Health Service, or even how to run anything today in Britain – seems to have become of major concern . . . The Hospital Internal Communication project seems to suggest that there may be virtue in seeking escape from our grosser torments by Action Learning, rather than by the external advice of academic theorists or commercial consultants.

> . . . by working together, those who have to run complex organ-
> isms like hospitals, learning with and from each other as they go
> along, and treating their daily problems as the occasion of that
> learning, may achieve their ostensible goals more economically
> than hospitals which pursue more traditional and authoritarian poli-
> cies.[2]

Since the consultants were being invited to join programmes
which were based on a different design from that previously
experienced during 'management courses' it was considered
essential to make clear the nature of the programmes offered.
Introductory sessions were mounted in both cases and the following description given for Action Learning:

1   Participants learn most effectively from tackling problems
    and generating meaningful activities from their lives and
    their work. In this respect, an important distinguishing fea-
    ture is that the participants choose what they wish to work
    on, not the tutor.

2   All members of an Action Learning group are assumed to
    have the potential by way of experience, knowledge and
    skills to assist each other in their problem solving and
    development. That is, 'experts' are normally not required.

3   The tutor's role is mainly one of facilitator, helping the
    programme run effectively, particularly in influencing the
    way participants contribute and relate to each other.

To annul any suspicion that doctors do not learn through experience it should be said that the author has been gently chided on
more than one occasion by participants that, although Action
Learning might be a *new phrase* for doctors, their clinical training, 'on the job', bears great similarities. Perhaps, however, the
departure may lie in the extent to which there is choice in what
is learned? This point will be addressed again later.

Case 1 The newly appointed consultants

This programme evolved from one of the introductory management courses run for newly appointed consultants in the latter
part of 1986. At the end of this three-day course the participants
(around 16) were invited to participate in an experimental Action
Learning group. Eight consultants of the original group decided
to join. The contract agreed with the participants was that the
group would meet on four occasions, with a final meeting to

evaluate collectively the content and outcomes. The meetings were to be arranged at about six-weekly intervals, between the hours of 3pm to 9pm. (In the event a further meeting was arranged at the participants' request.) The following is an account of the content and the evaluation outcomes of these meetings.

My previous experience of running Action Learning groups for a range of people (for example, NHS managers, unemployed executives, personnel practitioners) strongly suggested the need for an initial integrating event where participants could be helped to get to know each other, to share each others' concerns and needs, and to practise and test their skills of listening and confrontation. This latter aspect is particularly important since it profits no one in an Action Learning group if there is poor listening and feedback. Accordingly, the first part of our initial meeting was devoted to these aspects (a somewhat longer session would have been needed if the participants had not already known each other from the earlier programme).

The format for all later parts of the programme was the same, in that participants first listed the issues they wished to work on, followed by each individual taking turn in presenting and receiving ideas, challenge and feedback on their specific issue. These issues varied in nature and complexity, some being helped or solved quite quickly, while others were more intractible (a problem rather than a puzzle as Revans suggests) and spanned the life of the project. What was particularly striking was the openness and readiness the participants gave to addressing the issues raised during these meetings, a characteristic not always found in their managerial colleagues in similar circumstances. A summary of the types of issues which they addressed, collected under four main headings, is as follows:

1 Self management/development

- coping with feelings of being threatened/isolated
- developing and practising assertiveness
- building self-confidence in dealing with management and colleagues
- reducing 'Type A'* pressures from the working environment

2 Colleague relationships

- introducing change in the face of opposition
- separating friendships from professional relationships
- negotiating in and between committees
- negotiating teaching sessions
- negotiating work-load commitment
- managing approaches to research

3 Management relationships

- managing the political and economic environment
- clarifying the roles of doctors *vis-à-vis* managers
- challenging a perceived undemocratic management decision
- negotiating the content of a job description
- role clarification in hospital reorganization

4 'Small m' management

- 'time and motion' study in clinic
- dealing with low staff morale
- balancing work priorities
- developing a working strategy
- managing the clinical and support team
- bed utilization and numbers
- apportionment of study leave
- design of wards

*Briefly, susceptibility to heart-related diseases. See, for example, Friedman, M. and Rosenman, R. H. (1959).[3]

While this typology of learning needs, constructed on the basis of participants' declared issues, may be reasonably representative of newly appointed consultants, it should not be taken as a prescription for any standardized programme. Such an approach would run entirely counter to the philosophy of Action Learning, whereby participants generate their own agendas.

It may seem surprising that no clinical issues were raised. This, of course, might have been because the programme was seen as part of a 'management course' and alternative forums were available for discussing clinical issues. On the other hand, it might have been because, as more than one participant put it, 'Clinical work is the easy part of it.'

The term 'small m' management evolved in the group particularly to help the consultants distinguish between what they customarily viewed as 'big M' management (for example, hospital managers) and those aspects of their job which although managerial in nature were not normally described as such by those practising them. A clear exception to this distinction, however, may be found among those doctors who are responsible for large service functions such as radiology – a 'big M' responsibility by most standards. Perhaps, too, those interested in the practice of 'big M' management might discern some interesting similarities in all four of the areas given above with many of the models of management practice. In answer then to the often-raised question 'Do doctors really manage?', the simple answer is 'yes'.

What then about the outcomes and benefits of this programme as seen by the participants? First, participants were asked in the evaluation stage (a group-designed event) whether any changes had been made in the work place which could be attributed to the programme. The responses reflected the list of issues given above.

The self-management/development aspects were relatively highly represented in the area of developing increased levels of assertiveness; for example:

> More assertive and looking at 'lateral' ways of achieving my aims

> Self-assertion – reason for lack of it were tackled – successfully

Linked with this was the area of colleague relationships which was clearly an important issue for some participants, particularly in learning how to deal with more senior consultant colleagues; for example:

> I have relaxed more, I realise others share my problems, and [I] find it easier to talk with more senior consultant colleagues.

The area of management relationships was highlighted most frequently, with a variety of outcomes; for example:

> Much clearer contact with my managers, leading to a useful working relationship . . . I now actively seek them out . . .

More vocal in my complaints about management – to Region, District Management and colleagues

More aware of the way managers want to deal with consultants

Perhaps a more acute observation of the system and some insights into those within it. Hopefully an increasingly sophisticated view of how mechanisms are/can be manipulated

And finally, two participants referred to their 'small m' outcomes:

Instituted a quality control study in Out-patient Clinic

Taken on new responsibilities in controlling my team.

The nature and usefulness of the Action Learning approach to this group of consultants were examined in the evaluation process by asking them whether there were any benefits from the programme that they had not envisaged. Their responses highlighted the learning community aspects of Action Learning; for example:

Enjoyment of working with others and commonality of problems leading to increasing confidence in the work situation

Been able to talk about difficulties and trust the participants to be neutral in their attitudes

Learning from the difficulties and responses made by other consultants in the group. Realizing that we all have similar problems

Whilst other comments focused on the problem-solving aspects:

I gained more benefits than I had expected, that is, analytical approach to problem solving

I have learned to be more analytical of the motives of others

Action Learning groups vary in their length and in the frequency of meetings, and participants were accordingly asked for their thoughts for any future programmes. The popular view was that five to six meetings at a frequency of around six weeks was about right.

Perhaps most informative (and gratifying for the organizers), in response to the question 'If you knew at the beginning what you know now, would you still have joined the programme?' the unanimous response from these newly appointed consultants was 'Yes'. Linked with this were comments reporting more favourable responses to this form of training compared to the conventional, externally-set repertoire of subjects experienced elsewhere in their careers.

Case 2 The established consultants

This second case study concerns a rather more ambitious programme, fundamental aim of which was to provide a group of 18 established consultants with the necessary skills and experiences to carry out management training for their junior staff (senior registrars, registrars and house officers). In addition, the programme's objectives stressed the opportunities to explore both personal and more general managerial issues. As with the first case study Action Learning was at the core of the design.

In this case, though, two residential 'start-up' workshops, each of three days duration, were provided – one as an introduction to management (and getting-started period), the second as an introduction to training methods and techniques. There followed six one-day Action Learning session at monthly intervals (three groups of six participants plus a facilitator). At each session during the first half of the day the participants worked on issues arising from their training project activities in their hospitals. In the afternoons there were group-designed sessions involving external experts. The issues raised during the Action Learning meetings and the subjects chosen for the afternoon session of the programme included the following:

- evaluation of training
- presentation methods
- assertiveness
- relaxation techniques
- programme design
- are doctors normal people?
- inter-personal skills
- persuasion
- time management
- career planning
- sharing progress reports
- trying out ideas on each other
- managing the department
- understanding the strategic and tactical issues

- personal presentation
- making deals with managers

These items were collected via facilitators keynote recordings during Action Learning sets, and also by participants in their group-designed evaluation questionnaire and in their free account descriptions of their 'journeys' over the six months.

As with the newly appointed consultants, what emerged during the programme was a wide diversity of needs and gains from the programme. Again, there is a similar pattern of issues. As illustrated below, the opportunities provided to (a) work on issues of personal development and (b) explore roles outside the conventional consultant role were clearly valued (although these aspects were not envisaged as being the prime purpose of the programme). Greater diversity in activity and interest came from those objectives and outcomes relating to the 'training the trainer' aspects. This diversity may be explained partly by reference to those participants who did not see their role (or their use of the programme) as to do with delivering management education and development (MED), and partly to do with the prevailing lack of clarity about the practice, nature and organizational place of the MED role for consultant staff. This is perhaps not surprising in view of the pioneering nature of the role.

In order to illustrate these points, extracts from the 'journey accounts' written by each participant at the end of the programme are given below. They are necessarily selective, but an attempt has been made to give a fair indication of outcomes. At a summary level they may broadly be classified as to do with the following issues:

1   An interest in management as an activity which is seen as an intrinsic part of the consultant's job ('big M' or 'little M').

2   An interest in relating the consultant role to that of management, and understanding the processes and practices involved.

3   An interest in training junior staff and/or peers in management skills, methods and techniques (it should be noted that the programme's objectives related to 'junior staff' as the target population).

4   An interest in personal development.

It is also worth noting that this group raised more strategic issues, perhaps reflecting their more senior status; for example

I have run seven workshops for staff at my hospital and have seen all 16 members of the junior medical staff for discussion of progress/problems/training needs . . . In a general way I don't think that the achievements of the programme can be overestimated . . . I have personally encouraged and assisted about 30 doctors to develop their own management skills . . . we now have a small section on management topics in the library . . . members of staff frequently discuss their own further training, potential initiatives and problems with me on a regular basis.

I foresee a role [for me] in the experiential type of training and I have begun to take small steps towards this end . . . [and] feel more competent as a manager of my own clinical service.

The course gave me time to focus on the needs of junior doctors both in my dept and the NHS generally . . . [to recognize] the importance of communication and workforce . . . the insights gained have helped me in my work as director and as consultant member of our hospital management group . . . I hope to have the opportunity of passing on present skills to trainees and developing my own further . . . have had preliminary conversations about setting up some sort of management training for medical practitioners along these lines.

So against the advice of the Ivory Tower shouters, Red Riding Hood eventually met the Big Bad Wolf. Actually, other Red Riding Hoods had already told her that the Big Wolf was only as bad as you thought he was . . . More than the little things Red Riding Hood learned, and they were many, she became more and more convinced that to survive in the Forest where the Big Wolf ruled she had to know his ways [a reference to the new management regime].

The programme was altogether helpful because it brought me to regard my project as a true and central part of my working life rather than a peripheral and extra one . . . it has been a frustrating, exhilarating, time-consuming, educative experience for me. The project has got off the ground well and is running well, but it has taken a great deal of time and effort and continues to do so.

The main benefit I derived was through the Action Learning sets where I was able to obtain a lot of support completely unavailable elsewhere . . . some of the best advice was that I should stop 'owning' my project entirely on my own . . . with the help that I received we now have a firm programme for pursuing the issues of consultants in management . . . I think we have obtained the best possible structure for any solution to emerge.

I agree 'the best answers' for me 'are within' and since I am usually able to find within the resources I need, I should be able to manage. Should needs arise not within me I feel I would know where to seek.

My project was targeted at my consultant colleagues rather than junior staff . . . [as] the group I most wished to influence . . . unexpected 'spin offs' from involvement in management training have led to a recognition of my role in training doctors in my unit . . . [and] an invitation to join a multi-disciplinary management development forum . . . Without this course I should not be doing what I am doing in the management field now, and my hospital unit and my life would have been the poorer.

I have benefitted a great deal from this training . . . the project may get done . . . within the next academic year rather than within this one . . . a change is the realization that I don't have to do it (yet) and I do not feel guilty . . . the methodology which I had originally intended to use is now recognized as flawed . . . but my expectation for outcome is more patient, and I'm sure is more realistic than it would have been before I attended this course.

Now I am involved in the DGM's think-tank looking at district-wide problems. I am close to the point of deciding whether to come off the fence and move further into management . . . I would like to spend more time in management.

I am more aware of where the problems lie . . . I am much more aware now that I can control my time . . . very difficult issues have been raised and aired . . . hearing the achievements of others gave me a clearer idea of where I should go.

Some qualifying thoughts

In case it is thought that these programmes always ran smoothly and to the total satisfaction of all participants at all times, some indicators of the less satisfactory issues are necessary.

One participant referred to an initial 'destructive tendency' in testing out his work on self-assertion, another to being more aware of the frustrations of the work situation, while a third guardedly reported 'none which are as yet apparent'.

Another criticism concerned the lack of 'gel' in one of the Action Learning groups of the second programme, which was linked to the rotating-facilitator approach employed (the three facilitators shared the role across the three groups). With large programmes which form more than one Action Learning group the decision has to be made about how best to carry out the facilitator role. There are pros and cons for having the same person for each group, and for rotating the role. The former has the advantage of stability and greater knowledge of individual and group processes; the latter offers the possibility of a different style and the value of the 'naïve question'.

Some criticisms were made of colleagues who did not make regular appearances. Action Learning groups work best with five to seven people who are committed to attendance and involvement. The loss of a couple of people can be very disruptive.

Four participants expressed the view that the second programme lacked purpose and cohesiveness towards the end, and that a residential ending would have been useful. This point has been made on similar programmes where participants value the opportunity to bring the programme to a graceful end: residential events seem to help in this, particularly when the start-up is residential.

One participant referred to the lack of 'grass roots experience of the training staff' which, it was felt, handicapped them in their understanding and potential helpfulness in the realities of the consultant role and the demands of general management. This point is sometimes made by participants in Action Learning groups, although the facilitator role should not need to include content knowledge – indeed it could be argued that this is a distinct disadvantage.

Some participants raised initial concerns and feelings of guilt over the self-indulgent use of their time at the expense of their duties in the hospital. For example:

> Could I afford the time to attend? . . . Contrast between the loose free-flowing structure of the group with the hard realities of my management job, was it worth going on if I wasn't sure where we were going . . . in the end it was worth it . . .

The attraction and appropriateness of Action Learning for doctors

What seems very clear from these accounts was the diversity of issues raised. No strictures were placed on the participants to confine themselves to the subject of managerial issues, yet this was a dominant theme. However, two further themes may also be discerned. The second concerns issues relating to self-development, and this was explicitly referred to by over half the participants; for example: '. . . recognizing the importance to identify action plans for personal needs and their development' . . . 'I am much more able to say "no, that is not for me" '; 'I have learned to be a better listener . . .'; '. . . also helping to develop

and grow as a person'; and '. . . it has widened my horizons with
regard to personal development'.

The third, and linked, theme concerned the attraction of
Action Learning. All participants reported a favourable reaction
to the programmes, perhaps because of the flexibility of the
Action Learning approach which was specifically given favourable reports by half the respondents in their accounts. Key words
used were 'addictiveness', 'supportive network', 'safety', 'listening and being listened to', 'stress reducing', 'respecting colleagues', 'group cohesion', 'trust', 'reassurance', 'kinship', and
'confidence'. Several participants referred to a sense of surprise
that involvement with their group should prove so beneficial.

The question remains: why did this form of learning design
seem to be attractive to these doctors, who were perhaps atypical
of the doctor 'body corporate' in volunteering to attend a course
on management? They were atypical, too, in attending a management course which was designed in a way deviant from the
norm. At the time of writing, management courses in the NHS,
particularly those organized by management, are still viewed with
suspicion by many doctors. ('Going over to the other side' is a
common, taunting, rebuttal.)

The loneliness of the long distance doctor?

Has it to do with the very rigid and strict training regime for
doctors? This starts at around the age of 16 with a requirement
for excellence in three science subjects, followed by 20 years' of
training and regular selection procedures with that final qualifying acceptance by peers, seniors and self not appearing until the
average age of 37. The final struggle for appointment is won at
the consultant grade – 'the light at the end of the tunnel', as
more than one participant put it.

During this lengthy period, few opportunities for development
of the self, as opposed to development of the role, are formally
encouraged (or thought to be acceptable behaviour). Perhaps
now, for the first time, the doctor has the legitimate means to
exercise personal power and autonomy, and to express awareness
of and to address some of these unfulfilled issues? A time which
also coincides with a new and largely unfettered freedom to
explore new directions, both clinical and non-clinical. These are
early and speculative thoughts, but they are also reinforced by
my experience of over 200 personal counselling sessions with
doctors, following (and stimulated by) personality questionnaire

feedback. The personal issues dominate with a force distinctly different from other groups in my experience.

Perhaps it may be worth pondering over Revans's revisiting of his work with colliery managers in 1953:

> Cannot we learn with and from each other what is wrong with what we are trying to do, and the manner of our doing it? What can those who do not sense our responsibilities (because they do not need to bear them) tell us about our own personal behaviour as leaders of this complex and kaleidoscopic army?

References

1 Griffiths, R. (1983) *NHS Management Enquiry* , Letter to Secretary of State for Social Services, October
2 Revans, R. (1982) 'Action Learning Takes A Health Cure' in *The Origins and Growth of Action Learning*, Chartwell-Bratt.
3 Friedman, M and Rosenman, R. H. (1959) 'Association of Specific Overt Behaviour Patterns with Blood and Cardiovascular Findings', *Journal of the American Medical Association*, 169, pp. 96–106.

Acknowledgements

My co-facilitators in these two programmes were Helena Waters (Cases 1 and 2) and Helen Jones (Case 2), whose partnership and dedication to the programmes was greatly appreciated.

14 Action Learning in an academic context

Richard Thorpe and Maggie Taylor

The issues discussed in this chapter derive from our experience as members of a course team running a Master's level programme geared to management and organization development. The story of the development of the programme goes back several years to when Manchester Polytechnic, with the North West Regional Management Centre, set out to devise a programme to help managers learn and develop whilst tackling a strategic work-based problem. The result was the introduction of an MSc in Management.

Unlike traditional Master's programmes in Management, this one is based on Action Learning principles, incorporating many of the ideas discussed elsewhere in this book. However, in common with other academic institutions, we are required to justify all elements of the programme, offering an appreciation of the theory underpinning it, and constantly monitoring the progress and performance of the curriculum, students and staff.

The term 'Action Learning' has been around for some time now and, as Boddy points out, has been used increasingly to describe a wide variety of approaches to management education.[1] Some give greater emphasis to the practitioner's experience and perspective, others lean towards the use of models to be found in the academic literature. The Manchester Polytechnic Master's programme holds a balance between the theoretical and the practical and brings the practising manager and the academic perspectives together.

Originally our market had an industrial base but this has shifted as management development became more pertinent to the public sector. On all intakes small business has also been represented. The programme has attracted both men and women, although in some years the latter have been under-represented.

The outcomes for participants include rapid career development, both during and after completion of the programme. For some, their national standing within their profession has been advanced. For client organizations, some have attributed the success of divisional, regional or corporate initiatives directly to the programme. We are encouraged by 'repeat purchase' patterns of some employers each year and requests for consultancy services from members of the course team during and after the programme.

The structure of the present programme is set out in Figure 14.1.

The MSc in Management by Action Learning takes two years on the basis of one day a week. In the first year, participants undertake a project. This has to be a real organizational problem or opportunity, agreed between the course participant, their client and the Polytechnic. The focus of the project is essentially practical. Theories and models used at this stage are to inform action. Participants are expected to achieve some degree of implementation on the premise that the important aspects of strategic management are about power, politics and the ability to influence and make changes. Without implementation, such aspects are rarely appreciated or developed in managers.

In the second year, participants reflect on their project experiences. Using wider conceptual frameworks, they seek to make sense of theory and practice, and explore alternative perspectives. Their experience is used to challenge and comment on the literature, but the literature is also used to illuminate experience. There are various 'models' for the dissertation. One type focuses on an individual's performance and development. What abilities did the manager demonstrate in executing the project and how might they be developed or improved? Other types include the conceptualization of one or a number of aspects of the internal or external environment in which the organization or manager operates.

Both these stages are subject to academic requirements for a project report to be submitted at the end of the first year and a

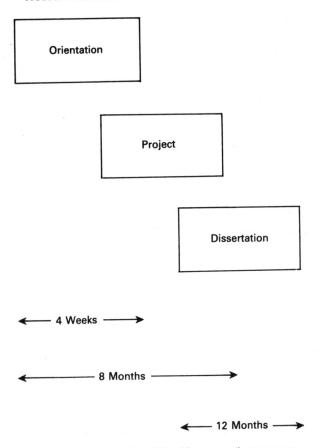

Figure 14.1 Outline of the MSc (Management) programme

dissertation at the end of the second. There is also a viva voce examination for all candidates at the end of each year. Academic requirements appear to supersede client organization interests here!

But what are the problems of introducing action learning into an academic environment? Can they be overcome? Can academic programmes employing this philosophy be made to work? In the following sections we address these issues from our experience, concluding with pointers to others in education considering this philosophy and approach.

Problems with Action Learning in an academic institution

Action Learning as a vehicle for management and organization development at Manchester Polytechnic has not been without its critics – not least some colleagues who see the method as challenging a hard-won discipline base. Those questioning the approach have claimed it is not sufficiently rigorous to warrant the award of a higher degree and is not in the 'academic tradition'. Advocates on the other hand have often not helped their case by claiming the method is more innovatory than it actually is.

Academic institutions exist for the development and dissemination of knowledge. Their value systems and career structures reward excellence and expertise in research and teaching, measured in terms of publications, conference papers and pass rates. The role of the 'expert' teacher or researcher is embodied in an institutional language emphasizing a dependency relationship, as in 'centres of excellence' or 'such and such a person, a leading authority on . . .', and even 'reading for a degree'. In many institutions staff are noted for their preference for research rather than teaching – or helping students learning. Teaching has 'nuisance' value, as the financial and promotional rewards are derived from such activities as research contracts, publications, book chapters and royalties.

In recent years pressures on educational institutions to deliver services efficiently have often meant reducing inputs. This has advanced the cause of traditional teaching, larger class sizes and distance learning rather than riskier, resource-rich student-centred approaches.

In such a context, proponents of Action Learning are inevitably involved in attempts to establish credibility and acceptance within the institution on professional, intellectual and administrative grounds. At Manchester, the task has been to secure the recognition of Action Learning as a credible philosophy underpinning the whole of a Master's level programme. It involved enabling staff to shift from a 'teacher-expert' role to one of 'learning facilitator', where students are permitted to make mistakes without it being seen as the 'fault' of the tutor – or seen as loss of control.

Changing the culture at an institutional level and departmental level has perhaps been the most difficult task of all. However, over the eight years of the running of the programme there have been a number of measures of success, meeting academic, participant and employer criteria.

One is most certainly the calibre of the applicants who enrol. The support and encouragement of our external examiners has been another. Student and client feedback and the promotions gained by participants have provided further confirmation of the value of the programme. Over the years we have undertaken close monitoring and evaluation and developed an academic justification for the components of the programme we offer. We have also seen our ideas incorporated in other programmes nationally, and have been involved in workshops to help other institutions implement the approach.

How has this been achieved? The answer lies in recognizing the difficulties associated with a problem-centred, learner-centred approach to management development; for example:

1 *Loss of skills* Management educators genuinely fear that involvement in such programmes devalues their skill and knowledge base. This is something that throughout their careers they have valued and which has traditionally been the measure of success.

2 *Fear of not being the expert* Tensions arise within educators when the role requires them to be quiet and allow other members of the group to come forward with their experience and expertise. Even on occasions to be the ones who make the formal academic 'presentations' to other members of the group. Fear of not being the expert relates to a problem of loss of control.

3 *Devaluing old skills* This relates to a reduced opportunity for demonstrating particular skills of the tutor, for example, in the form of lectures or workshops.

4 *New skills* Clearly the role of facilitator requires completely different skills. Preparation for classes is difficult and teachers often go into the situation apprehensive and nervous, and therefore fearful of the situations which they might find. It is common to find set advisors anxious in the face of a great deal of uncertainty.

5 *Changes in the student/client expectations* We have found that for a certain type of manager the type of approach to learning we offer is well received. These managers search for relevance rather than knowledge for its own sake and enjoy the problem-centred/learner-centred approach. But there is also a high expectation that we will deliver, and any slippage in the process of sharing the responsibility

for learning is often heavily criticized. The process they experience therefore is important in shaping their expectations.

These problems have been tackled by means of staff development and attention to the development of an 'open' and cohesive course team. Changing the 'lecture culture' has involved a paradigm shift from teaching to learning, as shown in Figure 14.2.

The change necessitated a complete reappraisal of the role and skills required of the lecturer, together with the attendant risk and worry of being found wanting in the area of process, rather than content delivery. Changing the culture of the institution required a major investment of time and energy developing a credible philosophy for the programme, underpinned by research of how managers most effectively learn, and how organizations can be influenced and developed.

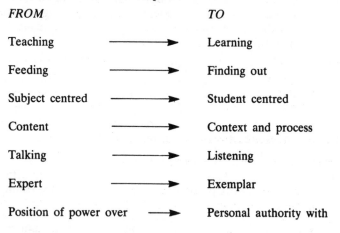

Adapted from a model developed by John Hughes.

Figure 14.2 A new paradigm for management education

The development of managers and their organizations

Managers on the programme are, typically, experienced and in mid-career. The problems they tackle are strategic but not everyone is strategically positioned in their organization. Those who are not learn quickly that they need to influence their organizations from the bottom.

Whatever their organizational position, the programme

encourages managers to release themselves from day-to-day operations and begin the process of developing a longer-term view. This involves getting to grips with the realities and uncertainties of an organization and its situation.

These complexities increase and as Spender confirms, the broader a manager's responsibilities, the longer term the view.[2] We believe managers need the skills to gather information and process it properly so that they will be aware of the consequences of various courses of action. However, unlike tactical problems they are much more likely to find strategic information difficult to collect and when they do, difficult to analyse. As a consequence an important managerial skill is 'judgement.' Judgement differs from analysis in that analysis implies finding the answer hidden in the data whereas judgement often requires practice and experience that is acquired not by formal methods of teaching but through simulation, interaction with peers, and project work.

It is for this reason that our programme aims to assist managers to bring judgement to problems as well as offering the various techniques for analysing the kind of data which managers might consider. This, we believe, is a quality for strategic management, and they will gain their insight and have their judgement assisted by using the reference frames of the people with whom they work in a set to help them move forward.

How can Action Learning be made to work?

Preparation, publicity and recruitment

From our experience we have found that Action Learning will not work without shaping the expectations of course participants and clients in advance of joining the programme. In order to achieve this the teaching team have responsibilities beyond class-contact hours allocated. The role, perhaps, needs to be more ambassadorial rather than evangelical. All members of the team are involved in the recruitment process and this requires a complete awareness of pre-course requirements.

Our advanced publicity takes the form of course brochures, supplementary papers and any journal, article or conference papers that are current. We recognize, as with the marketing of any service, that part of the key to success is to market ourselves. Notwithstanding the formal approaches to recruitment, we have found the most successful source of new recruits is through the personal recommendations of past and present course members.

Interviews

On this programme we interview all applicants. The general format of an interview is an explanation of the programme by a member of the course team followed by an explanation by the candidate of their management level, the extent to which they have already gained some formal management training and their individual career aspirations. As the first year project is crucial to the programme, an exploration of the area the participant might tackle is an essential part of that first meeting.

For participants to work effectively in sets, applicants are required to have a broad knowledge of management theories and concepts. Our expectation is that applicants will have either completed a post-experience programme in management and business, or a relevant undergraduate course or professional qualification with a substantial management content. If managers do not have appropriate formal qualifications we have used an assignment as a means of assessing candidates' descriptive and analytical capabilities. If the candidate appears to be able to benefit from the programme they are asked to write a project synopsis which provides the basis for discussion between the candidate and the organization client at a later date.

'Contracting' with clients

Client interviews are the second stage in the decision process. Normally, two course team members meet with the prospective student and their client. The philosophy and approach to the programme, the roles and processes involved and provisional broad development plans for the organization and participant are discussed. The intention is to establish a common understanding of the project area and gain agreement on organizational support for the participant. The value of this to us is appreciation of the organization context, for the client a better understanding of the strategic nature of the work to be undertaken and the extent to which implementation is seen to be an important part of the programme. Only when a viable project is agreed with all parties is a person accepted onto the programme.

Building a learning community

The programme consists of three interrelated phases:

1 The orientation phase – duration four weeks

2   Problem centred project (Action Learning phase) – duration eight months

3   Dissertation write-up and consolidation phase – duration 12 months

In the orientation phase the intention is to build a mature learning community as quickly as possible whilst generating appropriate knowledge, attitudes and skills for the action-centred project. Broadly, the objectives of this phase are:

1   To transfer certain information thought to be important for all participants to successfully complete the programme (that is, the nature of Action Learning, various approaches to research);

2   To allow participants to experience and value a mature approach to learning;

3   To create a supportive approach in the programme community;

4   To help participants (re-)examine their strengths and weaknesses;

5   To develop basic knowledge, attitudes and skills which will allow participants to analyse their own and their organizations' development needs with the aid of available resources.

In our approach participants are seen as major resources in the learning process. Initially, staff design and deliver specific 'content' elements (P) considered essential. Priority is quickly given to team building and the development and recognition of the significance of the pool of experiences and knowledge within the group. Our justification for this is that managers are used to having time pressures impose a structure on their day. We recognize that during the orientation phase any attempt to transfer participants with this 'reality' into an unstructured learning environment before an understanding of the learning-centred approach would probably result in adverse reactions. Responsibility is increasingly shared with participants as a mature learning community develops.

We have found that course members benefit from initial training and exposure to participative learning approaches in order to appreciate the roles, responsibilities and processes involved in the programme. So a primary aim of the orientation phase is to complete a mini-project related to the main project topic as a vehicle for this participative learning. This mini-project facilitates the development of approaches and skills for diagnosing and analysing problems and implementing solutions, and often highlights important aspects of the main project.

Format of the orientation phase

We have found that a wide variety of learning methods are appropriate during orientation. These include inputs, experiential exercises, self-directed study and discussions.

Broadly the orientation phase is divided between the Polytechnic, a residential venue and each participant's organization as follows:

Week 1	Week 2	Week 3	Week 4
		Mini-project	Mini-project
College	Residential	Participant's	Participant's
	Venue	organization	organization

Week 1 In College, deals primarily with 'hygiene' factors, initial introductions, the resources available and foundation knowledge, skills such as the Action Learning approach, models for internal consultancy, issues related to research and methods that might be employed.

Week 2 In a residential venue, the aim is to create and develop a supportive climate, allowing participants to re-examine their development needs and to experiment with new skills and behaviour. Initially, indoor exercises are used to achieve this, culminating in an integrated outdoor exercise over a day and a half. The use of the outdoors has proved a most successful medium for team building and providing the opportunity for members of the course simply to get to know each other better and begin to remove the protective layers of organizational status.

Week 3 Each participant is based in their organization with one day in college, working on the mini-project and developing insights into how best the main project might be approached and tackled.

Week 4 At this stage findings are presented to the set and project supervisor, and feedback received for the first time.

The problem centred project (Action Learning) phase

By this stage in the programme, participants should have developed considerable freedom for direction and control of their own learning. This freedom, together with support and encouragement from members of their learning set, their set adviser and their project tutor, will provide the conditions for rich learning.

During the early stages of the programme, each participant will have prepared a research proposal which, in essence, is a diagnosis of the organization's problem and an action plan for tackling it. The objective is not only to give focus to the first year's work, but also to provide a yardstick as to whether the proposed approach will satisfy the requirements of the client.

As they tackle their organizational project, members are concerned with the identification, diagnosis, analysis and exploration of theories thought to be useful and the experimentation, implementation and evaluation of improvements related to their organization's problem and their own development needs.

It is normal practice throughout the project phase, for participants to keep an account of their experiences and insights, using a journal or log book. This is so that ideas and insights are captured and not lost for the second more reflective part of the programme.

Learning sets

Sets normally consist of up to eight participants together with a set adviser. More than this number would, we feel, prevent proper interaction taking place. The primary functions of the set are to support and encourage each participant through the project task and associated learning. Gaining personal insights and being challenged normally involves:–

- Sharing experiences and problems and helping to rationalize them.

- Helping with the identification and diagnosis of organizational and personal needs.

- Exploring theories and approaches.

- Discussing programmes for action.

- Exploring processes of evaluation and experimentation.

- Developing and evaluating plans for implementation.

- Providing feedback on the competences and progress of each participant's efforts.

- providing feedback on each participant's interpersonal skills.

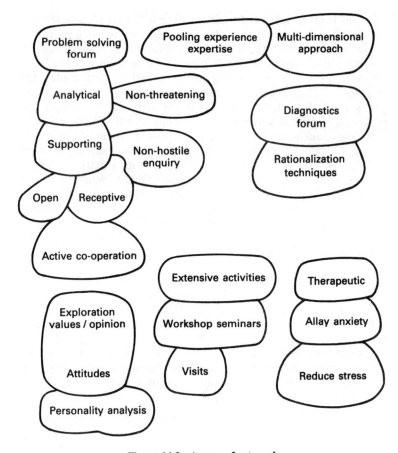

Figure 14.3   A map of set work

One student represented the usefulness of the set to him in the diagram set out in Figure 14.3.

Dissertation write-up and consolidation phase

This phase is intended to further develop skills in reflection and conceptualization. Managers are often weak in these areas and many are apprehensive about the difficult demands this phase of the programme will make on them. A major requirement is for them to read more widely than perhaps they have ever done before. Notwithstanding their initial reluctance most managers express a benefit from the process and confirm that strengthening conceptual skills is important in managing their own self-development.

During this phase, reflection often results in many project experiences being explained, new insights often being achieved and concepts recognized and developed. The dissertation takes the form of a reflective commentary which records, analyses and evaluates project experiences and the learning resulting from them at a variety of levels. At an instrumental level, reflection might show better approaches or techniques than those adopted on the project. At a higher level the whole nature of the project might be reconsidered in the light of a reflective assessment of the organization and its environment. Considerations relating to management development in this case would take a different direction.

Skills in analysing, evaluating, expressing and presentation are also developed during the dissertation phase. Before this phase, there will have been discussion on the requirements and assessment criteria for the dissertation. By this point in the programme, the ability to reflect and conceptualize should be well advanced and participants will have been encouraged to document each stage carefully as they progressed.

The regular meetings with the project/dissertation supervisor continue through this final phase of the programme. The discussions between the participant and supervisor will probably now focus upon methods of analysis and presentation, and ensuring that the dissertation is progressing satisfactorily. They will also deal with the criteria which the dissertation must satisfy.

With the emphasis on self-direction and control, participants are expected to include a thorough evaluation of the insights and the learning processes they have experienced, and the implications for their future development. Goals relating to their personal and organizational needs have the opportunity to be recorded so that changes in direction and progress can be evaluated.

The discipline of reflecting on, analysing and presenting their experiences during the action-centred phase can produce further insights to be shared by members of the learning set. Sets continue to meet to share problems and give support, but due to the pressure of presenting a Master's thesis, meetings are often less frequent and held at the discretion of the members.

Occasionally, managers face disruption to their studies, for example, a promotion, or a job change. However, providing the project has been completed to such a stage that it is possible to prepare an acceptable dissertation, the manager is allowed to continue. Extensions of up to six months are granted for participants with severe time pressures.

Set formation

Action Learning sets are formed to provide as rich a diversity of talent, qualification, experience and organization as possible. We make no use of psychometrics to produce 'balanced' groups, but rely on a personal knowledge of our participants and their performance during the orientation phase. There are some rules. No two people from the same or competitor organizations go into the same set. Set members will not have their project supervisor as their set adviser and so on.

We choose the sets, and so far there have been few problems. If there are severe personality clashes, then the problem will be tackled. Harmony is important, for after the orientation phase the set becomes the course and, once split, attempts to get a full group back together often fail.

The skills of the set adviser

The kind of skills required to be developed by set advisers are as follows:

The development of listening skills

- The ability to keep quiet.
- Avoid putting words in the mouths of others.
- Process consultancy.
- Hearing what is *not* said, as well as what is said.
- The ability to stand apart from the action – in order to bring to the surface the process issues.

Understanding group processes

- Through experience and formally through reading (including formal learning, for example, T Groups).
- Involvement in the total process.
- Feedback skills.

A broad understanding of management theory

- Expertise in a particular area is helpful: *but* dangers exist in over-use in interpreting events.

- Superficial knowledge of other disciplines area is good particularly:
  - Processes of management;
  - Power, politics;
  - Influencing strategies and networks;
  - Organizational change;
  - Decision taking.

Personal characteristics

- Good listener.

- Unobtrusive manner.

- Willingness to confront (done sparingly) and give feedback.

- Conceptual recognition of roles.

- Judgement as to when to direct the set's attention away from the task and on to the process.

- Willingness to be involved in the total process which includes selection, project meetings, induction and assessment.

Role of the set adviser

This role involves sharing the experiences and learning of the participants, whilst acting as process adviser when necessary.
They will be responsible for the following:

- Assisting the set members in developing a group climate and ethos within which open, effective communication can occur.

- Helping set members develop the skills of giving and receiving knowledge, opinions and experience.

- Helping Set members clarify the various processes involved in the Action Learning programme. These include processes of:
  - organization change;
  - project management;
  - group development;
  - self and career development.

- Helping set members to treat their experience of these processes as sources of learning.

- Assisting set members to assume responsibility for their own learning and development.

- Acting as a link between set members and the learning resources available within colleges offering the programme.

- Liaising with the course leader, project/dissertation supervisors, workshop tutors and the course committee on the arrangement of workshops, inputs, and so on.

From our experience, we have learnt a number of lessons about set advising. Firstly, no two sets are the same, a flexible contingent approach often pays dividends, sets are not necessarily teams, however much you wish them to be so, and set advisers are not necessarily equal members. Finally, effective sets more often than not begin with an effective common experience and we have found the outdoor exercises ideal for this purpose.

A typical set meeting

Typically, meetings take place weekly. The first few meetings are normally held in college and thereafter increasingly at members' organizations. This not only improves appreciation and understanding of that organization but also gives the organization member the opportunity to use the multiple skills of the set to help research the problem on site.

During meetings members might outline progress, indicate what they have discovered between meetings and outline what conclusions have been drawn. Opportunity then exists for colleagues to question how those conclusions were derived, methods of analysis used and, in the light of their own experience, to check the validity of assumptions made.

Workshops and special arrangements

The most common sources of learning will be the experiences and knowledge of members of the Learning set, the project/dissertation supervisor, the formal inputs and relevant reading. From time to time learning needs will be identified which cannot be adequately covered from these sources and for which other arrangements will be needed.

Alternatives that we regularly provide for students are as follows:

- Attending relevant lectures on other course programmes.

- Learning programmes/programme packages.

- Visits to organizations to see and discuss particular developments or applications.

- Special workshops where sufficient interest has been identified in a particular topic.

- Distance-learning materials available on a variety of subjects at whatever level.

During the project phase of the programme there are a number of specialized workshops. Although initiatives for these workshops or special inputs come from the course participants, by the very nature of the projects being undertaken we have found that a number of common themes recur each year, for example:

- Qualitative methods of data collection and analysis.

- The marketing of services.

- Implementing change – the role of the internal consultant.

- Financial management.

- Corporate objectives and the development of strategy.

Role of the project supervisor – the importance of contracting

Throughout the project and dissertation phases of the programme regular meetings take place between participants and their supervisor. Discussion centres around the participant's approach to their projects with a view to meeting the programme requirements and those of the client organization. The supervisor may also advise on technical or specialized aspects of the projects which the learning set does not have the resources to handle.

The term 'Supervisor' is certainly at variance with an Action Learning philosophy. Its continued use in our vocabulary remains problematic in the expectations it creates. The result is a range of interpretations and models of the role.

One model of the role involves the following responsibilities:

- Helping each participant with the discipline of planning and progressing project work.

- Helping each participant to reconcile any difference in interests or requirements between the programme and the client.

- Helping to identify learning needs and to suggest relevant reading.

- Liaising with set advisers, the course leader, workshop tutors and course committee, on the arrangement of workshops and other special events.

- Helping each participant to evaluate the significance of problems or potential problems, and to advise on approaches and sources of help for coping with them. Any problem which is likely to affect the progress or quality of a participant's submission should be reported to the course committee.

- Advising each participant on the programme requirements and the presentation of their dissertation.

The pace of the programme and personal commitment

Although there is a great importance placed on personal responsibility of the learner in this programme, there are nevertheless certain mechanisms whereby the pace and direction of an individual's progress will be monitored.

Firstly, the structure of the programme is quite explicit in terms of how long the orientation phase lasts, how long the participant can expect to take over the actual project work and exactly when the final dissertation has to be handed in. The programme structure therefore provides a basic timetabling framework for the participant.

Secondly, each participant has their own personal project/dissertation supervisor. The role of the supervisor includes not only providing guidance and advice on technical methodological issues, but also on the very practical issue of time management.

Thirdly, the learning set also provides a context within which the relative progress of each participant will be visible to every other participant. Should this not provide sufficient motivation, it would be accepted, and indeed encouraged, practice for set members to comment on the possible slow rate of progress of one of their colleagues.

Individuals are also visible in their organizations as they undertake important project and development work. Part of the progress is to seek and obtain top management support, and continuing goodwill rather than resentment from peers. At a personal level, then, the participant stands to gain relevant managerial experience, together with a recognized high-level qualification.

Each of these factors tends to produce high levels of commitment from each participant to completing the requirements of the programme.

Outcomes

We believe that the outcomes of the programme justify the input. Tangible outcomes include a project report submitted in the first year of the programme, and a dissertation submitted in the second. Both documents are subject to a viva conducted by one external examiner and two internal examiners. Vivas offer the opportunity for course participants to explain aspects of their work in greater detail and engage in a defence of their particular stance or approach.

In development terms, we have had many reports of the developments for which the programme has been responsible, both individually and organizationally. Repeat business from clients and recommendations by past participants reinforce this sense of success.

In terms of organizational development we have had some notable successes attributable to the programme – the commissioning of a new hospital, the introduction of a new staff development policy and a reduction in manning involving a £1.5 million budget cut.

As far as individuals on the programme are concerned, there have been promotions and new appointments which have at times led to envious comments from staff.

Conclusions

From our experiences at Manchester, we have learnt a great deal about the kind of things needed if programmes of this kind are to run successfully.

Action Learning makes for effective management development because it recognizes that in order to develop an organization there is a need to develop managers, and the problem-centred, strategy-driven approach of Action Learning is ideally suited to accomplish both.

By exploiting the power of learning on the job, it develops high level management competences in a social context that encourages both openness and a positive questioning attitude that leads to a true change experience. Managers are challenged with a number of relative perspectives, probably in a way they have never been before, by other programme participants. The strangeness of the situation, the process of reflection, and exposure to wider frames of reference of other managers and the literature provide a rich learning experience.

It is our own experience that managers who attend the programme are not initially aware of the likely effect such a process will have on their personal development and attitude to management. For those considering Action Learning in an academic environment, there are a number of lessons that seem important if maximum advantage is to be gained from the programme:

1 Build up the group of managers into a learning community in as short a time as possible. Action Learning emphasizes the importance of the social process in learning. Group or team development exercises, or even the use of the outdoors as we have described, can be useful to this end.

2 Ensure that the correct balance is struck between organization problem solving and personal development. Personal development will always be a consequence of the problem-solving process. The converse is not always the case; individuals need to be working on a real organizational problem.

3 The chosen problem needs to contain sufficient complexity and uncertainty for a variety of different solutions to be possible, not just one 'correct' solution as with a puzzle. Judgement should be brought to bear on it, not just analysis.

4 The organization needs to be committed to finding a solution, and the individual needs to have the support of someone in the organization who will sponsor the work being undertaken.

5 If the greatest potential for management development is to be realized, the problem should include the implementation of a solution. Effective managers need to understand aspects of politics and power, and need to develop strategies to influence effectively. Ironically, one way to really understand how an organization works is to attempt to change it.

6 Where programmes take place in academic institutions, and particularly when they are award bearing, care needs to be taken so as not to lead with too much programmed knowledge (P). Programmed knowledge will be useful to guide the manager at all stages of the project and provide a framework for conceptualization and reflection, but it is the ability to question (Q), challenge, synthesize and evaluate in order to understand, that is the heart of the action

learning process. This implies a need to encourage individuals to recognize talents and ideas that emerge from the group and exploit them.

7   Organized properly, Action Learning programmes in academic institutions can conform to the requirements thought to be important if maximum learning is to take place.[3]

Learning = O (Opportunity) + C (Challenge) + H (Help) + F
          (Forgiveness)

Where O represents a real organizational problem to be solved; C represents a problem that stretches and challenges the manager by either being in a new area or an environment where ideas are challenged; H represents help, provided primarily by a set of managers and additionally by academic or industrial supervisors; and F represents a measure of forgiveness if the project should fail to achieve the desired results.

References

1 Boddy, D. (1980), 'Putting Action Learning in Action', *Journal of Education and Industrial Training*, **5**, (5).
2 Spender, J. (1989), *Management Receipts*, Oxford: Basil Blackwell.
3 Compare: Handy, C. (1989), *The Age of Unreason*, London: Century Hutchinson.

PART III

ACTION LEARNING ROUND THE WORLD

15 Helping US human resource professionals into Action Learning

Nancy M. Dixon, Larry Hales and Richard Baker

General Motors has historically employed a cadre of human-resource development (HRD) professionals with the expertise to teach middle managers competences identified with successful performance. Such competences are represented by the 'P' in Revans's formula L = P+Q. However, in more recent times, top Human Resource management at General Motors has come to recognize that to meet the new leadership challenges – continuous improvement, customer satisfaction, teamwork, empowerment and personal responsibility – an additional competence is required of middle managers. That competence is the ability to think in new and fresh ways about existing problems. Such competence, which is referred to here simply as 'Q', has been variously labelled critical reflection, context shifting, reframing and paradigm shift. The essence of the competence is 'the capacity to dig below the surface layer of perception to examine taken-for-granted assumptions and values in order to determine whether or not one is addressing the right problem'.[1] Thus, to meet the challenge of a rapidly changing General Motors, top Human Resource management saw a need for the 'P' competences which human-resource professionals had traditionally taught to be balanced with the 'Q' ability managers could use to ask fresh questions.

To respond to this need General Motors set up a development

team of individuals from three organizations: a professor with a working knowledge of Action Learning from The George Washington University; the president of a management consulting firm, Baker & Company, with a reputation in the training industry for innovative learning designs; and several General Motors HRD professionals with long-term experience consulting with and teaching middle managers.

Action Learning was identified as one of the appropriate methodologies to develop 'Q' in middle managers. The initial vehicle for implementing Action Learning was three week-long leadership courses to be designed for newly promoted first and second level supervisors and third level managers. Specifically, the course objectives were as follows:

- to introduce managers to the ability to shift contexts, develop new perspectives and reframe assumptions within a challenging global environment;

- to facilitate the ongoing development of management knowledge, skills and insights; and

- to empower managers to utilize each other's cross-functional skills in action sets that would meet, following the initial training, for the purpose of solving complex real-world problems facing their business.

The development team was assigned two tasks: 1) to create the initial five-day courses for each level; and 2) to prepare the HRD professionals for their role as facilitators in both the initial classroom experience and later as set advisers.

The primary focus of this chapter is the second of those two tasks. In a sense this chapter is itself an instance of Action Learning. It is a reflection on the experiences of the development team as it attempted an unfamiliar task, that of assisting the HRD professionals at General Motors to gain the new skills, roles and attitudes necessary to model and facilitate 'Q'. We are sharing our experience in order that others who undertake to help HRD professionals switch from 'P' to 'Q' have the opportunity to learn from our reflection.

Difference in the skills needed for 'P' and 'Q'

The first task in the development of the facilitators was to delineate how the skill sets for the two learning processes, 'P' and 'Q', differed in order to plan the assessment and development process. These skills are as follows:

Skills and knowledge needed to teach 'P'

- Master the subject matter on which the instruction is based.
- Understand the task environment in which participants function in order to build connections between the content and their work.
- Explain the content in terms of practical guidelines or procedures which participants can employ when addressing problems they face on the job.
- Design and implement exercises that allow participants to gain proficiency in applying the guidelines or procedures.
- Ask questions that will lead participants to discover the 'correct' answer for themselves.
- Manage any resistance to the ideas off-line or in ways that are the least disruptive to the learning of others.
- Make the training a positive experience for participants:
  - keep things moving;
  - keep things light;
  - be seen as personable, likable, friendly;
  - 'save face' for participants by paraphrasing incorrect responses so that they more closely represent the correct answer;
  - reinforce correct responses;
- Avoid situations or topics in which lack of expertise might lessen instructor credibility.

Skills needed to facilitate 'Q'

- Design opportunities for participants to find their own answers to problems
- Design opportunities for participants to learn from each others' perspective, mistakes, and successes
- Encourage a climate where participants will both support and challenge each other
- Refrain from displaying one's own knowledge and understanding
- Challenge individual and group assumptions both about the back home environment and about the action that is on-line

- Give difficult feedback to participants
- Ask questions that assist participants in exploring the reasoning behind their assumptions
- Raise difficult issues even at the risk of participant's becoming annoyed with the facilitator
- Acknowledge facilitator mistakes publicly, framing them as learning experiences

In constructing such a list it became clear to the team that although the two skill sets varied greatly, the most striking contrast between 'P' and 'Q' was in the assumptions about learning and instructor responsibility that formed the basis for each.

The assumption on which traditional 'P' is based is that participants will be better managers if they learn and apply the skill and knowledge which management experts have developed. In the classroom it is the HRD professional's responsibility to see that participants understand and value those skills and ideas. Since HRD professionals have no line authority over the participants they must rely on their credibility as subject-matter experts and their skill in creating a positive classroom experience to accomplish these goals. If participants are resistant to the ideas which are proposed, HRD professionals are likely to see themselves as having failed in their task.

The assumption on which 'Q' is based is that managers learn best from working to resolve real problems. However, to do so they must get beyond the limits of their current assumptions. The facilitator's job, then, is not to provide answers but to assist in removing the 'blinkers'. Removing blinkers requires facilitators to challenge current assumptions and contexts. Even when accomplished with caring and concern, having one's current assumptions challenged is often a disconcerting experience. Facilitators must expect that at times participants will be angry or upset with them. With 'P,' facilitators' credibility is based on their knowledge of the subject matter. By contrast, 'Q' credibility comes from facilitators being able to 'walk their talk', that is, being open to seeing their own limiting beliefs, contextual perspectives, and ineffective reasoning.

The development team hypothesized that facilitators, in attempting to facilitate 'Q' rather than 'P', would be faced with the same challenges as the managers they would be helping; that is, they would need to remove the blinkers of their current assumptions in order to act in new ways. The difficulties they would face in facilitating 'Q' would entail not only using different skill sets, but also modifying their assumptions about the role of expert knowledge in learning and about the nature of the responsibilities of the facilitator.

Further, the team hypothesized that, as with managers, the support and reward system within which the facilitators functioned would affect their success. For example, when teaching 'P', the HRD professionals had traditionally paid close attention to: the ratings on participant reaction forms completed at the end of the course; the number of participants that were attracted to the course; and the respect participants tend to bestow on those who display subject-matter expertise.

Preparation to facilitate 'Q'

To test these hypotheses and to begin the facilitator assessment and development, a two-day meeting was designed for prospective facilitators. The objectives of the meeting were: 1) to model the facilitator skills; 2) to explore the concerns of prospective facilitators; and 3) to provide prospective facilitators an opportunity for self-assessment of their own skill level.

The meeting produced a mixed response from the prospective facilitators. They recognized that the 'Q' process was clearly going to bring to the surface uncertainty and paradox related to business issues. They acknowledged that they felt more immediate comfort leaving such issues alone. Yet at the same time, they felt that it was critical to General Motors for managers to be freed of their current assumptions in order to think in new and innovative ways about the business and its challenges. In addition, they welcomed the opportunity to exercise more facilitative skills than they were able to use in traditional courses.

The concerns which the prospective facilitators expressed about the 'Q' process are summarized here under three headings.

Concerns related to protecting the participants from themselves

- Asking participants to deal with their own assumptions may cause them some pain – they may leave the workshop feeling badly.

- This feels like sensitivity training – a lot of people got hurt with that.

- How can we help participants save face in class if we are confronting their assumptions?

- If we teach participants to think in this way they may find themselves penalized when they go back to work and try to use these ideas.

Concerns about the consequences to facilitators

- If we are confrontative our ratings on the participant reaction forms will go down. As HRD professionals we have traditionally set great store by those forms.

- People want answers, not questions, in the courses.

- People in the courses may not tolerate this kind of probing, they might just walk out.

Concerns about making mistakes or being seen as less skilful

- When we team-teach, one team member might turn out to be more skilful in this than another and hurt feelings might ensue.

- If we engage in lengthy discussions we will not cover all the material. We are likely to be criticized for that.

- It would not be fair to some of us to have to learn and practise these skills in front of our more adept colleagues. We should be given an opportunity to learn these skills in private, away from the organization.

In addition to the concerns listed above, the self-assessment revealed that the current skill set associated with 'P' was so automatic that prospective facilitators had difficulty setting it aside in order to use the new 'Q' skills. For example, they demonstrated:

1 a tendency to use questions to bring participants around to an answer the facilitator had already formed in his/her own mind rather than using questions to help participants explore their own ideas;

2 a tendency to try to persuade participants to the facilitator's point of view rather than attempt to understand the participants' reasoning and assumptions;

3 a tendency to avoid rather than confront difficult and contentious issues;

4 a tendency to act in ways that saved face for each other and the participants.

Finally, the self-assessment indicated that the prospective facilitators were often embedded in the same assumptions about the organization that the managers held. They were therefore unable to be helpful in identifying the manager's assumptions in order to raise them to a level at which they could be examined.

As a result of the assessment, the prospective facilitators devised a process to help each other gain the new skills by working together in teams, so that each could provide feedback for the other. There was, however, an unwillingness to commit fully to the 'Q' methodology as long as they felt it involved the risk of a negative consequence to themselves. In particular, the prospective facilitators wanted assurance by their own management that if the ratings on participant reaction forms were lower as a result of the 'Q' methodology they would not be held responsible. Realizing that traditional success indicators would need to be viewed differently for 'Q' learning to proceed, General Motors' HRD management offered the required assurance. The prospective facilitators, however, continued to express concern about how they would be judged.

The development team proceeded with the design of the initial courses and with plans to begin action sets following the courses. The first course, which was piloted at the supervisor level with externals facilitating, achieved mixed results. Before arriving, participants had talked with others who had attended earlier versions of the courses and therefore came expecting a very different kind of course from what was offered. They were, as well, new to their jobs and, as the prospective facilitators had anticipated, were 'looking for answers'. This need was particularly strong at the first-line supervisory level. Despite this, most participants achieved breakthroughs in their own thinking and left with a desire to continue the exploration. The course was seen as frustrating but beneficial.

As the process moved forward the internal HRD professionals took over the task of facilitation. Several activities were built into the design of the programs to provide feedback to the facilitators about how the group was doing and how they felt about the facilitators. These activities, initially seen as high risk for the facilitators, came to be valued as a source of useful information. With the use of such tools and with strong management encouragement, the facilitators gained both skill and comfort. However, as expected, their existing assumptions and beliefs remained a hindrance to switching skill sets. In some instances the development team altered the facilitator tasks to provide more 'P' and less 'Q' to increase the comfort level of the facilitators.

Action sets

As the time came closer to implement action sets, new issues arose. One related to the structure of Human Resources within US organizations. In most US organizations, 'Training' is responsible for providing 'P' through scheduled courses that often bring together participants from across the US. A separate branch of Human Resources, 'Organizational Development', is responsible for working with managers on-site through the use of small group activities that are problem solving oriented. Since action learning overlapped both 'Training' and 'Organizational Development', it was unclear which area should assume responsibility for the implementation of action sets.

A second issue, also related to the way many US decentralized organizations are structured, is that HRD typically does not have the authority to implement programmes in plants or divisions. At General Motors mechanisms were lacking to describe and promote the Action Learning concept to line management, whose support would be essential to the successful operation of Action Learning sets at the plant/office locations of the organization.

The Action Learning process is sufficiently attractive, and so greatly needed, that progress continues despite such formidable roadblocks. It remains to be seen whether Action Learning can enter an organization in the US through the Human Resources function; and further, whether it can be successfully facilitated by HRD professionals. In any case, from the lengthy experiment some lessons have been learned.

Lessons learned

HRD professionals experienced in leading 'P' learning often come to expect a well-thought-out instructional design complete with leader's guide. 'Q' processes, however, require a minimum amount of pre-design because of the situational nature of the learning event. The ambiguity and lack of explicit learning objectives associated with 'Q' requires HRD professionals to make a significant shift in skills as well as assumptions.

Because 'Q' facilitation demands considerable openness as well as a willingness to examine one's own mistakes publicly, not everyone should be encouraged to become a 'Q' facilitator. The selection process for identifying personnel for the 'Q' role should clarify what is required of a 'Q' facilitator in terms of both behaviour and values.

In the US, the traditional reward system for both the HRD professionals and the Human Resources department supports the use of 'P' rather than 'Q'. Human Resources departments are often budgeted according to the number of participants who have attended. HRD professionals are rewarded for the positive response they receive from participants. Major changes in the reward system for HRD are required to support 'Q'.

Through this experience with Action Learning, as well as with other learning efforts that are being implemented at General Motors, there is a growing realization that the distinction between 'Training' and 'Organizational Development' is in many ways artificial. Many at General Motors have come to understand that the typical US organizational structure which separates the roles of 'Training' and 'Organizational Development' may need to be redefined or abandoned for the full potential of Action Learning to be realized.

Having externals on the development team, in this case the professor and consultant, brings a perspective to those learning 'Q' that helps them to reframe their own assumptions about the new role of the HRD professional and the environment in which they are functioning.

The preparation of 'Q' facilitators who have been mostly involved in facilitating 'P' learning requires a very thoughtful process. This process is probably most successful when a master facilitator is assigned the tasks of teaching, coaching, and mentoring experienced 'P' facilitators as they learn the new skills.

Action Learning and the 'Q' learning process are difficult to promote or explain to action oriented managers in the US who have come to think of learning as separate from work. The 'Q' process, questioning insight, is often initially seen by managers as the stuff of philosophers or, worse, 'idle dreamers'.

Regardless of the ambiguity or situational nature of 'Q' learning, success indicators need to be identified by the facilitating team. Success indicators may be determined through discussion, consensus and critical reflection on the part of the HRD facilitation team.

Senior managers appear to value 'Q' more and to be more receptive to it, than supervisor-level managers. There appears to be a greater willingness on their part to reflect and to seek the perspective of others.

Although the act of challenging taken-for-granted assumptions of managers is a critical element in the learning process, it is helpful only if it is accomplished in a climate of support, trust, and openness. It is the combination of challenge and trust that facilitates 'Q' learning.

Reference

1 Marsick, V. J. (ed.) (1982), *Learning in the Workplace*, New York: Croom Helm, p. 5.

16 Action Learning at Digital Equipment

Doris Adams and Nancy M. Dixon

Action Learning has been a component of a management development effort at Digital Equipment Corporation's manufacturing facility in Burlington, Vermont, for the past one and a half years. Approximately fifty people in management positions in the plant, from executive staff to supervisors, have been involved in the two cycles of the nine-month programme called World Class Leadership. Participants either entered the programme on a voluntary basis or were selected by their managers. The programme combined two-day and three-day workshops, usually one per month, spread over the nine months, with Action Learning sets which met on a weekly basis during the last four to five months. A variety of topics were included in the workshops, ranging from the history and future technologies of computers to the specifics of total quality control and coaching techniques. The sets provided an opportunity for participants to apply the techniques and ideas from the workshops to the solving of real organizational problems in the context of a small group.

Design of the programme

The goals of the Action Learning sets were as follows:

1 To learn problem-solving skills which are data driven and to concentrate on problem framing.

2   To discover and change rules which are taken for granted (underlying assumptions, stereotypes, norms, perceptions, and so on), and which impede effective group problem solving.

3   To develop the ability to reframe problems and situations.

4   To develop a high-performance team.

5   To develop coaching skills.

6   To learn consultation and project-management skills.

7   To resolve business issues.

Each Action Learning set had five to seven participants who represented different levels of management and various organizational functions. The heterogeneity was introduced to ensure that problems were approached from diverse viewpoints.

The organizational problems for potential set consideration were generated by the plant executive staff and the programme participants. Participants identified the problem they would like to work on and sets were formed around individual interest in the problem area.

In the second cycle of the programme a set adviser or coach for each Action Learning set was used. The self-managed sets in the first cycle in most cases proved ineffective in producing the level of learning desired and in developing implementable solutions to business problems. Participants had not developed, and were not supported in developing, the skills to be able to work through group conflict successfully and align around a common compelling goal. These steps seem to be critical to achieving the desired outcomes.

Coaches for the four sets in the second cycle of the programme were selected for the strength of their interpersonal skills. Argyris and Schon define the skills desirable for resolving organizational problems as Model II skills.[1] These include the need to spend time clarifying problems from diverse viewpoints and looking at the underlying assumptions which are operating in the situation. This involves the skills of inquiry, a willingness to suspend judgement until all ideas are considered, and openly confrontating conflict or disagreement.

The designers of the programme chose these primarily interpersonal competences for coaches rather than a knowledge of the business, project management expertise or specific knowledge of the problem. Following Revans they believed that the coach who was naïve about the problem itself might ask the kind of difficult questions which would be useful in framing problems alternatively.[2] The role of the coaches was also to teach these interpersonal skills to programme participants. Since the perfection of these skills requires practice over time, the set and a skilled teacher/coach became keys to their development. The sets were encouraged to call in experts to obtain information useful for problem identification and solution.

The Action Learning set component of the second cycle of the World Class Leadership programme began as each set convened to determine meeting times and dates, establish operating rules, clarify roles of members and establish goals related to learning and the business problem. During the programme's three-day workshop on coaching, sets began clarifying the nature of their task or project. They obtained initial sponsorship from organizational representatives who were seen as the customer and person with the resources or authority to implement the change. The sets then identified the customer's requirements and standards for successful completion of the projects. Examples of rules (norms) developed for group operation were as follows:

- to determine if a leader is needed and what the leader's role will be;

- to challenge obstructive behaviour and process, and to find ways to redesign it;

- to obtain group consensus around the process to be followed;

- to build in a critical pause;

- to state your position and reasoning, and to be willing to have it disconfirmed;

- to listen to everyone equally;

- to bring people up to speed who miss part of the action;

- to raise difficult issues for discussion.

The sets then met weekly at the plant with their set coaches to implement the action planning process which they had developed. Full group meetings occurred at the mid-point and end of the Action Learning set experience. During these meetings, the groups shared progress and what they had learned and obtained comments and ideas from the larger group. The reflections of the four sets were presented and discussed in the final public forum of the programme.

The remainder of this chapter will discuss the nature of the learning and business results of the four action learning sets in the second cycle of the programme, and will review the revisions in the process which are being considered for future cycles. First, the experience of the sets.

Experiences of Action Learning in four sets

Set A solved a business issue related to waste elimination, particularly in terms of reducing unnecessary computer reports and person-hours required to produce the reports. They won a plant-wide contest for a poster supporting the elimination of waste (especially paper), and will extend their set activities until the last of their recommendations are implemented.

This set struggled for several weeks before they could answer the question: 'Why are we here?' Even though they had an area of focus when they formed – waste elimination – they took some time to arrive at a specific project that was compelling for the group and that had a clear sponsor. In the process they lost two group members who, in the face of more pressing work in their area of responsibility, chose not to persist in the effort to arrive at a common goal.

Pausing to work through the group conflict around member commitment and an unclear task led the members to disclose their thoughts on matters that they had not felt 'safe' in sharing earlier and which were preventing them from progressing on their project. They spent time reaching a good understanding of the group's process to date and the difficulties they faced related to the problem. Out of this discussion, the specific problem/task the group wanted to address emerged, a specific sponsor was located, and the group began practising the type of communication which would lead to collaborative action.

In their final reflections, they recognized many of Argyris and Schon's Model II skills as the key skills which led to their effectiveness. They asked questions to understand the other's view, bringing out for public discussion what they were thinking and not saying. They tested the assumptions that they were making about others' meanings, and stated their view with an invitation for feedback. One member said, 'It is more effective to say "this is what I think . . ." and test it with others versus asking "what do we want".' The set found they had to slow down action considerably in order to develop the community of inquiry which led to having full information about the problem and the thinking of members of the group. They also adopted the view that members needed a free choice about set participation, and that varying levels of participation were acceptable; and they established a norm in which set members declared their commitment to action with the expectation of accountability by the group.

The coach and co-coach were invaluable to Set A's project and process accomplishments. The co-coach (a programme participant from the first cycle) brought effective project management skills. The coach introduced the issues that were blocking effective group action, provided the group members with 'on-line' feedback on whether their actions conformed to the new norms set by the group, and reinforced the emergent skills in communication and problem framing.

The cross-functional team was critical to solving the problem, as differing views were used in the process. In addition, implementing the solution across functions was facilitated.

It was important to the set's success that a sponsor be found who was clearly interested in the project and who would ask for information and check on progress. This sponsor also shared the activities of the set with the executive staff of the plant.

Set B developed a plan for improvement of the financial reporting process. Like Set A, they too identified as key elements to their effectiveness the struggle for defining a clear goal, and also the conflict that occurred prior to obtaining this direction. Their initial goal had been productivity improvement, and the specific project emerged from dealing with the conflict around the question: 'What is our goal?' This set also emphasized the importance of coaching to their learning and movement as a group.

The Action Learning set experience produced specific content knowledge for Set B in the area of finance and assessment of customer needs. The former learnings were made possible by tapping the expertise of one of the set members who assumed a teaching role in the set.

As the goal of the project became more and more specific, it became clear that accomplishing a number of small improvements was a valuable contribution to improving organizational effectiveness. Initially, this set's members thought that the outcome had to be of major significance. This belief created tension because of the competing pull of work responsibilities and the time it took to become an effectively functioning team.

The set experienced the tension between process and content (or task and maintenance activities) fairly constantly. Some set members argued strongly that the process must be effective to be able to produce the desired results, and they, therefore, wanted to spend time discussing how the process was going. Others wanted to spend time on the content, learning about the financial area, and identifying and solving the problem. This 'battle' was waged openly, and occasionally the set resolved the dichotomy using process techniques to act on content issues. The dilemma was not fully resolved in this set. However, members pointed out that they will return to their daily work groups with an appreciation of the tension, and some ideas about how to handle both group process and content issues more successfully.

There were differing levels of commitment among members of the set. A core group did most of the work on the problem. This core group developed the ability to be more open with one another, discussing undiscussables particularly related to the issues of content vs. process and commitment definition.

Set C addressed the most specific and initially compelling problem, developing a model for becoming competitive in the manufacture of one of the plant's products. The set formed around four members who were on the operations staff for this product, one of whom was the executive staff member and three who were in other businesses. Its pattern of development was somewhat different from that of Sets A and B.

Initially this set was goal-directed, had clear communication from its sponsor and was committed to developing the action plan necessary for implementation of the model for competitiveness in one product line. The group spent time pooling its information and establishing the additional sources of information it would need to address the problem.

As in Set B, a set member from finance helped the whole group develop the knowledge necessary to frame the issues involved in developing a plan to reduce the cost for producing the product. This was seen as a valuable lesson for the group.

About six weeks into the process, this set experienced the influence of external factors on a project team's goal and level of commitment. The first influence was felt as the set lost the member who was the executive level manager. He left the set when he assumed some additional responsibilities. This member had exerted strong leadership within the group and his leaving left members struggling with role definition. Secondly, the perception began to grow that the set's business focus was no longer going to be a priority in the Burlington plant. Based on this assumption, another set member who was most passionate about the initial set problem began looking for a position outside this business. After attendance at set meetings began to dwindle a core group of four members and the coach began to perceive what was happening and the next steps which the group needed to take to move forward.

The group members recognized they were in trouble – if they continued with the project and it was not valued by anyone then they would feel they were wasting their time; if they did not continue, they felt that they would be quitting and would be viewed as incompetent by their peers. Discussion of this problem led them to realize the importance of synthesizing where they were in terms of the project and of delivering what they had learned to the project sponsor in order to obtain direction regarding next steps. This would involve testing their assumption about shifting business priorities. In a meeting, the group synthesized what they had learned and prepared a report to be delivered to their sponsor as soon as possible. The group was thus able to reevaluate its goal and flexibly define new work in collaboration with the project sponsor.

In facing the breakdown, the group also began to recognize how their very goal-directedness had led them to suppress information which would have been helpful both in slowing down their process and in predicting and dealing with the changing business goals at an earlier point in the process. Several group members came to the realization that they were operating with underlying beliefs similar to those which led to the suppression of information. For example, one common thought pattern that guided behaviour was: 'When I am in situations where there are issues that are not being discussed and I fear there will be retribution if I share my view, I collude with the others by keeping my view private or contributing in a passive way.' In this situation the group avoided looking at their action, which prevented them from understanding and altering it.

In the end the group felt that they had achieved significant learning, about how to address projects and communicate effectively within groups, to take back to their work environment. For example, they became aware of the tendency of groups to use filler activities, such as presentations and reports, rather than deal with difficult issues, and of the strong tension between doing and planning, between acting and reflecting. The action often kept the group from spending time discussing and understanding its purpose, which led in turn to ineffective action. As the group began to raise issues, and members became willing to reveal what they were thinking, they became aware of powerful new tools for effecting business results.

Set D had the most difficult time with the Action Learning process. They eventually disbanded without even agreeing on a project goal. This group started with the aim of doing something with the customer integration programme. The set members identified several possibilities for action but did not agree on a project.

The project sponsor was not actively involved in assisting the set in establishing a specific project. Almost anything the set wanted to do was agreeable to this sponsor. Left to set up its own project, the group raised several possibilities, but no project achieved group consensus for moving forward. Without a clear goal, the group had no incentive to stay together, and the longer it took to arrive at a clear goal, the more difficult it became to maintain commitment to the group. Attendance diminished, and some members began taking action on their own to investigate or act on project ideas.

The set failed to suspend judgement in order to discuss each option openly, to bring up all the information about the potential project, and to assimilate each set member's reasoning related to the projects. Members who had an investment in a particular project maintained the position that their idea was the best one without testing its validity with the group. By the time they attempted alternate communication strategies, these win/lose dynamics had polarized the group, and members did not believe that alternative approaches could save the set. At the finish, members felt as though they had failed in the completion of the task and were concerned that they had not learned a sufficient number of skills to work through the group breakdown.

Conclusions

Significant issues facing Action Learning sets emerged from the experiences of the participants in the World Class Leadership program at Digital Equipment Corporation in Burlington, Vermont. The successful sets, in terms of achieving business results for the organization and defining learning for themselves, developed an effective process of communication and a clear and compelling goal to which the group members were committed. Members were able to discuss openly the underlying assumptions they held about the problem, the group process and each other. They aired conflicting views and discovered a collaborative view through the process of consensus. Out of this emerged the group's goals. Working through intra-group conflict and the emotional response to task demands was essential if the group was to find effective ways to address the task, and to actualize what they had learned from this process. The process seemed to lead to the set members' commitment to the goals which emerged. At the same time, skilled coaching also seemed to be necessary if this outcome were to result. Unfortunately, in the course of conflict, some group members and one of the sets disengaged from the Action Learning process.

The pressure of the work environment was a powerful factor to deal with during this type of learning experience. The tasks of the sets were viewed as non-essential activity in comparison with the 'real' work evolving in the plant. Some members did not find support for their participation in the programme from their managers, peers and subordinates, and those members found it most difficult to remain active in the set activities. In the instance of the development of a competitive business model, the uncertain priorities of the plant led to a wavering commitment of set members around a problem which potentially was no longer significant.

Additional factors which contributed to set success were in the areas of sponsor support, team composition and expertise, and coaching relationships. Sponsors who monitored the set's progress and took an active interest in the set activities motivated the sets to persist in their activity. Effective solutions and implementation strategies emerged from cross-functional teams that shared different perspectives and had contacts in their organizations to support the implementation of cross-functional solutions. Set members learned from their expert members who had content or project-management skills. Co-coaching arrangements in two sets led to more effective coaching, as co-coaches assisted each other in reflecting on their practice and developing their coaching skills.

In general, each set participant found that much of the communication and problem-framing skills, as well as learning about group dynamics and content knowledge, was usable in their work environment. Also, the ineffective patterns of action demonstrated in the Action Learning set were not unlike those enacted in the work environment.

Currently, an evaluation of the programme is being conducted. Interviews of managers, peers, and subordinates of programme participants who were part of the core groups of the Action Learning sets in the second cycle have revealed that the participants have transferred behaviour learned in the sets to the work setting. Participants also recognized the expansion of their net-

work of contacts. They described the programme as having supported their ability to span functional boundaries in their thinking
and action.

The design and evaluation team is considering future alter-
ations to the programme and its Action Learning set component.
One of the changes contemplated is to integrate the theory and
techniques of world class manufacturing (total quality control
and just-in-time) and action science more specifically with the
Action Learning set experience. The purpose of this change is
to improve the relationship between real work and the Action
Learning set process, by using these techniques to address actual
business cases. Participants would come into the programme with
business issues from their work area. The work of the sets would
be to consult with each other to solve the business issues of set
members, and in so doing, learn a new set of skills. In addition,
an intact work team or project team might enter as a set to deal
with the business issues they face and integrate this learning
component into their work.

In the future, at the onset of the Action Learning set component of the programme, each group will be taken through an
outward bound/ropes experience which will help break individual
barriers to change and build the trust level in the team. Other
individual work may be instituted to assess participant needs,
support personal development during the set experience, and
provide performance coaching and assessment as follow-up to
the programme. A rigorous course will also be given to develop
expert coaches for the sets. Several persons who have completed
the World Class Leadership programme are candidates for this
course. Finally, certification and credit for this programme are
being explored.

The Action Learning sets at Digital Equipment Corporation
in Burlington, Vermont, provided the participants in the second
cycle of the programme with a rich learning experience which
transferred to the work environment. The plant benefited from
solved problems, and from a new level of skills in communication, problem framing and team development which was exhibited by its management-level employees.

References

1 Argyris, C. & Schon, D. (1974), *Theory in Practice: Increasing Professional Effectiveness*, San Francisco: Jossey Bass.
2 Revans, R. W. (1983), *The ABC of Action Learning*, Bromley, UK:
Chartwell-Bratt, p. 16.

17 Learning from action in Australia

Charles Margerison

I have been seriously involved in Action Learning for only five years. However, I have known about Action Learning for the last twenty-five years. Knowing and doing are very different.

Therefore, I shall summarize what I have learned from direct involvement by asking questions and considering the answers. I trust this article will encourage those who know about Action Learning to apply it and for those that already do it to continue to do so effectively. I say this because for many years I did not apply what I knew. I concentrated on knowledge and skills programmes rather than action. There is a big difference. The following cases provide some example of how I have tried to implement what I know about Action Learning. They are not necessarily the way others should do it. I offer them only as illustrations for sharing and comparing.

What are the major Action Learning projects in which I have been involved?

I was invited in 1985 to meet with a senior executive of a company employing over 20 000 people. His job as manager of Human Resources was to facilitate the introduction of new approaches for managing people effectively. He told me that despite working long hours, travelling considerable distances, and receiving warm receptions from line managers, little change had occurred. He therefore asked my advice.

My instinctive response was that he was working too hard and his clients were not working hard enough on the issues. He immediately sat forward in his chair and said: 'Yes, that's true, but how do I set up a way of changing that when I don't have direct line authority?' So began a major two-year assignment on Action Learning.

The steps we took to get the project going took about six months. They involved the following stages:

- A meeting with the Executive Board and myself at one of their annual workshops to lead a session on management development. Instead of giving them a talk I asked them to identify the major management strengths and weaknesses they saw in the company. After forty-five minutes they conceded that of all the points they could identify 75 per cent were weaknesses. I proposed they establish three Action Learning groups to investigate their assumptions and report back within ten weeks.

- The Board agreed and we set up a steering committee involving four executives and three of my team to plan the programme. This was crucial to gaining internal political support below Board level and establishing sets that were seen as representative.

- The three groups were then formed and we had a workshop at which: we outlined the Action Learning approach; had clients outline the projects; did team development work; discussed action research methods; and prepared everyone for the work ahead.

- Each group had a set adviser. One of the groups conducted a study on how people in the top 400 managers felt about management development at their level. Another group conducted a similar representative study of the next 400 managers below the senior group. The other group visited 13 different companies to discover what they did to facilitate management development.

- At the end of the ten weeks the Executive Board convened to hear the reports. Each group had one hour. After that the Board met by itself for three hours to discuss the findings and recommendations. They then made a presentation to the groups saying that they supported their findings and would allocate over $300 000 in direct funds to implement their proposals.

This was the beginning of a real Action Learning initiative; yet it had taken approximately eight months just to get this far. Therefore, the first major learnings for me were that to be successful:

- Action Learning needs a lot of senior political support;

- this takes a long time to achieve and requires internal support and validation;

- as a facilitator I had to set up a structure outside the normal day-to-day operations in order to gain commitment; and

- patience and persistence were vital ingredients – and in this case as I was flying 1 000 miles each way to and from the client headquarters, which was demanding.

For the next two years, until the company was taken over, many important Action Learning projects were undertaken. These included

- Organizing the arrangements for moving four small factories with four different unions and four different ethnic groups from separate sites to one site.

- Developing a supervisory training system.

- Improving the export of a product which had surplus capacity on the home market.

- Developing a more effective production management process for bottles.

Each set had three or four people. We insisted that senior management clients not only prepared the brief with us but personally attended the programmes to discuss their requirements with their set. Finally, all clients had to attend the presentations and report on what had been achieved.

Again, I learned a lot about the role as the chief consultant. On such a large project I found it could only succeed on the following conditions:

- that I had a network of external and internal advisers who were co-ordinated to work together;

- that I had to provide a script of expectations for set

advisers, clients, participants and their managers so everyone knew what was happening; and

- that instead of teaching I spent most of my time co-ordinating the contributions of others – very much like a conduc-
tor of an orchestra.

On this assignment I had the good fortune to work with my
colleague Dick McCann who shared the co-ordinating role on
what was indeed a complex assignment. Much was achieved in
economic terms, but equally valuable was the improved communication that occurred both within and between groups, as we
deliberately had mixed sets of people from production, marketing, personnel, finance and research working together.

The ICI Action Learning management programme

While conducting the above assignment I was asked by ICI Australia to put forward a plan for developing a number of their
high-flying specialists who required an understanding of management. They had in mind people like senior scientists, the corporate lawyer, engineers, finance and other staff people aged
between 28 and 38.

In essence, they wanted an MBA programme but did not have
the time to send so many people to a business school for up to
two years. Therefore, I developed with them an in-company
Action Learning programme that covered the same ground in 18
months.

My colleagues at The International Management Centres in
the UK, together with those in Africa and South East Asia, had
been developing such programmes since 1983 so we had a lot of
experience to draw upon. Nevertheless, each assignment is different and this was no exception. Before we could begin there was
an extended period of discussion through a steering committee
we established, then with senior management who would act as
clients, and later with the participants who we called associates.
In all it took nearly 12 months from the initiation of the idea to
starting the programme.

Fifteen people participated on a model that involved the following features:

- Following two five-day off-site start-up weeks (separated
by a month) the associates met one day every fortnight for
set meetings.
- During these meetings they were introduced to key con-

cepts in marketing, finance, operations, human resources and strategy over a nine-month period.

- In each of the above areas the associates had to develop an Action Learning project and apply the concepts to their work situation.

- They were assessed internally by making presentations and externally through a written action case of 4 000 words on each of the areas.

- Once beyond the nine-month stage 13 participants continued to the second half, when they conducted a corporate overview on action required plus a dissertation and literature review on individual major projects.

- Throughout the members met as a set, and learned with and from each other how to manage change.

The intervention was successful as judged by the participants and the company. It was, however, a radical departure from normal practice. Associates were given an opportunity to conduct major reviews on company practice from which they and others could learn to improve performance. Instead of being confined to their own area they were encouraged to cross boundaries and develop a wide managerial overview of company operations. Instead of leaving the company to go to a business school we, the faculty from IMC, went to the company.

Once again, I learned many things from this intervention, not least of which were:

- The difficulty of managing an assignment over 18 months when the participants have other pressures of job and home and the faculty have to keep an ongoing involvement with a complex action process.

- The need for sound organization structure between the company, its managers, the clients, the associates, the tutors and the administrative staff.

- The need for a clear intellectual educational design that is both firm yet flexible to meet all the problems that real action throws up.

- The personal persistence and determination to keep it going, and in this I had support from people like John Little, Geoffrey Prideaux, Barry Smith and the tutors on our team, and John Watt, Bruce Rowe and the steering committee on the ICI team.

The management for safety set

As a final example I shall outline briefly an innovative approach to improve the management of safety in an organization concerned with agri-business fertilizers and chemicals. They compared themself with the Dupont safety standard and concluded they needed to improve. However, standard lectures and policy statements did not do the trick. Therefore, I was asked how Action Learning could help. Again, there was a lengthy period of discussion with the safety committee and the establishment of the conditions for genuine consultation at various levels. This resulted in the setting up of various Action Learning groups – we have now had over 25, each with four managers as set members participating. The programmes ran as follows:

- We chose the theme of improving safety through auditing.

- Each set was assigned by a client an action area to audit and in which to produce improvements.

- To start the process off we had four sets at a time spend three days working out how they would conduct the assignment, during which time we provided tuition on team work and Action Learning approaches.

- Thereafter, the sets met under their own agenda with an in-company set adviser who we had trained to pursue the objectives.

- After a period of eight to twelve weeks the sets met with senior management to report on the results achieved and plan the follow up steps.

- The range of assignments tackled included identifying how: to make the transport of toxic chemicals safer; to improve the safety level amongst apprentices; to improve systems for self-audit between transport drivers on load safety; to review audit procedures on various equipment and improve performance; to improve fire prevention methods and process. These were a few of the many vital safety improvements tackled.

In the process we all learned a lot, including:

- how many improvements could be made in what was already a very safety conscious company;

- how much teamwork was vital to success in the Action Learning process;

- how a team could influence so many others to become safety conscious by getting people together and asking questions and being willing to act on what was said; and

- the importance of senior managers setting the assignments and following through on implementation.

What have I personally learned?

All of these Action Learning assignments and the others I have done have been very interesting. However, we should all learn from the action and my conclusions are as follows:

- People don't learn from action *per se*. There has to be a disciplined system of review. This I have done by getting associates, clients and senior managers together to review both content and process. Getting everyone together is a difficult task, but unless it is done you will have action without learning that can be transferred to the next stage.

- There is a need to push for process outputs. I have now become tougher in asking for written records of what has been achieved. I typically give managers key questions, such as:

  1 What did you do?
  2 How did you do it?
  3 What did you learn?
  4 What were the costs and benefits?

This has to be written up in 1 000 to 2 000 words and provide the basis for presentations. Managers do not like having to do it but afterwards acknowledge the value of clarifying their thoughts based on action. In this way I believe managers will become intellectually sharper in what they do.

- There is a need to be well organized in co-ordinating the complex issues and roles and structures. Action Learning is not just a simple matter of giving people projects. It is a political as well as a business and educational involvement and if you don't get political support from the key players you will not achieve the business and educational objectives.

- Selling Action Learning is the hardest educational process or product I have ever sold: it is not easily tangible; it has to be sold to many people simultaneously; it has to be costed when so many variables are unknown; it is time consuming; and, most frustrating of all, it is not a product that can be easily re-sold as you have to start again with new clients, projects and associates.

Summary

Given the above points, I now understand more clearly the frustration often expressed by Reg Revans. He has over many years seen the power of Action Learning in action. However, for all his success, and despite his eloquence, he has had difficulty in converting people to do likewise. I should not of course be surprised for it took me over 20 years to move from conventional teaching, albeit in an experiential mode, to an Action Learning approach. I heard the words, I read the books, I debated the issues and at times thought I was genuinely involved, but it is only in the last three years that I have come to grips with the real problems and opportunities of Action Learning.

In short, it is a challenging and exciting area in which to work. Equally, it is the most difficult and complex area in which to work because of the reality of dealing with political, financial, organizational and people issues face to face. By its very nature, Action Learning is trying to do two things at once. It seeks to improve individual and organizational performance while learning individually and collectively. At one level it seems so obvious to say to managers, if you want to improve, study your own work and your own organization. In reality it can be a painful experience that adds more work to an already full day and stretches everyone to the limit. If it did not do so, then we would not learn. For all the problems I believe Action Learning is the way to go, and I go forward to seek more opportunities.

18 Applying Action Learning in several Australian settings

Warwick Rowell

Early days

My involvement with Action Learning began in the early 1970s when I started establishing problem-solving groups to design and implement computer systems. Since then it has been such a pervasive part of my work as a management educator and consultant that I find it difficult to separate the ideas of Action Learning from the way I conduct my life on a day-to-day basis. Writing this chapter has led me to reflect a lot on the successes and failures of my attempts to use Action Learning techniques, theories and philosophies.

Mastering Action Learning

After being instrumental in getting Reg Revans to Australia in 1976, I went to England myself in 1978, to spend time with my wife's family and to pursue post graduate studies in Management Education. I will never forget the two days we spent at Reg's house in Altrincham. The incredible energy that Reg still has and his contacts with a wide range of people led to my enrolment in the first Action Learning Masters programme in England, which started just three weeks after my visit.

The structure of this MSc programme was one worth imitating for anyone trying to get an Action Learning approach through an academic maze. It required an intensive residential four-week common-learning programme, then eight months on a full-time management project, with one day a week devoted to meetings. Half a day was the Action Learning set meeting, and the other half was a continuation of the core programme.

The Manpower Services Commission had been providing seed funding for Action Learning programmes around England, and wanted to evaluate their progress. They needed someone who was familiar with Action Learning techniques, but independent of the network, so this Australian that Reg recommended must have seemed ideal. It was certainly a magnificent opportunity. Moving around England and spending time with the top management educators; looking in detail at their work, why they were doing it, and what results were being achieved was the most sustained intellectually stimulating experience I have had.

After writing up all the reports of this experience, it was time to do a thesis. One of the problems that I had discovered in my travels was that Action Learning takes many forms, and that while the original structures proposed by Reg may be modified, there was a 'deep structure' that seemed to interfere least with effective learning from action. My thesis therefore attempted to illuminate these deeper structures, based on an exploration of the literature, and testing what was read against the experience I had had of thirty-nine different programmes. A brief summary of what turned out to be nearly two years of exploration is as follows:

1   A situation needs to be structured so there is time to distance oneself from day-to-day activity on a regular basis.

2   Enhancing an individual's personal methods of coping with the stresses of problem solving is far more important than training in problem-solving techniques, which is still necessary.

3   The contribution of the set adviser is enhanced immensely if the person filling that role has the ability to take on and swap roles with ease and flair, whilst ensuring participant comfort: from lecturer, to coach, to counsellor, to learner.

4   Learning from action is increasingly effective in smaller groups: more than five or six people tends to result in shallow and so less effective intervention and assistance by colleagues.

Action Learning used in Australia

On my return to Australia in 1981, I spent some time at the Institute of Administration, part of the University of New South Wales. I was advising them how they could redesign their courses, based on what I had seen in England. It is interesting to see that some of these ideas are still in use – they have withstood the test of the market place for nearly ten years. The major programme they run is a four (now six) week residential management-development programme. This programme has personal learning groups of four that meet daily. Each individual has an opportunity to consult any member of staff about a concern.

Action Learning in a big company

The major practice of Action Learning in which I was involved over the following five years was in a self-management exercise, for a group of trainers, educators and consultants, in CSR, a large Australian industrial conglomerate. CSR at that time had about 90 separate business units, chiefly throughout mainland Australia, but also in South East Asia, New Zealand, Hawaii, and a small presence in the USA.

With the huge amount of travel any one individual undertook (100 or more nights away from home each year at least), and the range of knowledge that was required it was essential to provide mechanisms for support, learning, clarifying directions, and information exchange. We found that the easiest way to do this was through an Action Learning approach.

The first week of each month was never programmed. Within that week, as far as possible, no one programmed any activities away from Sydney. Sometimes the meetings were spread through the week, sometimes we had one or two days full time, depending on the nature of the task we faced. Certainly, there were many opportunities for one-to-one conversations.

To provide a degree of external support, we invited outsiders to join key meetings, as advisers, information sources, fellow learners and supporters: line managers involved in a particular assignment would ensure practicality; senior managers confirmed their ideas while ensuring a match between our direction and theirs; outside experience provided refreshers to our own skills, contributed to a project, and tested our ideas. As this was an opportunity for them to test and market their ideas, many provided this service in exchange for one of us doing the same for them. Others went on to become key external resources for the whole company. Mike Pedler and Per Rangaard from Norske Hydro are two from overseas who contributed much to the group, and the company.

Once a year we had a full week away from the office to plan and budget for the next year. Again, outsiders were used for specific skills training, but generally we all took turns acting as adviser/process manager for the group, as well as later being the 'line' manager for the technical production of our key marketing document for the year, the training programme. One session that we all found very powerful was Barrie Blicharski, a very experienced psychodramatist, who helped us build our skills at role swapping. We felt that we needed this to assist us in sharing more profitably the lessons from our own previous practice as (CSR) managers and now as learning facilitators. The annual arguing, and sharing, and clarifying of values and directions provided a very clear set of goals for the group, and defined individual responsibilities for managing tasks, which allowed a group support style of management. These all contributed to an organization that performed at an outstanding level for five years.

Action Learning in a medium-sized company

This led me to attempt the same design at a family company which needed help. They were manufacturing furniture, with a turnover of about $30 000 000 a staff of 40, and wages employees of about 100. Family members were joint managing directors, and other family were employed in various roles at various levels. Many of the in-company sets which I advised achieved substantial results, the largest of which was a complete revamp of the annual new-product design and launch process.

One highlight of the activities of this particular set was the use of a team-building tool, described below, which I have used subsequently to great effect.

A human critical-path design

Each of the (fourteen in this case) individuals involved in the process writes on a separate piece of paper every bit of advice, information, or output he or she requires from others before they can do their bit of the process, and the name of who can provide it most readily. They then similarly identify each of their outputs, and who uses them.

In a large room, they mill around for as long as it takes to get the pieces of paper placed on the floor as a giant critical path network of what actually happens now.

At this stage, review, analysis, argument and discussion identify overlaps, gaps, key decision points, and where management attention is needed to ensure faster action. Many decisions for change were made there and then by altering the relationships of the bits of paper.

This process clearly identifies the difference between decision-making responsibilities, and taking responsibility for the process of managing to get to a decision point. It was here that the Action Learning approach broke down in this company. Four of the key managers could not step out of the role of expert decision maker. They could not surrender control to others: they were 'stuck'. They were also unwilling to define where they most needed to learn – that is, where they had made mistakes. Before I was engaged, this had got to the stage where subordinates were keeping notes of instructions, for the sole purpose of avoiding blame for being the ones that were mistaken. This illuminates one of the paradoxes of Action Learning: a manager enthused about Action Learning approach probably does not need it, and vice versa. One of Reg's more profound statements, that is so simple that we tend to forget it, is also relevant here: 'The most important question for a learner is "What is an honest person, and how can I become one?" '

Action Learning in an academic setting

A source of inspiration to our practice in CSR was the activities in the Agriculture School at Hawkesbury Agricultural College. The staff there have been running a full Degree programme for many years now, with many of the features of Action Learning.

After one semester in an open-ended exploration of what is available from staff and other resources of the school, students define their own areas of interest, and then design their programme of study. They also define their own criteria for assessment, through negotiation with staff. One of the expected forms of assessment is detailed critiques by external practitioners. Another is by a portfolio of action research studies, and reports on their work experiences through the course of the year. A section of their portfolio describes what they have learned.

The major work of staff is to come to grips with multiple roles, and for some no role at all – the basic practice of the school is to give the students autonomy, and so staff act as true advisers, but only when asked. The most important safety net they provide is the role of mentor. Each staff member has a number of students who are studying an area outside the expertise of that staff member. Their job is to support and encourage, to nag and to defend. They can only do this well if they are learners too: learning about the individuals and their learning tasks.

Action Learning as an organization development tool

I returned to Perth as an independent management educator and consultant. One of my first assignments in my new role was to 'improve the communications' in a large brick-manufacturing company. Perhaps here I was more cautious than in the family company described above. The programme started with a structured three-day residential workshop, that was built around mini-lectures, experiential exercises, and lots of rumination about managers and learning styles, why learning organizations succeed, and how there is a continual process of action and reflection going on in management. This led into a shared definition of the prime purpose of the company, and the start of defining functional areas, and where the natural task boundaries occurred.

It was only after this process was completed by the individual teams for a follow-up meeting that Action Learning was raised as a design option: 'We could continue to build our overlapping skills of learning, problem solving, communicating, leading and managing by tackling this problem you have defined as urgent and important. We could meet once a fortnight and review progress, and plan what to do next.' This option was taken up by the senior management team, one production facility, and the transport group. The senior management team addressed the problem of how to get out of what we called 'suicide corner'. They had a small market share and old plant. This gave them low margins, and so little profit to invest in new plant, which was needed to maintain market share with more competitors coming into the market. The key problem they defined was how to get the output levels and product quality of an investment of $100 000 000, from an investment of only $20 000 000. In turn, this progressed to many creative solutions in terms of plant optimization and marketing campaigns, which have nearly achieved the result.

One carefully planned action was to ensure industry visibility of their series of well-managed steps. This has been one factor in delaying the establishment of a threatened rival company by over two years. The visibility aspect was one of the unexpected outcomes from a long and detailed discussion in the group when they reviewed their weekly progress. They talked about real action and visible action; and another form of action they discussed under the heading of 'all the lights on, no one home', that is, all surface, no substance.

Action Learning in government/citizen group interaction

A huge problem facing more and more areas of Australia is soil degradation. Recent enquiries have delineated the problem, and have concluded that in most cases the problem can be best addressed by self-help groups. Through several workshops last year, I was able to introduce the basic ideas of Action Learning to three-quarters of the 89 Land Management Committees scattered throughout our 250 000 000 hectares of land in Western Australia.

We have a further programme planned for later this year to test the use of an Action Learning approach further. Key issues will be: its perceived acceptability to groups of local land users after brief explanation; its ease of implementation in terms of using existing facilities and skills available to local groups of farmers; and its use of scarce government resources to achieve the maximum implementation rate of planned local actions.

It has been a major step forward to convince the bureaucrats that it is no longer possible to plan and fund elegant scientific experiments to prove the efficacy of one technique over another, when outcomes may not be really visible for thirty or forty years, and the problem is worsening by the year. This was achieved by highlighting the difference between research problems (P) and political problems (Q).

Permaculture design and Action Learning

A recent interest that is becoming a part of my work is permaculture. Let me describe permaculture and some of its principles, and see if you agree that there are many parallels between permaculture and Action Learning. Briefly, permaculture is an evolving process of consciously designing agricultural systems to meet human needs in a sustainable way.

Looking at the key words more closely:

Evolving As needs change the system will change; as the system changes, needs will change.

Process Permaculture is not a thing; it is an active experiment with living.

Consciously We cannot do permaculture by habit; we must carefully attend to what is being done, and the results that action brings.

Designing The only verb in the definition to highlight the fact that design precedes all other actions.

Systems Complex dependencies and interrelationships of sets of elements and subsystems mean it is difficult to define cause and effect relationships, and the meanings of events are always capable of re-interpretation.

Meeting human needs The people in the system have needs that must be clarified and continually redefined to ensure their compatibility with the needs of the system of which they are a part.

Sustainable way Sustainable is defined by enhanced durability and resilience, rather than increased permanence or sameness. This implies redundancy of elements (each function is performed by many elements) and redundancy of functions (each element performs multiple functions).

The educational design role is interesting because, like another discipline I know reasonably well, the chief exponent of permaculture is a charismatic leader who can, through intimate knowledge and total conviction, successfully communicate the fundamental importance yet the essential simplicity of his ideas whilst addressing very complex issues. This has sometimes led to impatience with the fumblings and reinterpretations of those who follow. Attempts to clarify the issues and sort out what is happening often leads to books like this.

We have spent much time with practitioners and students developing courses and modules aimed at meeting particular needs, and using sets solving real problems to illuminate good practice. Reflection and careful observation are built into the programmes, which are currently being examined by other experienced designers, before being offered as an enabling framework for other educators.

Action Learning about ethical investment

The ethical investment area of my work is again one where I am currently establishing an Action Learning group of those who are involved in Western Australia. We have a practical concern, as many of us have become investors in a company about to become a major provider of ethical investment funds.

We need to learn a lot about how ethical investment is managed by others around the world. Before this, though, we need to clarify our own objectives, or we could drown in the seas of information available.

Are we talking about providing options for investors; or establishing a group to examine the ethics of the providers; or assisting those who want to obtain ethical funds; or providing general investment advice; or helping organizations become more ethical? What is 'ethical' anyway? Is it an ethical product, or an ethical process, or ethical people we want? How will we decide, if there is a proposal for an ethical product, like recycled paper, but the owners exploit their work force? Who will decide?

Questions, not answers

There are all provocative questions. Perhaps they can best be summed up in the question that seems to continually engage me since I became involved: 'How do I do this ethically?' Many times the answer has come back: use the philosophy of Action Learning. Temporarily satisfactory answers will only come from careful scrutiny of planned action in the world; the continual effort to integrate learning and action.

19 Quality service in New Zealand

Eric Schlesinger

> Squareness is not the absence of quality; it is classic quality.
> Hipness is not just presence of quality; it is mere romantic quality.
>   . . . classic quality is the parent, the source of all subjects and objects.
>   . . . quality, or its absence, doesn't reside in either the subject or the object . . . peace of mind is a prerequisite for a perception of that Quality which is beyond romantic Quality and classic Quality and which unites the two.[1]

Quality and Action Learning

As quality programmes fly round the world in shiny packages, the techniques seem to gain over the consciousness of pattern, form and design. We need to grapple with that problem, particularly as thinking about quality is changing.

There appear to be four stages of quality:

1 Conformance to specification.

2 Satisfaction of customer needs.

3 Quality of work and life.

4 Quality of action itself.

Stage 1 was well on the way by 1955; stage 2 by 1970; and stage

3 by 1980. We are now at Stage 4. How can we do and learn at the same time? The hard reasoners and facts merchants pursue Pirsig's classic, square quality – and miss it because it is so simple and direct. Romantic hipsters just want to feel it – they do not miss quality but they can be dismissed as finding it wherever they like. The notion of quality requires Action Learning to tackle it.

I never went through the full rigmarole of learning to run training courses based on job descriptions and similar engineering approaches. A background in group dynamics helped. The notions of trouble, failure, support and tackling real problems slowly came together. I first heard of Reg Revans in the late 1960s; became intrigued and then confused; came back to the issues in the early 1970s and got going.

Action Learning seems to be the appropriate form for tackling issues of quality service. The principles of Action Learning assert that the learning cycle and the management cycle are fundamentally similar. Learning principles include:

- People learn only when they want to.

- People learn when they face up to intractable problems (we change and engage in fundamental learning only when we are in trouble).

- Learning is a co-operative, social process.

- Learning as behaviour change starts when we receive inputs about the outputs derived from action.

- Learning often consists of the restructuring of what is already 'known', rather than the acquisition of new knowledge and facts. Mental set can be a potent barrier to change.

Management and supervision is probably best seen as a problem-solving process. Problem-solving principles include:

- The most critical stage of a problem is finding the right one, rather than solving it. This means finding the right questions to ask.

- The best people to find and solve real problems are those who live with and are responsible for the results.

- Problem finding and solving through teams is superior to the efforts and wiles of 'experts'.

- Problem solving happens only when we rehearse, direct and control action in the real world.

These principles of action learning were applied in the quality service programme at National Mutual of New Zealand.

The quality service programme in National Mutual

These issues were debated during a series of interventions in a large insurance/financial services organization. National Mutual is one of the main financial services companies in New Zealand. Amalgamations, diversification and de-regulation have all created an environment of change, uncertainty and discomfort. Paternalistic and traditional styles of management had become unsuited to new conditions. The growth of specialist services and the loss of long-serving personnel served to create a confused, fragmented culture. Attitudes tended towards dependency, isolation and stereotyping and rules were either slavishly followed or ignored. Middle management had little formal power and rarely saw meaningful budgetary information. People were friendly but did not display innovation and purpose; there was a tendency to throw 'dead cats over the wall'. Finally, there was a good deal of ignorance about company policies and about the work of different departments; location in over a dozen separate buildings did not help.

A series of changes in 1986 seemed to require responses in the use of human resources to back up structural and personnel changes. To borrow a phrase from Morris and Burgoyne, what was needed was 'resourceful humans' as well as human resources.[2] Marketing moves placed a growing emphasis on sales and service. People-intensive, interactive and high-value added qualities were far removed from the more traditional life insurance world. What would distinguish National Mutual from its competitors would be only partly financial performance; much would depend on the quality of service. It was calculated that every time a client or potential client contacted head office or any sales office or agent, there were more than 10 million 'moments of truth' every year. The sales package consisted of many intangibles and peripherals; the whole was the quality of service that we could deliver.

In terms of training and development, the first major intervention was to introduce team briefing in the latter half of 1986. Team briefing is a simple exercise in communication that ensures everyone in the organization knows what is happening and why

– from top to bottom. A core brief is created monthly by the Executive, covering policy, progress, people and points for action. All managerial and supervisory levels below the Executive are briefed by their superior. Each level creates a local brief to complement the core brief. Briefings are carried out monthly in company time. Briefs are written down, conducted by the manager or supervisor and communicated face to face to the entire team. Full understanding is ensured through questions and summaries. Discussion or debate about an issue is not encouraged; such issues are noted and pursued in a variety of ways after each team briefing. The entire process goes from top to bottom of the organization inside 24 hours. Answers to any questions asked must be given within 48 hours. The entire process is monitored by team leaders who are strongly encouraged to 'walk the job'. Personnel Division have a holding brief for the entire process, including training in the processes and mechanics of communication.

Team briefing has three objectives:

1   To strengthen the role of management and supervision.

2   To reduce the effects of misunderstanding and the grapevine.

3   To lay foundations for the development of commitment.

By early 1987 it was clear that the process was beginning to work. Briefs were being communicated with commitment and care. Where managers gave team briefing thought and attention, it was noticeable that employees responded. The issue was complex. How could the organization build on these foundations? How could there be assistance with the push from being product-driven to market-driven? How could the quality of service be improved? Did this have anything to do with morale and the quality of work experience, or was it all to do with systems and management services? If you cannot run an information and knowledge society with a shovel and pick, then how do you win the hearts and minds and skills of all in a common venture?

Market research had established that service to the customer was critical to image and performance in the financial services sector. Head office in Australia had established a mission statement to this effect. It was clear that the New Zealand branch needed to make its moves. Following a meeting with the newly-appointed General Manager for New Zealand, Personnel was given six months to launch a comprehensive and effective service programme. The General Manager was asked to revise the mission statement to suit local conditions, to agree to the appointment of a Quality Service steering group with senior manager representation, and to lead internal and external publicity. This was immediately agreed to, with some insightful additions. It is interesting to reflect that this was the only occasion that the General Manager was directly involved in establishing authority and leeway, apart from an opening workshop before the pilot stage.

Objectives, meaning and charter

The steering group was critical to winning support. Its role was to develop policy and advice, information and support, training and administrative procedures. This was crucial in developing a persuasive and influence-broking approach to all levels of employees.

Three broad goals were set:

1 To implement a planned approach to develop service standards and performance.

2 To use the talents of people to improve their work.

3 To create a long-term strategy to shift the values, style and practices of the organization towards a service culture.

From this, two specific objectives were developed for a quality service programme:

1 To improve the quality of National Mutual New Zealand service for all our clients.

2 To improve the quality of work life of National Mutual staff.

It was a key value that people could not be coerced to work in Quality Service teams and that participation had to be made attractive. It was also insisted that all employees had customers, and not just agents. For example, Personal Business were a client of Systems Support just as much as a company with a superannuation scheme was a client of Actuarial Division. It would be impossible to treat our people indifferently and then expect them to give quality service to an external client. Internal markets were at least as important as external ones.

Defining (or rather interpreting quality service) proved to be immensely difficult. Robert Pirsig got closer than we did; we interpreted it to be:

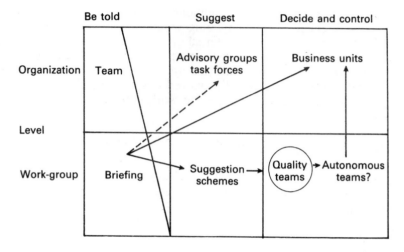

Figure 19.1   Involvement

> Understanding what services our clients expect, and providing our clients with service that is equal to, or beyond their expectations. Service is attempting to hit a constantly moving target.

We worked on an approach that endeavoured to mesh the organization and the individual – and to suggest the transformation of the one by the other (See Figure 19.1)

The discussion of the eight members of the steering group bore personal testimony to both the risks and need for genuine participation. The need to strike out in new ways for a different culture required us to face ourselves – how much risk and honesty could we display?

The notion of a charter appeared when we attempted to bridge the mission statement which asked us to 'provide consistently high quality service to all our clients' and the 'coalface' action of employees. It took thirteen versions to produce a series of simple and powerful statements. These covered such values as:

- Being flexible, caring and responsive.

- Promptly resolving problems that hinder client service.

- Providing autonomy for employees.

- Recognizing and rewarding energy, initiative and results.

- Learning from all experiences, including failures as well as successes.

- Being open, honest, friendly and sharing.

- Being positive, progressive and innovative.

It is interesting to note that we had produced a good example of what Peters and Waterman term 'simultaneous loose-tight properties'.[3] We also attempted to learn from our own behaviour and to be 'bureaucracy-busters' and 'service champions'.

The four components of the quality service programme

These were:

1 Individuals

2 Teams

3 Training

4 Ideas Bank

Individuals can be rewarded through work on a Quality Service team, and further through performance review. Managers were given a budget allocation for discretionary rewards for this purpose. In addition each Quality Service team could nominate a member for an individual award.

Quality Service teams were to be formed on an own job/own organization basis – at least initially, so that they could more easily manage issues within their control. Teams tackle a project. A project can come from anywhere and anyone. It can be set up by almost anyone, provided that a relevant client and sponsor are found. Projects are submitted on a simple form that is vetted by the steering group. A project has to fulfil the following criteria:

- Subject to management approval.

- Aimed at improving performance.

- Important to team members.

- Within the control of team members.

- Achievable within three months.

- The project must be specific.

- The project must be cost effective.

- The project must be likely to succeed.

- To do with quality service to clients.

A typical Quality Service team has the following characteristics:

- It meets voluntarily on a regular basis – perhaps once a week for about one hour on company time.

- It consists of five to eight people who do largely similar work.

- It takes from two to three months.

- It has a trained leader, backed by a facilitator and Quality Services co-ordinator.

- It produces its own report under the clear understanding that the recommendations are robust and able to be applied.

Management receive a presentation where the report is subjected to careful scrutiny. A rapid response is essential – either acceptance with immediate implementation, or rejection/modification with clear reasons.

The training for this process is important. We discovered from other analysis that employees needed considerable help in managing tasks, processes and procedures. Accordingly, the training uses a mix of participation and simple models to help explore and explain the quality of service philosophy and its practice. Participants are team leaders who face leading a project for the first time. The three-day programme is a combination of realistic and reality-based training, balanced between process and techniques. The former includes team dynamics and creative thinking; the latter includes Pareto, fishbone diagrams and meeting management. A part of the programme is also devoted to a very simple model of problem solving and decision making, built on Revans's System Beta. As the programme has developed, we have found that the content can be reduced and simplified considerably. The key points are extremely simple and need the minimum of explanation.

Trained leaders in turn become the facilitators of other team leaders, so that each learns from the other. A full-time Quality Service co-ordinator assists this whole process, as well as the publicity, support and administrative functions. The facilitators meet on a regular basis to learn how to help themselves.

Finally, the Ideas Bank committee, a traditional part of the organization's operations, has been absorbed into the process. Suggestion schemes continue to play their part in rewarding people for innovative *ideas* applicable to areas *outside* their area.

Progress to date

Failure often starts with an over-reliance on PR. We decide to start with a one-day workshop for selected managers and supervisors assisted by an external consultant – the only time we resorted to external help. The General Manager and the Quality Service steering group attended. Commitment was sought for and gained; projects were called for and six were selected. By December 1988 five out of six of the projects had successfully been completed. Full scale launch with full publicity and amended procedures was carried out early in 1989.

So far, over 60 Quality Service teams have been formed. The vast majority have successfully completed their tasks in the allotted time. Own job/own organization projects have predominated, spread widely throughout the company and covering diverse problems, which include calculation procedures, the model office, complaints procedures, systems specifications, audit procedures, agent/head/sales office relationships, and sales and operational manuals.

I never went though the full rigmarole of learning to run training courses based on job descriptions and similar engineering approaches. A background in group dynamics helped. The notions of trouble, failure, support and tackling real problems slowly came together. I first heard of Reg Revans in the late 1960s; became intrigued and then confused; came back to the issues in the early 1970s and got going.

The learning has been particularly powerful in projects involving people covering two or three levels, or across two divisions. Notable achievements have been the projects involving inside staff and outside agents where serious blockages have been tackled in procedures and stereotypes.

Some objectives were set at the major launch; these included:

- Development of team member skills and talents.

- Supervisors and managers as leaders of their own Quality Service teams (happening in about 25 per cent of possible cases).

- Quality Service teams indistinguishable from daily work (in a few cases; there is a long way to go before the culture changes to this extent).

- Quality Service teams form for cross-functional work as naturally as for natural work-team activities.

- All people find an appropriate balance between individual and team recognition (only about 40 per cent of staff have experienced a Quality Service team). However, performance review procedures have been changed to explicitly reflect Quality Service performance; many other forms of training and career planning relate to Quality Service values; business plans must now explore how Quality Service approaches will be used in the search for improved performance.

- All people deal with each other as they deal with external clients and customers.

- People constantly knocking on the doors of the next level up (this is beginning to happen at supervisory levels, but much needs to be done at middle and senior levels).

In addition, mentors are beginning to emerge and help each other, people are volunteering for second and third Quality Service teams, and many comments are heard about the power of teams and co-operative action. The programme is widely known. However, few quantitative measures are available as yet.

What has been learnt?

We have learnt that several issues are critical, as follows:

1 The greatest resistance to change does not come from the 'coalface'. Corporate concrete is strongest at middle management levels where stopping power can be insidious, in the form of non-response, strange delays, reactive concerns and apparently reasonable explanations. Apart from working on these issues as they arise, a strategy is evolving of squeezing these problems between moves coming down from above and pressure for change emerging from below. Other and more drastic measures can be considered when the commitment of top management is in danger of being diluted. Moves to involve middle managers in strategic planning and budgetary processes should assist.

2 The power of the reward structure cannot be underestimated. Rewards systems speak louder than words. A great deal of time was devoted to devising appropriate and *acceptable* rewards, and to relating rewards for managing change to ongoing performance in mainstream activities.

There is often a subtle interplay between publicity, recognition and financial reward.

3   Problem solution is vastly easier than problem finding and selection. Yet the latter is crucial – at least half the problem lies in defining it. In at least half of all projects the problem has had to be re-defined in scope or in its essence before useful progress can be made. Prescription is dangerous if the diagnosis is faulty. More time will need to be spent in future on learning quality control techniques for analysing problems.

4   Reappraisal of what is being done is essential on a continuous basis. Things change and evidence needs to be collected from all manner of sources and in all manner of ways.

5   The definition of quality used may be too subjective and relative. Are there classical absolutes in quality, and how do we operationalize them at the level of quality of work, life and action itself?

6   It may be that relatively senior/older managers may need a different sort of learning arrangement from other managers and supervisors. Braddick and Casey suggest that this group may need reflection learning on a less frequent basis, compared to Action Learning on a more frequent basis.[4] This change to a more personal development may relate to the more open-ended and uncertain role of senior management.

7   All learning is personal. The greatest barrier to change is not a lack of knowledge. We all know more than we know. It is our understanding that is the problem, not our ignorance. David Casey has quoted Khalil Gibran to the effect that it is breaking the shell of our *understanding* that is crucial.[5] How else can we reinterpret our past to manage our future than through some form of Action Learning?

References

1 Pirsig, R. (1976), *Zen and the Art of Motorcycle Maintenance*, London: Corgi.
2 Morris, J. and Burgoyne, J. (1973), *Developing Resourceful Managers*, London: IPM.
3 Peters, T. and Waterman, R. (1982), *In Search of Excellence*, London: Harper and Row.

4 Braddick, W. and Casey, D. (1981), 'Developing the Forgotten Army – Action Learning and the Top Manager', *Management Education and Development*, **12**(3) pp. 169–80.
5 Casey, D. *see* ch. 25.

20 Self-improvement in Chinese joint venture companies

Zhou Jianhua

In July 1987, a self-improvement group of senior managers working in enterprises with foreign investment was set up in Wuxi, in the eastern part of China. The twenty-three members came from different joint ventures and each was a senior executive, such as chairman of board, managing director or general manager.

The group – called 'The Wuxi Association Of Chinese Managers In Enterprises With Foreign Investment' – has very clear purposes: the managers would be able to exchange information frequently; help each other to solve problems and work out right policies; and run the ventures successfully.

The co-operation group was sponsored by Shen Renyong, the first person to be appointed by the Chinese side as general manager of Sino-Swed Pharmaceutical Corp. Ltd (SSPC). SSPC is the first joint venture in China's pharmaceutical industry and comprises five Chinese corporations and five Swedish companies. Mr Shen was opening up a completely new business and, being short of experience, he had to learn by doing. Since he met so many difficulties he had to seek help. He called on his colleague, Meng Ke, the managing director of China Jianghai Wood Products Corp. Ltd, which is the first joint venture in Jiangsu province and was established a little earlier than SSPC, and wanted to discuss some problems with him. Instead of making a direct response Mr Meng described what had happened in his own firm and what measures had been taken. He told Mr Shen that he also was puzzled over many aspects. But both of them realized that the Chinese managers of joint ventures should be organized and help each other. Their proposal was sent to all their colleagues in Wuxi and they had soon got positive reply.

At that time there were 23 approved joint ventures in Wuxi. Of these, only seven had started production and very few had made a profit. Although most of the Chinese managers had long experience, they had similar troubles to Mr Shen and Mr Meng. It seems more difficult to run a joint venture.

At first the members of the group met once a month and took turns playing host. They worked out a two-step programme: The first step was to find out what problems or difficulties they really had, and the second step was to study what measures should be taken to solve the problems. They listed the major problems they met as:

1   *Cultural discrepancy* Partners come from different nations and have different cultures, traditions and customs. Foreign managers have different decision-making processes and estimating standards from Chinese managers. What culture should be formed in a joint venture?

2   *Cooperation with foreign managers* General managers are separately delegated by Chinese and foreign sides, and strive for their own employers' interests. It makes cooperation between managers very difficult.

3   *Control of investment* Price goes up dramatically and the costs of buildings, machines and materials always exceed budgets.

4   *Balance of foreign exchange* A joint venture must make balance of foreign exchange by itself so that it can buy materials and new machines abroad, and pay foreigners' salaries and profit; that is, firms cannot buy any foreign currency from banks.

5   *Export of products* The government requires the products of joint ventures to go towards exports. But production costs in China are so high, even over the sale prices of the international market, that foreign partners are not interested in export.

6   *Control of import channels* Most joint ventures import machines and materials through foreign partners. Some

foreign partners are not very honest. They force up commodity prices and infringe upon the interests of joint ventures.

7 *Shortage of materials and energy* In China a lot of materials are supplied on the basis of the national plan, but the demands of new enterprises cannot be arranged at all. Another problem is the frequent power cuts.

8 *Recruitment of skilled workers* Many people hope to work for joint ventures since the firms pay higher wages. But it is very difficult for a new company to recruit skilled workers and engineers who are competent.

9 *Designing a salary and wage structure* The average wages of joint ventures can be 20 to 50 percent higher than the state-owned firms and the ventures have more autonomy to decide what wage structure they take. But the traditional wage system based on the length of service and the trend of equal treatment have such deep and widespread influences that companies have not defined their wage policy.

10 *Low efficiency of officials* There are so many official barriers to get through before a new business begins that due dates often have to be delayed.

In October 1987, two lecturers of the National Centre For Management Development at Wuxi took part in the group. They had just finished MBA course and spent a half-year in western companies. When one of the lecturers, Zhou Jianhua, was in Britain in the first half of 1987, he met Prof. R. W. Revans, the father of Action Learning. They discussed the possibility of introducing the theory into China and believed that it would be greatly beneficial. The other lecturer, Rong Zonghua, met Action Learning in Manchester Business School in 1984 while he was a member of a research group from China's management education circle, studying modern management education of western countries. After they came back, they tried to translate *ABC of Action Learning* into Chinese and introduce the theory to business world.

Action Learning and Chinese practice

When the members of the Wuxi group understood the theory of Action Learning, they were very surprised that they felt so familiar with it. The managers thought that it should be taken up as a major approach of management education. There are three reasons to explain why the theory should play an important part in China's management education.

The first reason is that the former president of the People's Republic of China, Mao Tsetung, who is the founder of PRC and governed the country for several decades, had formed a similar theory. In 1936, Chairman Mao wrote a book titled '*The Strategy of China's Revolutional War*' which is very famous in China. The following paragraph on training of military officers is still impressed on most of Chinese:

> Not only reading is learning, but also doing. The later is a more important way of learning. Learning warfare through warfare – it is our major method.

In the 1960s, Mao further summed up 'Learning to swim through swimming' as the major method to train officers.

The more important reason is that sharing experience is the traditional and popular method of learning in China. In order to improve management, leaders would organize a meeting to exchange experience. Normally, the participants of such a meeting work in similar positions. Perhaps they work in a trade and manage similar mills respectively, or they are in one large company as department managers. At a meeting several persons who are quite successful at their posts would describe what they have done and how they have been successful. Then the participants would be divided into several groups and introduce what problems they have met. Finally, a few points which are key factors in making the best results would be summarized. Before the Cultural Revolution, exchanging experience was the principal way of management education in China.

The most important reason, however, is that economic and political conditions in China are considerably different from those of developed countries and the principles of western management cannot be directly applied. Since 1979 China has started to carry out a new development programme. Meanwhile, the principles of modern management have been introduced from western countries. In the past ten years, management education has stressed the popularization of western management principles. Most universities have set up management departments and hundreds of business schools have emerged providing management courses for both students and managers.

In recent years, however, managers do not believe that they can find ready-made solutions for their problems from western management theories. They have to solve these problems by themselves. A number of management institutes have changed past educational programmes. The new programmes include more practical and less academic courses, and an increasing number of managers are invited to have lectures in institutes.

After the managers learnt of the theory of Action Learning, they were more confident that this method of self-improvement was very effective, and therefore made a new plan. From November 1987 to February 1988 they spent one day a week going through the programme in the following ways.

Sharing experiences within the group

Each member of the group was in charge of a business and most of them had been on these management posts from the outset. At the group meeting managers described the development of their own ventures and the problems met. Everyone told the others what measures had been taken – maybe some were mistakes – and all had a strong desire to learn from the others. Individuals made helpful suggestions to their colleagues. Usually all of them concentrated on one main problem each time. The exchange brought an unexpected result: not only did the new managers learn from those with previous experiences in the same positions, but also the others drew on fresh ideas from new colleagues. Since then the managers meet monthly.

Making research in small group

In order to design a new wage structure, they formed five groups and selected five companies to investigate. Each group entered a company and interviewed staff, workers, cooks, drivers, salesmen, and so on. They wanted to know, comparing it with the wage structure of state-owned enterprises, what wage structure joint ventures really should have. Then each group reported the results to all the managers. The association didn't make any decision on it and just provided a chance to learn. It expected managers to adjust their wage structure in terms of the internal situation of their own firms. For example, most joint ventures provide free lunch, but Allied Textiles Ltd has not taken up such policy although its business is very profitable. Since the company is in the area of its mother enterprise Wuxi No. 1 Textiles Company, Mr Gu Dingyuan, Chairman of the Board, was afraid that a big difference of remuneration or benefits between companies would influence the morale of the employees who worked in the state-owned company.

Learning professional knowledge from experts

The group invited some professionals to give lectures. These included China Bank's staff, the auditor of Accounting Affairs Office, a lawyer, a customs officer, the Industrial and Commercial Administration Bureau's officer, and so on. These persons introduced in discussion specific principles and procedures in which a joint venture would be concerned.

Opening dialogues with officials

In China the establishment of a joint venture needs many official seals. The government either still controls the venture, or the venture needs the government's help in such matters as materials supply, power, employment, and export documentation. Since the planning system is still the major form of economic structure and most of the Chinese shareholders in joint ventures are the state-owned enterprises, the government controls almost every aspect of business development. Communication between joint ventures and officials is very important. The group invited officers of local government to talk face to face. The managers put forward proposals and requests, and the officials explained government policies. It greatly improved the relationship of joint ventures with local government and made the managers understand their business better.

Exchanging experiences with foreign partners

The association invited foreign managers to take part in the project and built up a close relationship with them. Foreigners were very interested in the project. Managers from various countries came together to discuss the difficulties that had been encountered and the measures that should be taken to resolve them. They shared a collective think tank. Kinya Iyi, the general manager of Wuxi Grand Hotel Limited, had forty years experience in hotel management. Under his control, the cost of construction of the hotel was a little below the budget. In contrast, the costs of new projects in other firms were all over budget by a big margin. Chinese managers therefore learnt much from Kinya Iyi. Foreigners also learnt from Chinese managers. Shan Yuhu, the general manager of World Interior Decoration Ltd, is a Hong Kong businessman and had had some trouble with employees. After communication was improved he had received sound advice from other managers.

Six months later the group had not yet planned to make any

formal evaluation of the programme as the members felt they were still learning, but the appreciation started to come from the outside. In April 1988, the local government asked the group to train forty managers who worked in firms which intended to set up new ventures. In the training course, Shen Renyong introduced the results of the self-improvement programme systematically and stirred up great interest among the managers. In the end twelve managers became members of the group.

Now the programme is facing a problem in attempting further development. Bao Yongchang, the leader of the group, said: 'The members are not concerned about the same points, because the firms are at different stages of development.'

PART IV

LAUNCHING ACTION LEARNING

21 The components of Action Learning

Alan Lawlor

There is now a good deal of practical experience of Action Learning in its many forms. Moreover, there has been continual variation in its use, one programme benefitting from another – Action Learning has been learning about Action Learning. The purpose of this chapter is to describe the practical aspects of Action Learning and what is involved in actually running a programme.

Main programme variants

Flexibility in programme design is endless but the following examples will give the reader some idea of how to choose the best model to suit his particular needs. All the programmes described are based upon the concept of combining the solution of real problems with individual/organizational development and each offers its own unique advantages. See Figure 21.1 for a model and Figure 21.2 for a description of programmes in output terms.

1 Part-time programmes. In these, participants continue with their own jobs while taking part in the programme. They are, therefore, cost-effective and enable people to learn as they work.

2   Full-time programmes. These are of the kind conducted by Revans in Belgium. They are obviously more expensive in terms of time and cost but also achieve more in individual development.

3   In-plant programmes. These have different advantages. They are a powerful medium for bringing about organizational change and though a higher cost per organization than external schemes, they are much lower per participant. On the other hand, external schemes inject fresh ideas into organizational thinking by bringing together people from very different backgrounds.

4   Combined schemes, which offer the advantages of the in-plant and external programmes.

The option chosen is obviously dependent on the needs to be met.

Full-time or part-time?

By full-time is meant that fellows are released from their normal job to be engaged wholly on the Action Learning programme, whereas on part-time schemes the fellows continue to do their own jobs. The full-time approach is generally associated with the so called exchange scheme pioneered by Revans in Belgium. Indeed, until recently it was assumed that Action Learning only consisted of full-time exchange schemes, but as noted earlier there are many approaches.

Though extracting managers from their jobs for a period of six to twelve months and placing them in an unfamiliar organization is a powerful development tool it is an approach that forms a small percentage of Action Learning programmes. For this reason most of my attention will be directed to the part-time method. It clearly has many advantages including lower cost and the fact that the manager is not lost from his job. But there is another reason for adopting this 'learn as you work' approach. Managers are discovering that they can find the time to deal with their real problems and at the same time contend with the alligators that have been diverting their energies away from draining the swamp. Equally, they manage to attend set meetings where they critically discuss the interaction of their jobs with the problems they are trying to solve. In other words, work, problem solving and personal development all become part of one ongoing process; it is not a course which is separate and apart from work but a way of studying and learning from our day-to-day

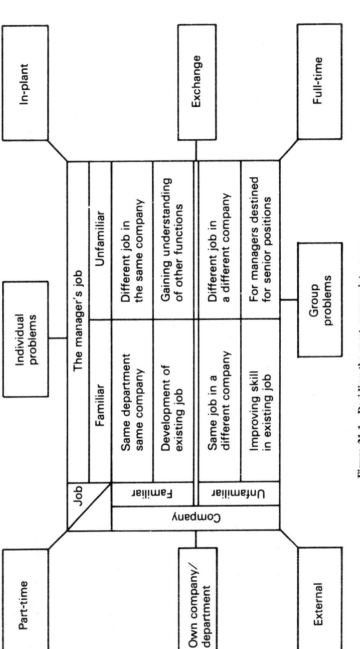

Figure 21.1 Deciding the most appropriate programme

What options are available?	What will they do?	Expectations
1 Own job	1 Will develop the individual and improve performance in his current job	1 Individual development
2 Same job in a different place	2 Will broaden the individual	2 Will expect promotion
3 Different job in the same place	3 Will develop and broaden the individual	3 Will be looking for promotion and more general management
4 Different jobs in a different place	4 Very high level of personal development	4 MD or senior management within two years
5 Common problems tackled by a group	5 Will develop individuals, increase morale and commitment, and will develop the company itself	5 Individual and organizational development in tune with both groups of needs, organizationally very powerful

In-plant schemes have greater impact on the company and are far less costly per participant.

External programmes yield high individual development with a lower cost per company.

Figure 21.2 The effects of various programme options

tasks. There is now little doubt that it is a cost effective method for developing managers and their organizations.

In-plant or external programmes

In-plant schemes tend to focus mainly on organizational problem solving and development. They will generally involve larger numbers than external programmes, numbers of over 100 are common, consequently the programme has much more impact on the total environment. In fact the 'client group' actually take part in the Action Learning sets. In-plant schemes differ from Revans' original model in that the set focuses on one common problem. Set members are all volunteers and come from the same organization although not necessarily the same department. The client 'owns' the problem because it his part of his everyday line management responsibility. Set advisers are recruited from the middle management group and are trained to advise. In this way the whole management structure of the organization becomes an integral part of the problem solving process. In more recent programmes this involvement has been extended to include the shopfloor.

The in-plant approach also achieves another and more difficult objective sought after by managers and trainers, to create a learning environment that maintains itself. There are several examples of in-plant Action Learning in this book and indeed this is one of the fastest growing forms. The current popularity of quality circles is also creating something of an overlap with in-plant Action Learning at shop floor level.

One example of the in-plant approach comes from Australia where Dr Roy Gilbert has introduced Action Learning as a way of running the Victorian State Housing Department. I said earlier that the aim of the part-time approach is to integrate work and learning into one process; however it is also possible for the whole organization to become involved – what Revans would describe as a learning community. If such conditions can be created programme length becomes irrelevant because learning is an ongoing process; a highly important aim when enterprises of all kinds are having to survive in a fast changing world.

The latest development has been to combine the advantages of in-plant and external schemes into one overall programme. Fellows on external sets get the benefit of the cross fertilization of ideas and at the same time help each other to launch their own internal schemes.

Designing your scheme

There are a number of issues to consider in designing your scheme:

1 How much time is needed?

2 What sort of preparation?

3 How big is an Action Learning set?

4 How often should the set meet?

5 Is the set adviser really necessary?

6 What is the role of the client?

7 How does learning occur?

I will now deal with these in turn.

Time involvement

The first dozen or so part-time schemes were of a six month duration with set meetings about one half day per week. Throughout the time that these programmes were conducted we were continually questioning their design including their planned time. One important question if we are to be concerned with the productivity of action learning is 'can we achieve the same results in less than six months?' If we can then the part-time approach becomes even more cost-effective.

Preparation

Action Learning is based upon the simple and natural process of learning from doing. Once the right conditions are created it should become self-sustaining. However, there is still the task of getting things started. The following points are equally applicable whichever type of programme is chosen and experience has taught me that the preparation phase is crucial to success. It can be divided roughly into three parts:

(i) *Gaining organizational commitment and understanding*: this would include getting commitment from the sponsors (generally the senior manager who nominates the fellows on the programme) and the fellows themselves. They need to recognize that while significant benefits are possible equally it requires active participation by all concerned. At this stage consideration of the problem to be tackled is also necessary, emphasizing that they must be real here-and-now problems that already exist irrespective of the Action Learning programme. This kind of preparation can be obtained with a combination of visits to each organization plus one or two planning meetings attended by all of the sponsors and fellows. This stage is spread over about one to two months with a total time of approximately two days. The time spent on this kind of groundwork is well worthwhile, because of its effect on the Action Learning activity that it precedes.

(*ii*) *Introductory workshops*: Views vary, both in the length of seminars to start programmes and on their content. Moreover, we can also consider the other option of having no introduction and instead just start the Action Learning activity immediately after the 'getting commitment' stage. I have now experimented with the range of approaches from nothing at all to a two-and-a-half day residential workshop. As a general guide where a group of fellows, or at least some of them, have some understanding of the way people work effectively together as a team, then an introduction may not be so important, at least for the social skills aspect. In this case perhaps a one day meeting to explain the programme may be all that is necessary. But this kind of appreciation, in my experience, is not common, so some form of preparation is necessary for the group work that is to follow. This belief is perhaps supported by the often expressed view from fellows that it took them some six weeks to really get the open and frank climate which is essential for Action Learning. It is an insight that also gives us a clue to the length of programme – if we can reduce the six weeks perhaps we can reduce the programme.

Arising out of the above observations a team development workshop on a three day residential basis has now been developed which enables the fellows to gain a practical understanding of the interactive skills required for a group of people to solve problems. The main emphasis is on a simulated learning experience which involves real products or services and the employment of 'outside employees'. Through this approach the participants have to set up an organization, learn to work as a team and manage a group of 'employees' in very real conditions. During the workshop the first set meeting also takes place and the fellows arrange and conduct a meeting with their sponsors. Thus, at the end of the three days the fellows are more aware of their own influences on group processes and have a mature view of how to create and work in a climate of critical questioning.

(*iii*) *The way problems are selected is important.* It goes without saying that problems have to be genuine and in need of attention anyway. Everyone is wasting their time if the problem has been invented to put someone on the programme. Accepting this basic requirement, the following methods have been used to select problems.

1   Sponsors make the decision.

2   Jointly agreed by sponsor and fellow.

3   Obtained during introductory workshops.

Methods 2 and 3 support the principle of involvement and ownership which is essential to an effective Action Learning programme. The sorts of problem which can be tackled are:

Attitude change:	We need to change attitudes; to each other, to our work, our markets and the competition. In a fast changing world we must learn to adapt.
Business audits:	We need to know where we are now. Where do we want to be? What are the gaps in these two conditions? What are our values, attitudes, standards and beliefs? What are our strengths, weaknesses, opportunities and threats?
Product development:	What should we really be doing? How do we integrate work and development into one on-going process? How do we create an effective organization which can make profits?
Leadership/ management development:	Are our managers really providing effective leadership? Do they really own problems and their solutions? How can we motivate our people, persist with the solution of the real problems?

Set size

How many fellows should comprise a set? Are there minimum and maximum set sizes? There are two factors which affect this decision. Firstly, the number of people necessary for effective social interaction and the necessary support to take place. Second, the time required to deal with the problems requiring attention. Experience suggests that a set of four is needed to meet the first requirement and that six is a maximum for the second. For instance, in a set of six, with six individual problems, where they meet one-half-day per week, on average the time per problem would be about half an hour. Consequently, any increase in set size beyond six will reduce the time to deal with problems. While for these reasons I have worked on the basis of sets of 4 to 5 fellows, innovations should be constantly in mind.

When Reg Revans and I visited India in 1979 to take part in the review stage of their third programme we were surprised and encouraged by their experimentation. The Calcutta group had only managed to get commitment from two companies and based upon my rough rule above this would have been insufficient to form a set. Instead we met a group of six very enthusiastic managers. The two fellows were busy senior line managers so to assist them in their investigations two young management trainees were assigned to them. In addition, a member of the client from each of the two companies attended set meetings. Hence what could have been a non-starter became a highly active set with the additional development benefits for the client and potential managers. Moreover, they had taken a further interesting step by running the first three months on a full-time basis for the fellows and the last three months part-time.

Frequency of meetings

As a general rule sets should meet every one to two weeks for a duration of a half to one day each meeting. However, a better guide is the needs of the fellows and the progress of the problem solutions. It is unlikely that pressing problems can wait much more than 2 to 3 weeks before receiving some kind of attention. This point highlights the alligator/swamp dilemma; the set creates its own momentum of concentrating attention on the important issues and minimises the distraction of the daily panic. But experience, as you would expect, has shown that problems do not want the same amount of treatment every week; sometimes it could be an hour and on other occasions only five minutes or no time at all. This blend of pressure and giving the time that is necessary is soon recognized by the set, perhaps with some guidance from the adviser.

An aspect of set effectiveness that cannot be emphasized too much is the importance of work between set meetings. If fellows do not get on with the investigation and implementation activities and therefore are unable to report progress, or even no progress, their meetings will soon become little more than discussion groups. If this happens momentum and commitment wane and the set will eventually disintegrate. This situation sometimes occurs when a fellow has an artificial problem or has no real willingness to learn. To prevent this the two previously mentioned prerequisites should be satisfied, that is prior commitment from sponsors and fellows; and selection of genuine problems.

Sponsors also play an indirect part in the frequency and quality of set meetings. As one sponsor said, 'fellows should be allocated one day per week to attend the Action Learning course!' Clearly though managers ought to be regarded as mature enough to make up their own minds if and when they go to set gatherings rather than be organized by the sponsor whose role is one of periodic interest in progress and support when it is needed.

A review at the halfway stage and the end of programmes, which necessitate a presentation to assembled fellows, sponsors and clients is another way of stimulating set activity and meeting regularity. While participants in Action Learning groups should plan and manage their own affairs, predetermined evaluation stages have the effect of motivating the principal people to get on with the inter-related tasks of problem solving and learning.

The set adviser role

The set advisers are the mirrors which reflect the learning opportunities back to the participants. They question, confront, encourage and support. These are the facilitators who help the group know themselves, try out different approaches and become more aware of their own actions.

The continuity of meetings and how well those concerned help each other is especially enhanced by the set adviser. Their role is a combination of tea maker, project manager, scapegoat, process consultant and a motivator. Views vary on how important the adviser is to the success of a set. But except for a few managers who already have the social skills to make a group into a good problem solving team, experience shows that the set adviser is essential, at least for the first few weeks. This does not mean that organizations cannot provide their own advisers. Of course they can.

The role of clients

I have already referred to clients and their importance to programmes. They can influence the development of fellows and if they desire the fellows can also help them to learn (what Reg

Revans calls the social process of problem solving) and they can decide if the problem is to be resolved or stay as it is.

Furthermore, clients can be keepers of the status quo or catalysts for change. They also represent the political system, the coalition of power, which has to be motivated and worked through if any kind of change is to take place. In other words, the client, or '*structure d'acceuil*' as it is called in Belgium, is a highly important part of change and learning. The problem in an action learning programme is how to get their continuing involvement and commitment. Though there is no simple answer to this question, experience has provided some guidelines. There are, in general, three means of involving the client;

1 The fellows, with the support of their set, seek out and try to persuade their client to solve the problem; over and over again, it is when the fellows endeavour to implement their solutions that clients commitment is put to the test.

2 Fellows on external groups form key members of their client into internal Action Learning sets.

3 Set up an internal Action Learning programme which involves a significant proportion of managers and supervisors in dealing with the problems that concerned them. It has now been shown that this is a very powerful means of bringing about organizational change.

The latest developments are a combination of external/internal schemes and for external programmes to form sponsors sets in parallel with those of their fellows. Again the advice is experimental, there must be many other possibilities for involving the client.

Feedback and learning

Insofar as the aims of Action Learning are in solving problems combined with personal/organizational development, learning how to learn is the real prize; it is one thing to solve the problems of the moment, whereas it is something quite different to learn how to deal with the unknown ones of tomorrow. Moreover, if what may be called a 'critical mass' of people know how to cope with what the future holds in store we could have that elusive animal the self learning organization. Many have expressed views on what is 'learning how to learn'. I think it is a trial and error approach to problem solving with the important requirement to learn from our experiments. Indeed, the idea of deciding in advance how we intend tackling a problem, trying it out in the real world and then learning from the results has always been the basis of human progress. Some people, of course, have a natural feel for this process! They are probably not conscious of it but they reflect on their successes and failures, are aware of their own actions and do not let past ways of doing things influence how they tackle new situations. The clue is feedback from the results of our own actions; an Action Learning set, fellows and adviser, puts a forced draught under this inter-related process of declaring in advance what you intend doing, implementing your decision through the client and learning from these two stages; a process which in reality is rough and ready with many 'U' turns, reversals and full stops. The set is the real life laboratory where feedback about real here-and-now problems can be better understood.

Feedback comes from four main sources:

1   *The set*: the fellows are without question best qualified to remove the bandages from each other's eyes and to shatter illusions about problems. Furthermore, what fellows propose to do and when they actually try and do it is more effective if feedback is provided as it all happens.

2   *Set advisers*: they help fellows to give each other their own feedback, encouraging them throughout the programme to experiment with different approaches to their problems and the way they organize their set meetings; taking the personal risks associated with testing new ideas and behaviours in the real world is the essence of learning.

3   *Clients*: the client groups which often consist of superiors, peers, subordinates and may include suppliers and customers have always been a good on-going means of managerial learning. The Action Learning set causes the participants to reflect on their interactions with these key groups of people.

4   *Review points*: feedback can be a part of the programme through the device of review meetings. These generally take place midway and at the end of the programme. This approach provides the opportunity for fellows, sponsors and clients to evaluate individual learning; the impact on the problems and the influence of both on the organization. Current developments include establishing a sponsor's set with the task of how they can help their fellows to use

Action Learning to solve their common problems – even experimenting with a fellow as their set adviser!

The way ahead

In a world which is changing rapidly, survival is now uppermost in most people's minds. Not so long ago, annual growth was taken for granted and we could sell virtually everything we made. Now that has all changed, the developing world can make our traditional products as cheaply and as well as we can while at the same time the micro chip is eliminating work in our industries. Hence a leaner and highly competitive market combined with raw material suppliers in the third world now wanting a bigger share of the added value means all our underlying inefficiencies are exposed. In such conditions academic irrelevancies have no place, organizational development has got to concentrate on involving people in the means of their own survival and that of their businesses. Unless we learn fast how to change, we shall fail. Action Learning is providing a secure foundation on which to cope with an uncertain future.

I have tried to show that Action Learning is not so much about specific programmes such as full-time exchange schemes or part-time external programmes as about furnishing a basis for changing the behaviour of ourselves and our enterprises and to solve our problems. Experiment with it, try new approaches; it will involve risks but the rewards will be tremendous.

22 The role of the set adviser*

David Casey

In Action Learning the prime source of help is the peer group
– not the set adviser. The set adviser is a special member of the
set, in some ways he is part of the set, in some ways not. His
role, in Carl Rogers' terms,[1] is to facilitate learning. He is not
a teacher in the sense of having a specific area of knowledge to
impart but he is a teacher in the sense of helping others to learn.
His locus is the set as a living community and not the projects
as technical challenges. When we began, we called him a project
adviser but this was misleading since his role is not directly
related to the projects themselves, so we then referred to him
as the project set adviser and finally we have come to think of
him as the set adviser since his role focuses on the set.

Not all set advisers focus to the same extent on the set, some
also contribute significantly to the projects themselves and we
have yet fully to exchange experiences among the score or so
facilitators who have worked on Action Learning programmes.
These notes are written from a personal experience of facilitating
eleven such sets and will, naturally, reflect my own view of the
role. I try to behave consistently according to a set of assumptions about how experienced managers learn. These assumptions

*This chapter is adapted from Casey, D. 'The Emerging Role of Set
Adviser in Action Learning Programmes', *Journal of European
Training*, vol. 5, no. 3, 1976.

are mostly based on Rogers and Revans and no doubt now contain something of me as well. (Rogers would have it so since, if I have learned in any lasting way by being a set adviser, the learning must have been self-initiated and self-appropriated learning.) Before stating my assumptions, a word of warning – it is very easy to agree with any stated assumptions about learning, without facing up fully to the implications of these assumptions. I have found recently in talking to management teachers that almost without exception they identify at once with stated assumptions about learning, but a large number will immediately contradict by their behaviour one or more of them. This contradiction may be as learners or as teachers – as learners they may ask for the gospel from 'the expert' and as teachers they may become infatuated by their own ideas.

The power of Revans's idea, which lies behind every exchange programme of Action Learning, shows up with great clarity when an honest attempt is made to live through the implications of whatever assumptions one makes about how managers learn. In Action Learning these implications extend into two quite separate arenas – the project location, where the participant spends four days a week by himself, and the set, where he spends the remaining day with his colleagues and the set adviser. My own assumptions and some of the implications, in both arenas, which I try to face up to when working as a set adviser, are as follows:

Assumption 1: Experienced managers have a huge curiosity to know how other experienced managers work.

This curiosity is the fuel which powers all Action Learning and it operates both in the project location and in the set. It is *not* matched by equal curiosity to know how management teachers think managers should work. Action Learning designs must therefore make *visible* and *accessible* the ways in which experienced managers actually work, so that the power of this curiosity can be tapped. These processes must be made visible and accessible in the set discussions as well as in the project locations.

Assumption 2: We learn not so much when we are motivated to learn, as when we are motivated to achieve something.

The implication of this assumption in the project location is obvious – a difficult and worthwhile task must be presented. In the set too, a difficult and worthwhile task must be presented – it is the educational task of helping the others.

Assumption 3: Learning about oneself is threatening and is resisted if it tends to change one's self-image. However, it is possible to reduce the external threat to a level which no longer acts as a total barrier to learning about oneself.

Left alone in the project location most individuals would react to opportunities to learn about themselves, by building instant defence systems to keep out any uncomfortable new information about themselves. The mechanism of providing a home base in a supportive set, one day each week, prevents these defence systems becoming too entrenched too soon – at least one day in five a participant can feel surrounded by support. However, this doesn't happen automatically, the set has to learn how to offer help in an unthreatening way.

Assumption 4: People only learn when they do something, and they learn more the more responsible they feel the task to be.

The responsible nature of project work is well understood in management training circles, and Action Learning projects must be carefully selected, just as in any other form of project training, to keep the element of responsibility sufficiently high. In addition, the highly responsible element built into the set arena is the task of helping other participants with their projects and in deepening their self-perception. What could be more responsible than that?

Assumption 5: Learning is deepest when it involves the whole person, mind, values, body, emotions.

The implications of this assumption will be clear enough in the project work, the whole person is inevitably fully involved in the project, which often takes a participant away from home to a strange location, with the daunting task of effecting some significant changes in an organisation busily engaged in a business about which he demonstrably knows nothing. But he needs also to be involved as a whole person in the intimate working of the set, and the set adviser must use the dynamics of small group work to ensure that he is.

Assumption 6: The learner knows more than anyone else what he has learned. Nobody else has much chance of knowing.

The assumption here is not that people always know what they have learned – but that the chance of anyone else knowing is very slim indeed. I find it very difficult to remain true to this assumption in spite of recurring evidence from Action Learning programmes and other activities. For instance, in one set recently one member found that he had learned profoundly about himself and about the processes of management, but after the programme was over he ascribed *all* this learning directly to his work in the field, doing his project. Another member said he learned much more of permanent value from the set discussions than from his project.

Tasks of the set adviser

His assumptions about learning are not the only assumptions which determine the tasks of the set adviser. Since his main job is to facilitate, he will see his tasks differently depending on what he thinks he is trying to facilitate, in other words what he thinks the set members are trying to do, both in their separate projects and during set meetings. So his facilitating behaviour will be motivated by two forces – his perception of what set members are trying to do, and his assumptions about how experienced managers learn.

These two forces mould the job to a particular shape and it would be possible to start from very different beliefs and turn out a different task for the set adviser. One could, for example, assume 'each participant will need guidance from an expert in the discipline on which his problem rests': this would lead to a task of *expert adviser*. Another assumption, 'groups work more efficiently if properly led towards their objectives', would give a task of *leadership*, and so on.

In my own work as a set adviser four distinct tasks seem to be emerging. These are:

1 　to facilitate giving;

2 　to facilitate receiving;

3 　to clarify the various processes of Action Learning; and

4 　to help others take over tasks 1, 2 and 3.

In explaining what I mean by each of these tasks, I will try to illustrate where possible with recent examples, changing only the names of those involved.

Task 1: To facilitate giving

This comes first, because it helps set members to get better at the most rewarding part of their work – and the richest vein of learning for them – that is, giving to each other. The most effective set, I believe, is one in which this attitude of giving permeates every question, prompts every comment, motivates every silence, sparks every show of feeling. The questions asked in such a set, as each project is discussed in turn, are phrased to give maximum help to the person questioned and not to satisfy the needs of the questioner. When John asked why Mike had decided to circulate a particular piece of information in his project company, the question was designed to make Mike think of alternatives, not to help John decide whether he should do it in his own project company, useful though this might have been for him.

Generous questioning is only one way in which a set member gives. He gives his opinion too – sometimes it is good news for the receiver, sometimes it is bad news – both have to be delivered effectively. He gives his feelings of the moment more openly as the set matures and he learns the value of openness. Here the set adviser often has to break new ground for experienced managers, who may well have spent their growing years as managers learning to hide their feelings rather than express them in the working situation. Sentences which begin: 'I'm not sure . . .' are heard more and more in set meetings. Expressing his current learning as it takes place is also difficult for the set member, but helpful to others – to say: 'I learned a lot from listening to you struggling with that . . .' helps others to express similar feelings and more and more the person being helped is able to select what he wants, so that quite frequently he is able to say: 'I'm not finding this whole conversation useful at the moment . . .' or: 'Yes, I see . . . that's helpful, can you go on a bit, Bill?'

The set adviser encourages members to give support; emotional support is often badly needed – projects can seem impossibly complex, dauntingly diffuse and at some stage every member of the set needs massive support.

I find it difficult to help members to give freely of their technical experience, they are at first diffident, and make the judgment themselves about the usefulness of their own experiences. I see it as my task to encourage them to give it freely and in such a frame of mind that the judgment about its relevance lies wholly with the listener. This dialogue from my notes in a recent set meeting illustrates this kind of giving:

> . . . I don't believe, from my own experience at X, that you get commitment that easily from shop stewards to looking at the terms of employment as a whole, I believe their commitment is confined to money!
>
> Really? . . . I find that interesting . . . but if you don't mind I'll store it in the back of my mind for now . . .
>
> Fine! I think I'm right, but it's your project!

Task 2: To facilitate receiving

The ability to receive help from others is not distributed evenly among the management population and very competent, self-reliant men such as we have on these Action Learning programmes, often find it difficult. For this reason I like to emphasize the first task of giving – when the set members are skilful in providing help for one another they more easily accept the possibility of receiving help too. Eventually I expect the members of the set to go after help, searching diligently among the diverse experiences they recognize within the group. But this comes normally at a later stage; they learn first to give, then to receive, then to go looking for help.

The advantage of developing this kind of searching attitude is that it allows the searcher to probe deeply without any suspicion of dependency. The traditional teacher-student relationship is abandoned – instead of the teacher persuading the student to accept his ideas, the student is relentlessly searching the mind and experiences of the teacher. In an Action Learning set both 'teacher' and 'student' are experienced managers and the relationship described can be built up by the set adviser if he facilitates the ability first to give, then to receive and finally to search.

Accepting the view of himself which others have is also a field of great potential for the set member. Recently when someone was seeking help in framing his questions within his project company, he received a min-lecture from a fellow set member who described in glowing terms how much effort he himself put into the questions he asked, ending with the statement: '. . . I put a very great deal of thought into those questions'. This sparked an immediate retort: 'Well, you've got a more political situation!' Lots of things were going wrong here. The giver of help was satisfying his own needs, and doing it in such a way that resentment was building up in the supposed receiver, so that he totally rejected the help offered. The other set members were allowing this to happen. I quoted back to the set exactly what had been said and we discussed the incident fruitfully for ten minutes. The outcome was a declaration from a different member of the group that he frequently felt the first speaker to be 'speaking down' to others. This was said so sensitively that it was accepted with these words: '. . . I'm horrified . . . do I do that? . . . thank you for telling me anyway . . . Painful, but useful to know. I'd like to know if I do that again . . .'

Another aspect of receiving is the ability to receive doubts expressed by others. Respecting the doubt expressed by another person is necessary if that person is to be encouraged to express his doubts more often, and here the set adviser who really is trying to reduce the external threat in the situation, in line with my third assumption, has to be able to express his own doubts too. I find there is a best time in the life of the set to begin to express one's own doubts and worries – too early retards the early growth of the group – too late and the opportunity to move from dependency to interdependency can be lost.

Task 3: To clarify various processes of Action Learning

Action Learning is not simple, although based on simple ideas. The two tasks discussed so far – facilitating giving and receiving in a group – are by no means revolutionary and much has been written of them in therapy and sensitivity training. The extra dimension of an Action Learning programme lies in the fact that there are several unique and important processes taking place, which the set adviser must reveal to the set. He cannot do this until the set begins to understand group processes in general and this understanding is gained at set meetings, within their own learning cell. His task then becomes one of transferring this new understanding to illuminate at least four important processes taking place outside the set.

First there is the complex process of change, embedded in the web of relationships which we call the client system. This web comprises at least three separate networks, the power network, the information network and the motivational network (this is what Revans means by 'who can, who knows and who cares'). The forces for change which the visitor must identify and use to get his project implemented – not by him, but by his clients – are already there within the client system and it becomes the set adviser's role to point out the dynamics of this system as the work of diagnosis and implementation proceeds. If the participant can learn, with the help of his set peers, aided by his set adviser, how to work this system effectively he will not only achieve the implementation of his project, but will have enriched his managerial abilities significantly for all time. In addition, the organisation in which a successful project is implemented will learn something of itself and how it goes about getting things done; there will be a new power released in such an organisation for getting things done more effectively in the future.

The second process to be illuminated is the process of the project itself. Here the task of project management is no different in essence from managing any other greenfield project. The lifespan of the project must be contained within the timescale of the programme and the action leaner must control the whole project just as any project manager has to. This means deciding on the project objectives, planning resources, monitoring progress and all the other normal activities associated with a major finite project. This will be a familiar process to some participants, but many will find it new and challenging.

Thirdly, there are the processes of the total Action Learning programme which include the interaction of the managing body, the managing directors or other forces of power, the management development specialists within the companies, the participants, the tutors, the various sets, the nominating companies and the client companies, and the total learning community which often comes together at important points in the timetable. There will be interactions between sets as well as within those sets. There are often interfaces between one programme and another.

Finally, there is the process of this particular year of action learning within the total career context of the individual manager. Here is something which only he can manage and which will have been highlighted for him before he makes his decision to come on the programme. Included in this process is the constant awareness of his re-entry problem for which he must bear personal responsibility, although many resources are available to help him to reduce the difficulties of his eventual re-entry, whether or not he returns to his former job.

The set adviser must ensure that all these processes are identified, separated and illuminated as human processes for the participant, using his learning of group dynamics derived equally from the dynamics of the set meetings themselves and from the discussions taking place in those meetings.

Task 4: To help others take over tasks 1, 2 and 3

This task, which I certainly give myself, may well be controversial among other set advisers. I aim to declare at the beginning what

I see my tasks within the set to be, and try to involve the set in its own process work as early as I can. To establish in people's minds as quickly as possible that I wish control to be shared, I tend to use symptoms and symbols of control as examples. I will refuse to take minor decisions about where, when and how we meet, how we use our time, what we do about visitors, what administrative and domestic arrangements are necessary and so on. I then move on to encourage process comment from set members and point out when it happens, and, if it does not happen, I will ask why not.

My experience so far is mixed. Some individuals in each set do seem to grasp quite quickly what I am getting at, others see it as some level of abdication of the set adviser's responsibility. My justification for encouraging the set to share in the facilitating role is that I believe it is an important part of a top manager's job to work on the process of the work he undertakes with his groups, as well as on the content. I think I would go so far as to say that, for the chief executive, the ability to think out what the process should be and to see it through, is his greatest personal asset. The dilemma is that not all managers have the necessary interest, although I believe that those selected for a senior Action Learning exchange programme should certainly possess most of the required personal characteristics to do the job of facilitator.

Results are always encouraging and by the time the programme ends several members of any set are considering the process quite naturally and automatically.

What makes an effective set adviser?

This question is being asked widely in management learning circles at the moment since Action Learning is making such headway. We do not yet know the answer, but some progress can be made by identifying a list of characteristics which seem to be valuable and a list of skills which seem to be needed and comparing these with some of the characteristics and skills needed for effective teaching in more traditional settings. My belief is that very many successful teachers could become excellent set advisers, since, by definition, they have what it takes. I am not so confident about the true academic. His commitment is to using his own mind; the real teacher's commitment is to using the minds of others.

I have described the tasks of the set adviser as I see them. It would be sensible now to move on from the tasks to consider what personal characteristics and skills seem to be needed to do the job.

Characteristics required

First the well known characteristics which all successful teachers have. Clearly sensitivity is needed – sensitivity to people and situations. Perception is needed and a quickness of mind. Conceptual ability too, to help others to conceptualize. But in addition to these qualities, which are widely distributed in the teaching population, we have come to recognize about five additional characteristics which may or may not be so widely distributed. These are:

1. Tolerance of ambiguity. Traditional teachers may like the security of a well prepared lesson given in a setting determined by themselves to a timetable which is known in advance so that their tolerance of ambiguity need not be high. The set adviser must live in a world of uncertainty and must be prepared to allow the learners to take control from him. Unless he enjoys this situation he is unlikely to enjoy the role of set adviser.

2. A quality of openness and frankness which is best described by Rogers as 'realness in the facilitator of learning'; this implies an ability to recognize and express one's own feelings in the learning situation, as they arise.

3. Patience. Endless patience.

4. An overwhelming desire to see other people learn. Unless this is there to a high level the sheer frustration of the work in an Action Learning set would drive some traditional teachers to distraction. The rewards of set adviser must be in seeing incremental learning take place very slowly and very personally over long periods of time. This is what all teachers look for, of course, but in set work the teacher seems to be doing very little, although inside he is in turmoil, endlessly interpreting and modelling what is going on within the group, but only declaring to the group what he sees occasionally, for fear of upsetting the value of the process itself. To use so little of his hard-won interpretations is only possible in someone who has an overriding belief in the method and in the value of learning.

5. Empathy. This quality of 'operating through the mind of

another person' is only enjoyed by those who can put themselves into other people's shoes and almost feel their feelings with them.

Skills required and not required

In addition to the characteristics described above there is, of course, a range of skills. First, let us look at some traditional skills which teachers have invested many years to perfect, because they have been an important part of their professional repertoire, and which in the role of set adviser would no longer be of any value, while in the role. In that simple statement there lies a worrying threat to many a practising teacher. Not only does the statement make his hard-earned skills redundant, it raises the worrying question of whether he has, or can develop, the new skills needed for the role. Some of the skills he will no longer need are these:

Skills not required

1 Presentation skill. From the Assembly in ancient Athens to the House of Commons, hundreds of thousands of orators have ingrained deep in our culture the value of making a convincing presentation – and the expectation among students that it is appropriate for teachers to do this, is just as deeply ingrained. Add to that, the sheer pleasure most teachers get from making a well-polished presentation, and we have two very good reasons why it is difficult to let this skill lie fallow.

2 Structuring skills. It is no longer necessary to structure the sequence of lessons and the sequence of material within a lesson and the sequence of lessons within a term to cover the material required by examinations. There is, of course, a design task to be performed but this refers to the whole programme and not to any one set. We normally have a steering group to discharge this role, for the programme as a whole.

3 Fluency. The ability to use the language in an oratorical sense. Excellence and clarity of delivery, the perfection of one-way communication.

4 The skill of preparation in advance of a teaching assignment. How much to prepare, how much to leave unprepared, when to ad lib, when to quote from authorities, and a host of other considerations.

Choosing to work in a new teaching role, which does not need these skills, built up painstakingly over the years, is not something that everyone can bring himself to do. Most teachers who work in a process way are young. This is no coincidence, it simply means they had much less to throw away. There is nothing to be gained by criticising those conscientious teachers who have deeply-learned skills on which they have based their careers. I believe many of them, with help, can develop new skills quickly for the new role. Many of them want to, they are intellectually convinced that Revans and Rogers are right, but emotionally there is an understandable blockage. It is important to establish that we are concerned here with the demands of a particular role. The learning assumptions in this article were stated with reference to a particular learning setting, with experienced managers learning from each other, helped by a set adviser. There is no reason why the same set adviser should not deliver first class lectures, in settings where lecturing is appropriate – and there are many such settings. The management teacher who has highly developed skills as a lecturer need not feel threatened by the challenge of working in the new role of set adviser, his lecturing skills will have to be shelved while he is in the new role, but since he almost certainly has the necessary basic characteristics required for the role, he can quickly develop a new range of skills to add to the old, and powerfully extend his total capacity as a teacher. With this wider range of teaching skills at his disposal he will be in a position to adapt more effectively to the challenges presented by different teaching opportunities. What are these new skills?

Skills required

One meets a snag at once. The old skills, no longer needed, are familiar and easy to identify. The newer skills are emerging, unfamiliar and not easy to describe. They lie somewhere in these areas:

1 Skill in timing interventions. Too early and the intervention is not understood, too late and the opportunity has passed.

2 Skill in asking what must be exceptionally good questions which make people think, but at the same time feel challenged and supported rather than criticized.

3 Skill in using the language of managers. To avoid speaking down, and resist the seduction of analysis and intellectualizing.

4 Selecting and applying the appropriate model to reflect processes taking place at a particular time. And skill in choosing the issue for examination which best relates processes within the set to processes within the projects.

5 The skill of saying nothing and being invisible.

6 Skill in hearing two or three processes at the same time, most of the time.

7 Skill in making statements truthfully whilst structuring the statements to be of maximum use.

The skills described are not very clearly differentiated from each other and ALP International is still working on compiling a better understanding of what various set advisers' skills are. Different set advisers work in different ways and there may well be several quite different roles which a set adviser can usefully play. These notes have emphasized the role of facilitator of learning because this is how I see it. Others add to this a further dimension of acting as environmental scanner for the set, encouraging the members to look outwards to an ever-changing world. Other set advisers contribute more than I do to the technical content of projects. By sharing our experiences we hope to learn too, in spite of the very real difficulty of ever being sure, from the outside, what is actually going on inside another set.

Reference

1 Rogers, C., *Freedom to Learn*, Merrill, 1969.

23 Developing the set adviser

J. M. Harries

In simple terms Action Learning theory states that managers learn most effectively with and from each other by working on real problems and reflecting on their experience. In a typical Action Learning (AL) programme groups of four to six managers meet regularly to help each other tackle these problems or projects. These sets, as they have become known, are autonomous learning communities.

Why then – given the formidable potential of such a peer group – do we find that most AL programme sets have an outsider foisted on them? This space-invader is usually designated as a 'set adviser' and yet surely the very notion of an adviser runs counter to Revans' concept of 'comrades in adversity' representing the most compelling learning environment? Is this role of set adviser nothing more than a management training lecturer's alter ego, a new nomenclature legitimizing his retention of direct involvement in a 'training' process? In a word, is the role of set adviser superfluous?

Any consideration of the training of set advisers should start by examining the need *for* them – only then ought we to consider *their* needs. The perfectly natural desire of trainers for involvement in Action Learning as a vehicle for management and organization development is not justification enough! What is it, if anything, that a set adviser can, uniquely, contribute to the set? For me the answer is simple – the adviser's *raison d'être* is to help the set members identify and capitalize on those learning opportunities occurring during the project work and in the set meetings themselves. This emphasis on the helping or facilitation of the learning process raises the issue of the correctness of the accepted terminology. I find the word 'adviser' misleading in that it conjures up images of expertness, and, by implication, leadership or authority. 'Facilitator', on the other hand, while more pretentious, conveys more accurately the essence of the relationship. I hope this will not be construed as mere semantic hairsplitting. It is important that those with responsibility for the development of aspiring advisers should not make the mistake of thinking that they are training counsellors or arbiters! Perhaps the key, as is so often the case, lies in the Latin root of the word 'adviser': one who helps set members to *see* themselves (and *for* themselves).

The fact that the adviser does not have a project (and therefore cannot be one of the comrades in adversity), far from being an insuperable barrier, is his greatest strength. He has no admission to the group on the ticket of project involvement, but is someone whose very detachment from the concentration on the task provides a perspective which, axiomatically the others cannot have. Thus, we arrive at a crude, but hopefully practical, statement about the position of the adviser. The sole (but vital) justification for his presence is the 'non-combatant' focus he can bring to bear, and his objective is to facilitate the learning process. If we accept such a statement we can start to make judgements about the operating range within which the adviser works, and hence how we might help in the process of developing aspiring advisers.

Managing and facilitating the life cycle of the set

My experience as a member of, and subsequently adviser to, a number of AL sets suggests that it may be useful to think of the adviser as having two continuous functions. These can be termed *managerial* and *facilitative*. The functions are complementary and synchronous in that the adviser never switches exclusively from one to the other. The terms are used to distinguish between what we may call strategic and tactical activities. The managerial or strategic function involves constant monitoring and appreciation of 'where a set is' at any given point in its life cycle (see Figure 23.1). The facilitative or tactical function encompasses the use of appropriate skills to help the set progress. This view of the set adviser's work presupposes an identifiable pattern of growth within a set, from its creation to its dissolution. At the risk of offending those who would argue that each set creates its own unique dynamic and determines for itself the shape of its development, I believe there *is* a model we can use to chart the significant stages of any set's growth.

Any working group with a finite life span passes through certain identifiable stages, each of which can be equated with generally agreed characteristics. The human life-cycle may be taken to illustrate this assertion.

Life can be viewed as a movement from immaturity and high dependence, through maturity and independence to 'supermaturity' and interdependence. Forget for a moment that periods of counterdependence may occur, or that one might add a fourth stage, senility, and reversion to high dependence (a set should dissolve itself before such a stage could occur). What seems to be important is that we can recognize such stages by the behaviours exhibited. It is a fact that some people never progress beyond a certain stage, and those who do move through the stages do so at differing rates. Anyone concerned with the learning process must take into account the stage which people (either as individuals, or as groups) are at, and adopt appropriate approaches and methods.

An AL set, then, can pass through specific stages of growth, or not (again, it is the rate of progress which is the variable). It therefore seems only logical that the adviser, or potential adviser, should be able to identify at any time which stage the set has reached (the managerial or strategic activity) and needs to possess the tactical or facilitative skills to expedite progress. Figure 18.1 shows a model representing the life of a set.

Each triangle illustrates the typical operating mode of a set during any one meeting at early, mid point and final stages of its life. Initially R and C activities will take up the bulk of available time. Each set member will report on his project – its nature and background, his terms of reference, the range of options available, and other such matters. His colleagues will seek clarification of these points to ensure that they understand the intricacies of the problem being tackled (or at least the individual's perceptions on that score) and the planned courses of action. Only when R and C have been achieved can the set fulfil its *main* purpose, namely the generation of support and pressure aimed at successful resolution of the problem (SP).

Inevitably each meeting will have some periods of R, C and SP, but as the set gells and members become increasingly familiar

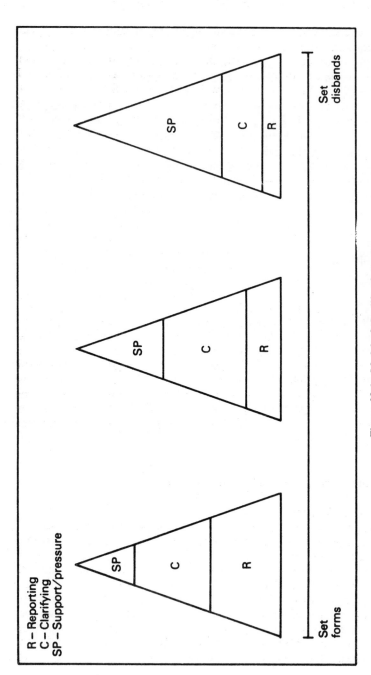

R – Reporting
C – Clarifying
SP – Support/pressure

Set forms

Set disbands

Figure 23.1 Model of the life of a set

with each project, the need for R and C diminishes, creating additional time and space for SP.

If we accept this model, then the adviser should have some responsibility for accelerating progress from a mode of high R and C/low SP to one of low R and C/high SP. This is not to deny that, as an autonomous group, the set members share this responsibility to a degree. Indeed there is high learning potential in the process of the set members grappling for themselves with the difficulties of moving from one stage to the next. Without help, though, some sets might get stuck in one particular operating mode. They might even do so through collusion if they find themselves in a comfortable or cosy situation! Since most AL programmes face practical time constraints, and opportunities exist for only a predetermined number of meetings, many sets could spend a disproportionate amount of time in any one stage at the expense of operational achievement. The *managing* activity of maintaining balance between the development of process awareness and the successful resolution of projects seems to me to be a legitimate responsibility of the adviser, and therefore of vital importance in his training.

It is not my intention here to concern myself in detail with the issues of the roles and skills of the adviser, both of which are dealt with elsewhere in this book. My purpose thus far has been to try and develop a framework of operating ranges within which the adviser is likely to function, and to focus on the two main activities in which he will be involved. From such a framework it should be possible to determine which approaches and methods, from the range of possible training options, best meet particular requirements.

Development approaches for set advisers

The remainder of this chapter sets out a number of ways in which advisers can develop, and draws on my experience as a tutor on two AL programmes, run by the Local Government Training Board, during the period 1979–81. The aims of the programmes, which were co-tutored by David Casey and also Tony Smith, a colleague of mine at the LGTB, were to help participants (all of whom were line managers or personnel and training specialists from local authorities) investigate the applicability of AL to their organizations, establish sets where appropriate and possible and develop the skills of set advising. David's considerable experience in the AL field was invaluable, as was

Tony's previous involvement as a member of a set. Nevertheless, when faced with the issue of devising a 'training programme' to develop the advisers, we struggled quite a bit, and while we tried *some* of the methods outlined below, others were either not possible at the time, or simply did not occur to us until we were reviewing the programmes after their completion.

The following list, then, is a pot pourri of tried and tested approaches, and, at least as far as my own experience is concerned, as yet unimplemented suggestions. The order in which they are discussed should not be taken as indicating prioritization since my growing conviction is that a thorough adviser training programme should utilize all of them in various mixes. The only pattern is one of moving from the more traditional didactic or cognitively based approach to the totally experiential (or, to use David Casey's typically perceptive phrase) 'whole-person' activity.

1 Traditional teaching methods

The current vogue is to question the effectiveness of this approach to training, including as it does such unfashionable adjuncts as 'books' and 'teachers'. As is usually the case with fashions, however, the pendulum over-corrects leaving a choice of extremes rather than the whole range between. I believe there is a strong case for a suitably brief formal introduction to Action Learning in an adviser training programme. Whatever the innate skills of the aspirant adviser, reading through an appropriate bibliography (see Appendix 2) will ensure that he has, at the cognitive level, an appreciation of the basic concepts underlying AL.

To build on this hardcore, inputs from respected practitioners are useful. Generally speaking, students of management tend to place greatest credence in those members of the teaching staff who have actually managed something or somebody sometime. Similarly, it can be illuminating to listen to and talk with those who have practical experience of designing and implementing AL programmes and set advising. On the LGTB programme referred to earlier we were fortunate to secure the services of such exponents as Alan Lawlor and David Sutton. At an early stage, therefore, our horizons were broadened. We learned about the diversity of applications of AL, the way in which set activities could be built into formal programmes, the possibilities inherent in the macro-project set (in which set members tackle different components of one major organizational issue) and the differing perceptions of 'successful' advisers as to the roles and skills involved. This learning we could not get from books alone, but would not have appreciated fully without the base knowledge gleaned from our pre-reading.

Neither books nor speakers can do much to *develop* the facilitative or managerial *skills* referred to. They will, however, provide the aspiring adviser with an *understanding of the need for the acquisition of such skills.*

2 Observation of a set in action

This is more immediate than the previous item, but still some way from whole-person involvement. There are two ways in which it can be done, either observing a set meeting 'live' or on film/videotape. Each has its merits and shortcomings. The major dimension which either adds to item 1 is the opportunity to *observe* the application (or absence) of the skills of which item 1 can provide only a cognitive appreciation. The main advantage of watching 'live' is that you begin to experience, albeit vicariously, some of the tensions generated within a set. You can also begin to practise your own skills of reading where the set is (in terms of R, C and SP) and make at least notional decisions as to which interventions you might be making if you were the adviser. These can be compared with what the real adviser does. The chief difficulty is arranging for this 'sitting in'. The confidentiality of set proceedings is absolute and accepting an alien is difficult; even if it is negotiated, the presence of the space-invader may, in itself, be enough to induce a certain artificiality to proceedings, at least initially. If it can be arranged, however, it is useful, particularly if the 'real' adviser subsequently talks the observer through what happened and compares notes.

Watching a filmed or videotaped set meeting may be easier to arrange, again with the approval of the set and adviser. While the immediacy of 'being there' is lost, the action can be stopped and replayed at will and the various interventions/non-interventions discussed and analysed. It is particularly useful in the training of a group of aspiring advisers, as opposed to an individual. All of them can practise their skills simultaneously – there is no way in which they could all invade the privacy of a set! We used the videotape method on the LGTB course, and, as the set adviser concerned, it was, in prospect at least, extremely embarrassing to have my performance subjected to critical public scrutiny. It was however an immensely rewarding learning situation and the constructive criticisms were gratefully received. The watchers and the watched gained equally!

One word of caution is appropriate here. There is a danger of modelling yourself too closely on someone who is perceived as a 'good' adviser. This can be disastrous! It has long been accepted that watching an acknowledged expert practitioner in action is a valuable learning experience. In the area of set advising, however, acting your way through and hence being false to your natural self is to invite (and almost certainly receive) retribution from your set. On the programme referred to it became readily apparent for example that Tony and I had quite widely contrasting styles of advising, both of which were different from those of David Casey. I was concerned about this until David pointed out that while he did it his way, *I* had to do it *mine*. Once this vital message is hoisted aboard, the observation process really begins to work – You are watching not on the basis of 'things I must remember to say and do' but 'how and when is X fulfilling his strategic and tactical responsibilities and what learning (in the sense of generalizing and applying) is there in it for me?'

3 Membership of an AL set as a participant

We cross an important threshold in moving from items 1 to 3. No longer are we observers/interlopers/voyeurs. We belong! We can get direct personal experience of the power of a set, both in terms of its supportiveness and (initially more uncomfortably) its challenging, bullying and pressuring. I would go as far as to say that set-membership should be a pre-requisite for aspiring set advisers, certainly those who have no previous experience as small-group facilitators. It is particularly helpful in developing the ability to check out the set's growth in terms of R, C and SP, and goes some way to creating the opportunity to practise set advising skills in a real situation. If, after all, one of the main aims of AL sets is to develop awareness of group processes, and interpersonal skills, then the more effective the adviser the more quickly set members take over some of his functions. One perhaps over-mechanistic way of catering for this is to set aside fixed periods of time within which set members take over the advisory role in turn. We tried this, with some success, on our programme – it certainly eases people in, in the sense that they have, say, an hour to practise in, which is real, and live and here-and-now, but know they are not carrying the burden for too long at a time and can always be 'retrieved'. With a sympathetic set, which we had, since everyone was in the same boat, this process of learning to swim 'in the water', as opposed to reading a teach-yourself book (but in the shallow end with a life-belt handy) can be most effective. Again the danger to be avoided is modelling your advising on that of your own set adviser.

4 Co-advising (shadowing)

This approach can be done in two ways. Firstly, co-advising, which involves having two advisers to a set, secondly, shadowing (this is not an 'accepted' AL phrase in glossary terms, but my own attempt to find an expression to make the distinction clear!) In shadowing there is only one adviser (the trainee) present at meetings but he has the services of the 'expert' as a sounding board, someone with whom he can discuss his performance.

A refinement of this which we tried was to have David Casey acting as our shadow under the following arrangements. Tony Smith and I were the set advisers but at certain intervals (say one set meeting in every three) David actually 'sat in' on the meetings. We were able to do this since all the participants accepted the usefulness of such an arrangement in terms of developing their own set advising skills. If I am honest, it was not totally successful for me. I began to resent David's attendance at meetings, since, whenever he was present, the set could not help but regard him as the expert (the sorcerer to my apprentice). I felt a loss of prestige, which perhaps reflects more on my own make-up than on the arrangement itself! Despite my own feelings of resentment, there is surely validity in a learning situation wherein a trainee adviser can receive feedback from an experienced adviser who is also present during the meeting. Such an arrangement should be of assistance in the development of both managerial and facilitative skills.

5 Doing it yourself

There comes a time when, after any or all of items 1 to 4, the aspirant must finally go solo. After all, if we accept Revans's assertion that the most effective learning arises from doing something and reflecting on the experience, the 'best' way of learning how to be a set-adviser is to do it for real. The parallel with flying training is too good for an ex-RAF man to resist! You can read all the books and manuals there are on the theory of aerodynamics and the handling characteristics and performance limits of the aircraft-type you are trying to master. You can observe your instructor as he demonstrates the art, you can even fly the aircraft completely unaided (but still in the reassuring presence of the instructor). Eventually, however, he steps out and leaves things to you. All the training you have received will certainly be needed, but only soloing enables you to experience the activity *for* yourself and *by* yourself. By reflecting on your performance – your attempts to cope with the problems and tensions encountered – you become more proficient next time round.

Conclusion

These then, are some ways in which the development of set advisers can be approached. Whatever we choose to do in this context, one thing is clear – the wide perceptual gap which currently exists between those who manage and those who 'teach' management needs to be bridged. The development of a cadre of set advisers from the ranks of such management teachers may represent one way of achieving this. I believe that project sets of real managers tackling real problems in real time will become more and more part of the management training scene. There will be increasing demand for such a cadre who, instead of confidently telling hard pressed managers what management is all about, will be able to help them learn *from* the management activity itself.

24 Another look at set advising

Mike Pedler

Apart from the preceding accounts there are numerous passing references and comments in this book on the role of the set adviser. Over the years many management teachers, trainers and consultants have taken up this role professionally – we use it to earn our living, to justify our time. We all agree that set advising is interesting, exciting, intellectually and emotionally demanding and, it goes without saying, crucial and important.

Reg Revans on the other hand has never said much about this important role – not much that is encouraging anyway – although he has said time and time again how interesting, exciting, demanding and important Action Learning is. We need then, first of all, to ask why we are so convinced of the importance of this role when the master remains dismissive? Here two somewhat polarised scenarios spring readily to mind. The first holds that Action Learning, as an idea beginning to grip the minds of all who manage, is an entirely satisfying and meaty host for the carpet-baggers who swarm around the corporation of management education and training. Hence, this argument goes, the rise of the 'professional set adviser' – a person who will help you implement this deceptively simple schema – at an appropriate professional fee.

The second scenario is kinder to us management trainers and runs something like this. Working in groups is one of the more important social features of the twentieth century. We spend more and more time in groups for the purposes of learning, work and living because ours is an age in which many of the tasks and questions we are addressing require group resources and support. This is nowhere more true than in management; that complex social art once seen as the property of imposing, individual gentlemen and now increasingly recognized as a shared contract and way of doing things in groups and organizations of people. Action Learning brings together the impulses of the work group and the learning group to tackle hitherto intractable problems. However, in the rich countries of the world, our experience and education is strongly individualistic and creates blocks and difficulties to the more diffuse group consciousness essential to the twin energies of support and challenge in the Action Learning set. It follows easily from this argument that we need skilled people – skilled in facilitating action and learning in groups – to ensure that the idea of Action Learning finds an appropriate form in a particular setting and gets a fair start in the life of that organization.

Unfortunately this argument is now uncomfortably close to that of the carpetbaggers in the first scenario, for even social artists, skilled in creating developmental forms like the Action Learning set, have to live! Once again, as so often in history and in management education, it becomes difficult for even the wise and the wary to tell the saviours and the confidence tricksters apart.

Whichever pole you incline towards, it is clear that Revans himself is strongly averse to the idea of 'professional set advisers'. First, the mainspring of Action Learning rests upon a distrust of the expert. Anyone can achieve and exercise expertise of a particular sort but the peculiar social warping that leads us to distrust our own judgements and feelings and dub others with the status 'expert' is the enemy and antithesis of Action Learning. Dependency infuses all who fall into the shadow of the expert. In Action Learning each of us must be autonomous and responsible for our own actions; each of us must be our own person.

Secondly, Revans points out that, as soon as it is clear that there is money to be made, educational advances assume a package quality. The short and none too glorious history of management education confirms this view and it can be said that whilst Action Learning aspires to the idea of 'continuous revolution' and requires a challenging or pioneering quality even, many professional trainers and educators still lean towards the structured and standardized forms which can thus be more easily propagated and 'sold'.

Thirdly, Revans makes the distinction between 'set advising' and 'set initiating':

> There was once, on a very hot day, a thirsty old tramp approaching a pub. He found it buzzing with bluebottles . . . 'Well Barman, I don't think much of this place. Why do you put up with these bloody flies?' 'Because I can't bloody well get rid of them!' 'Indeed? Well I'll kill every one of them for a pint of bitter . . . but first the pint, for I've walked a long way and need a short rest'. The deal was struck and the tramp enjoyed his beer. After half an hour, as the tramp seemed to be dozing off, the barman said 'What about killing the bluebottles then?' 'Certainly! That was my side of the bargain . . . Bring them to me one by one.'[1]

This is the tale of the Action Learning set pioneer and the set adviser and Revans speaks of the 'terrible injustice of the initiator sweating for six months for no reward to get a set together and then for the set adviser condescending to find a day to show the participants what they ought to do'. He assumes that the 'professional set advisers' will not deign or will not be able to afford to do the initiating as well. So, let us look at the role of the set adviser in the light of these three critical points.

Set initiating and set advising

Taking the last point first, it seems that in the distinction between initiating and advising, we have all leaned towards the latter role and borne the other with, at best, cheerful resignation. Examine the contributions in this book and you will find many a thoughtful disquisition and even some elegant conceptualizations on set advising, but little on the essential but dispiriting business of initiating.

In 1978, I was so demoralized with the whole business of initiation that I adopted the artful device of an 'initiator's set' in order to propagate Action Learning in and around Sheffield. I was fed up with knocking on doors and trying to sell something which people did not want or were not ready to buy. After initiating and advising three successful sets in 1976 and 1977, I was suffering from the failure of a set in Huddersfield established only after a year and more of effort. Apart from my own failings, significant factors in the collapse of this set were that people came for the wrong reasons which were usually related to the way their organizations were managed and the way those managers 'ordered' people to learn. In an admittedly jaundiced mood, I put this failure down to the unwillingness or unreadiness of most organizations to host such a potentially powerful embryo as Action Learning.

The initiators' set was therefore a natural bolthole neatly and reflexively applying the theory of Action Learning to the problem of getting Action Learning started. The set consisted of seven people whom I invited to join me because I knew them or heard of their interest in the method. The purpose of the set was to diffuse Action Learning more widely and to learn about the process of doing so whilst doing it.[2]

In the process of initiating five sets between us what we learned about initiating Action Learning boiled down to two major strategies. Type 1 strategies are the 'selling' ones using media, publications, advertising, door knocking and so on, to drum up interest in the product. In the field of management training and development a succession of techniques and methods have been unveiled over the years in this way. The weakness of Type 1 strategies for initiating Action Learning is that they tend to sell at the technique level with the idea already in pre-packaged form – you get your Action Learning complete with three day start-up, weekly three hour meetings, an experienced set adviser – all the trimmings.'

The alternative Type 2 strategies seek the right sort and sources of energy to harness to Action Learning, rather than trying to sell Action Learning to create energy. The way in which the initiators' set was brought together is itself an example of this type of strategy. All the people were known to me or made themselves known to me because the word was 'out' in certain circles. Type 2 strategies are 'joining' rather than 'selling' strategies; more opportunistic in a way, selective in their communication. They work through existing networks, colleague groups and associations and the rich infrastructure of 'speaking partners' to be found in our late industrial organizations. It is not a public seeking or communication in the normal sense of that word. Sometimes Action Learning can be brought to an existing learning, social or work group which wants to take the next step in its development; sometimes it is a question of who is around asking what questions or caring about which problems. Type 2 strategies tend to start from the situation and ask: how can Action Learning, at the paradigm or idea level, help here?

As you may have already guessed, I regard Type 2 strategies as the most appropriate for spreading Action Learning. For me this is the way to diffuse the essential idea of Action Learning whilst resisting and subverting the ossifying, packaging forces of 'dynamic conservatism'. Yet, this is surely too easy a dismissal of Type 1 strategies – often Type 2 strategies build on already 'warmed up' contacts of Type 1 approaches. Neither an easy preference of one or the other or the unexamined acceptance of both in partnership will do. We need to take the argument a stage further.

Both set initiating and set advising can be seen as phases of the same development and therefore as basically indivisible. In practice it is not as easy for the set adviser to reap the harvest from the initiator's toil unless they are one and the same. The analogy of the catching and the killing of the bluebottles falls down when we consider the true nature of the initiation process. The initiator is designing and creating a form for Action Learning to come alive and not just selling a package. This is perhaps to make a distinction between 'true initiation' and the 'warm up' or 'can opening' role which Revans himself has often played by inspiring first time listeners from a public platform. Beyond the analogy of the tramp and the barman lies the serious point. Revans is not warning us off trying to help groups and individuals to learn in whatever way we can, but that in exalting the adviser role at the expense of the initiator we fall into a new form of the old trap of distinguishing between the artisan and scribe.

In trying to avoid the initiating process for the more glamorous adviser's robes, I was making just this split. But if we conceive the role of initiator as designer and not as doorstep salesman, then we can rescue it. Perhaps there is more than one type of salesperson, for if Action Learning has something to offer managers and other people then we cannot entirely resist its packaging. However, we know that if Action Learning is sold merely as a package, then its life cycle will be as short as those other flavours of the month. The ideas of MbO for example are as distressingly simple and as difficult to capture and practise as those of Action Learning – indeed, they share some common lineage.

The initiator then is not just the despised doorstep salesperson selling the unprepared householder something he or she does not want, but also a sort of social artist who carries within her or him the impulse and essence of the Action Learning idea, seeking openings and opportunities to make that idea manifest in practice. We must, as initiators, stop Action Learning from too easily becoming 'AL' and resist for a while the loss of meaning which easily communicable but ultimately meaningless symbols bestow. To resist the pressure to package is then to prolong the life of the idea.

So how can this unpackaged Action Learning be communicated?

There are many different forms of Action Learning described in this book and they have proliferated from the original models taken from the mines, the hospitals and from Belgium. In virtually all these forms, the adviser is also the initiator, the person who takes the idea and gives it concrete form. It follows that advising cannot be done in isolation from, or in ignorance of, the initiating process. This provides some protection against packaging.

It is the non-packaged nature of Action Learning that makes it so difficult to communicate. I am not alone in feeling profound frustration when I have been unable to convey the treacherously simple idea. One reason for this is that discussions about Action Learning take place at different levels:

1 the idea or paradigm level – a way of looking at the world.

2 the theory level – a means of explaining or predicting certain events in the world.

3 the technique level – a method for doing something in the world.

The technique is the idea made manifest in the world; the vision brought to reality. However, the packaging process tends to present the technique as if it were the idea. There is nothing wrong with this development of techniques or specific forms, indeed I have referred to it as the artistic calling of the initiator, as long as these are not taken to be Action Learning. To make that error is akin to mistaking the landscape artist's representation for the landscape itself. At the theory level there are many elements to Action Learning – theories of scientific method, of organizational change, of experiential learning (systems alpha, beta and gamma) – which are intermediate links between the idea and its myriad possible forms.

The frequent experience of being unable to communicate adequately leads to one of the paradoxes of Action Learning; that of the historical and current dependence upon Reg Revans himself for the 'word'. The 'Reg-centricity' of Action Learning is both a bulwark against packaging and a block on the spread and growth of the idea.

Yet too many people have seen the light and the possibilities for Action Learning in the field of human organization for this to be the fancy of one man. The range and extent of the examples described in this book attest to the applicability of the ideas.

There are various efforts here to state the idea, theories and techniques of Action Learning in ways that can be easily understood. These attempts make it easier for managers to see what they need to do to bring Action Learning about and these efforts must continue to dispel the mystery and put the tools into the hands of ordinary people. However, against these efforts, consider the style of Revans himself who does not seek that kind of clarity for what he has to say. Like many great teachers before him he relies upon the story and the parable to carry the essential meaning. All attempts to directly describe Action Learning eventually founder upon the rock of the indescribable. Those things which we can capture and describe, and which we hopefully have done here, provide the P factor – the programmed knowledge which can be caught and communicated in the usual ways. The Q factor of Action Learning, the ability to ask the right questions and to get things done, can never be so described or communicated and will always remain to be discovered, lost and discovered again outside of any package. Distrust immediately, then, any programme which guarantees Action Learning or any person who says that he or she knows how to do it. Whilst you can 'buy in' programmed knowledge, you can only discover and invent the Q factor for yourself.

Where does this leave the set adviser?

The set adviser exists then somewhat uneasily between the tenets of peer learning community theory where there are no experts and the heretical but stubborn assertions of the practitioners about what is needed to 'make action learning work'. The role of adviser continues to persist well beyond the initiating stages and although it is theoretically possible we know of few examples where Action Learning groups operate without advisers.

There are three extant models of the set adviser role:

1   Reg Revans's own implied model of the *initiator* who withers away as the set begins to operate.

2   David Casey's *facilitator* (see Chapter 22) who encourages giving and receiving between participants and who makes explicit the learning processes.

3   The *managerial* role involved in steering the Action Learning group through the various stages of development from formation to mature action and learning. This role is apparent in several accounts contained in this book.

The various accounts in this book tend to support models two and three. Shaun Harries for example settles for a combination making the point that the role changes over time and with the development of the group. Alec Lewis' account implies a combination and suggests a move from the more active and managerial to the more passive and facilitative over time. Interestingly, although there are no accounts which support Reg Revans's preferred role, a number of them, including Casey's, suggest that set members should increasingly take over the facilitative or managerial functions as the set matures. In Appendix 1 David Pearce says:

> At its simplest, the set adviser's role is to help the set and its members to work on the problems and on their own learning. His secondary objective should be *either* to make himself redundant as quickly as possible, *or* to become a full, equal member of the set with his own declared project.

So, although at first sight there seems to be a divergence between theory and practice on the question of the set adviser's role, a more searching appraisal suggests that this is not so great as it may appear. Very few advisers would disagree with the ideal of the set members taking over the managerial/facilitative functions as part of their own learning and development; and most would agree that an adviser who does not seek this goal amongst others is probably falling short of what is desirable. There is perhaps less agreement on whether the adviser should become a full and equal set member with his own project.

Before nailing my colours to the mast on this one, let me summarize some of the points about the set adviser's role on which I believe there is broad agreement. First that the set adviser should be involved in initiating; that initiating is a noble art involving some selling and some learning design and that careful initiating is nearly always essential to the establishment of successful Action Learning groups. Secondly, that virtually all sets require an adviser in the early stages, and perhaps all through, to model and pass on various managerial and facilitative actions necessary to achieve action and learning. Thirdly, that advisers should not present themselves as experts either in management or learning and perhaps should seek active steps to divest themselves of any such tempting rainment that set members might seek to invest them with.

This third point is a crucial one because the temptation to collude with others in establishing 'expert' and 'dependent' boxes for the adviser and set members can be very strong. In the early stages of a group there are very strong predisposing forces towards this and the set adviser needs great inner strength to sit there in front of the proferred mantle awaiting the right moment to reject it. Too early a rejection may not be understood and may be interpreted as a lack of care – a fatal deprivation in the early stages. Too late a rejection will not be delivered or may create a double bind – I don't want to be King, but call me Sire!'

There is something of a riddle here which Torbert has referred to as the deliberate irony[3] of the adviser or leader trying to do three things at once: (a) being an equal and speaking the language of the other members; (b) being unequal, because of her/his actual greater knowledge i.e. of Action Learning processes, and therefore seeking to teach members a new language; (c) creating tasks, structures and questions which bridge the gap between the old (and less adequate in Action Learning terms) and the new and more adequate language. The availability of the knowledge of the adviser, of the 'new language' makes him/her an expert in that sense. Without great awareness, skill and determination, Casey's facilitator could very quickly turn into a full-blown social-science-cum-learning process expert.

No one is against expertise, only against experts. Expertise is a property possessed by individuals or groups apposite to particular circumstances at particular times. Experts are products of an extreme division of labour, of a narrow job description work culture, who arrogate a very partial and particular ability to the level of a general and universal embrocation. Action Learning sets, like other groups, need to avoid dependence upon quacks, but need to learn to use expertise when they specifically need it. This is one clue to the problem of the adviser and her/his expertise – it must be put on offer from time to time, but not delivered except at the right time and in the right circumstances. It cannot be delivered in response to questions which effectively say 'You set this up, where do we go next?' but only in answer to questions which leave the questioner free to reject these answers. It is only when the set or individuals in the set feel able to reject the 'advice' of the adviser that he or she can make this advice available. So the expertise has to be given in a certain way, as from a servant rather than from a master – on tap but not on top.

The irony lies in the impossibility of our understanding this sort of offer when it is first made to us – we cannot comprehend at one stage of development what we will not need to know at the next. Yet what we have to try and struggle to understand is what will provide the bridge to this new stage. This 'offer' appears to us as the leader being deliberately coy or mischievous in holding back and we withdraw in distrust or rebel in anger according to our style, yet this deliberate refusal to be the expert is what eventually enables us to act autonomously.

The set adviser as co-educator

We must, if we are to preserve the spirit and impulse of Action Learning, resist the professionalization of the adviser's role. In a way, we do the greatest damage to ourselves in assuming the mantle of expert. In the competence and omnipotence of universal expertise we cut ourselves off from humanity and from simple human aid for ourselves or for others:

> when ordinary men like hard-working managers are confused and uneasy, but nevertheless obliged by circumstances to get something done, it is not some intellectual explanation of their emergency that they seek, followed by a logical plan of action that will get them off the hook . . . At such times, borne down by responsibility, fear, confusion and helplessness, it is not argument one needs, but support, not analysis but example, not lucidity but warmth. . . . Once the simple human aid has been given and confidence starts creeping back, then may be the time to deploy the weapons of sophistication and dialectic.[4]

In order to preserve the capacity in myself to both receive and to give this 'simple human aid' I prefer David Pearce's second alternative – to aim at becoming a full equal member with a project. I seek to become a co-educator – to use a term coined by Freire[5] to emphasize the two-way nature of the learning process. As I write this I am well aware of the glibness with which these words go down compared to the struggle to achieve this seemingly modest ambition. It does seem to me however to be the best way of avoiding the trap of the expert, if I myself am struggling and failing at my project in the company of my peers. What work shall I do? Well, certainly there are plenty of opportunities around for me to attempt a little good. I can address my own role with the Action Learning group as my project provided that I open up my competence and incompetence (and therefore my struggle) for inspection and help. Beyond this, an effective Action Learning group creates action and learning in organizations which always leaves too much to do and not enough resources with which to do it. We can not predict what work you might wish to do as a co-educator, for it will be in line with your individual 'project' – ultimately the pursuit of your own identity or destiny.

This is really one of the things which has impressed me about Action Learning and those people who are involved in it. One reason why we have so much difficulty in defining the role of the adviser is because of the highly individualistic interpretations around us. The 'Reg-centricity' of Action Learning is only a constraint if we seek to emulate, to become a cypher. Most people I know have not approached Action Learning in this way, that is, they have not just looked for the 'right' way to do it. One of the first people I had much contact with was Alan Lawlor who, fired and committed as he was with the ideas, always brought some of his own make and mend Midlands engineering self in to create a unique blend. So it is with us all. For me, the avoidance of the mantle of expert, the desire to do my own work and the need to give and receive simple human aid all require one another. Action Learning is a way of working with managers and other people that enables our involvement well beyond the 'professional' level. We work with each other at a personal level and the adviser is first and last – a person – a co-equal, a co-educator.

References

1 In a letter dated 6 September 1980.
2 The initiators' set was supported by a grant from the Training Services Division of the Manpower Services Commission and the report was published as *The Diffusion of Action Learning* Occasional Paper 2, Department of Management Studies, Sheffield City Polytechnic, March 1981.
3 Torbert, W.R. (1978) 'Educating towards shared purpose, self-direction and quality work', *Journal of Higher Education*, Ohio State University Press, **49**.
4 Revans, R. (1980) *Action Learning: New Techniques for Managers*, London: Blond & Briggs, pp.289–90.
5 Freire, P. (1972), *Cultural Action for Freedom*, Harmondsworth: Penguin.

25 The shell of your understanding*

David Casey

Suffering and learning

It is a very old question. Is suffering necessary for learning? I have come to believe that suffering is sometimes necessary and sometimes not. In twelve Action Learning sets of five or six chief executives at Ashridge Management College over the past five years, I have watched half a dozen chief executives reach new heights of learning (for them) by crawling painfully through the most daunting jungle of pain and misery. On the other hand, in exactly the same setting I have seen an equal number of chief executives achieve what appeared to be equally significant learning for them, with no real effort – carried along on a light stream of joy and enlightenment, revelling in the sheer delight of their new insights. Learning is sometimes agony and learning is sometimes fun. Is it possible to identify which kind of learning demands suffering and which kind can be fun?

In my teens and twenties I was fortunate to experience at first hand two well tried systems of education – I was at school with the Jesuits and my first job was teaching with the Benedictines for three years. Here are two validated approaches to education,

*First published in the *Journal of Management Development* (1987), 6(2) pp.30–37.

both ancient in their pedigree and accepted across Europe over several centuries. At school I learned through suffering:

> To give and not to count the cost,
> To fight and not to heed the wounds,
> To toil and not to seek for rest,
> To labour and to ask for no reward . . .

Ignatius Loyola founded the Jesuits in 1534 and the grammar school I attended based its education firmly on the principles he established more than 400 years ago, and in its way it worked. There are penalties of course (as with any system) – for example, the weight of guilt and self-denial which all graduates of the Jesuit system carry around for life. But also implanted for life are the joys of intellectual exercise, the springboard of self-discipline, the stimulus of competition, the urge to self-reliance.

Four years later I found myself appointed as a schoolmaster in a Benedictine school. Benedict and Ignatius were poles apart in their thinking about education. Benedict believed in the power of love: not just as we all believe in love – his trust in the power of love was so rock-steady and universal that in his schools no place was found for heavy discipline, no corner for punishment, no coercive external force (other than love) was allowed to impinge on the young people being educated.

If survival is any test of a system, then these two diametrically opposed systems of education are both successful – they survive side by side today; you can send your son to Stonyhurst or Ampleforth, exposing him to two very different sets of assumptions regarding what will help him to learn. In one system the assumption is that learning is a relentless fight against our sinful propensity to indolence, in the other system the assumption is that learning is enabled only in an atmosphere of love. McGregor's X and Y come pretty close.

The dilemma facing any set adviser is no different from that facing every teacher; do you make the student work or do you cradle the student in love? Do learners have to suffer or can they get there on a surfboard of effortless exhilaration? And, most difficult decision of all, when do you push and when do you stand well back?

My work at Ashridge has reinforced in me the certainty that the ambience of an action learning set must be an accepting, supporting cradle of love. I have no doubt at all that producing this environment is one of the most valuable roles of the set adviser. When the set consists of chief executives, it is even more important (and difficult) to make the set a place where people feel supported, liked, trusted and valued. However, in the last few years I have come gradually to understand that such an atmosphere of love is necessary but not sufficient. There is another task to be added to the four tasks I offered set advisers in a 1976 article called 'The Emerging Role of Set Adviser in Action Learning Programmes'.[1] In the ensuing ten years I have found very little to change in that article, but now I want to add something.

The emerging role of set adviser

In 1976 I identified these four tasks for the set adviser:

1 To facilitate giving.

2 To facilitate receiving.

3 To clarify the various processes of action learning.

4 To help others take over tasks 1, 2 and 3.

The broad 'Benedictine' assumption behind these four tasks is that set members can look after themselves and can facilitate each other's learning, with a little catalytic help from the set adviser. The set adviser's role is assumed to be transferable to them, and since the skills required in the set adviser's role are not particularly exotic (and are widely distributed among management teachers and among managers too) transfer of set adviser's tasks to set members is a fairly straightforward business. And for the most part I still believe that. But in addition, I now believe that there is a rather special bit of the set adviser's role which cannot be transferred to set members in a month of Sundays. There is a fifth task, which only the trained and experienced set adviser can do and it conforms more to the confronting Jesuit model than to the benign Benedictine model. The Benedictine doctrine of all-through-love will get set members so far and no further. There is a level of learning, particularly about oneself, which can be reached only through some level of pain. And set members are not willing, nor are they able, to push each other through very much pain.

Kahlil Gibran wrote 'Your pain is the breaking of the shell that encloses your understanding'.[2] In the Ashridge chief executive sets many participants believe that their ignorance is the shell which encloses their understanding, so they come hoping to dispel some of that ignorance. They see the other set members as intriguing sources of *knowledge* and they are aware that they themselves are valuable sources of knowledge for the others. And so it turns out to be. They probe each other's experiences and knowledge by increasingly skilful questioning. They do learn to give and to receive. And certainly many shells are broken – but often they are only the shells of ignorance.

These participants find the programme useful and go away satisfied, with their ignorance reduced. Hard-worn knowledge has been traded. But Kahlil Gibran wrote that *pain* is the breaking of the shell of your *understanding*, not your knowledge; these participants have suffered no pain, so their understanding remains where it was when we started. Knowledge can be gained by breaking into shells from the outside, understanding can be gained only by breaking out from your own shell, from the inside.

My own nagging doubts as set adviser started when first I realized that many participants actually want more than extra knowledge – they wish to gain in self-understanding. I began to see that my 1976 model of set advising was not always powerful enough to help them. If the set adviser restricts himself/herself to the four tasks identified in the 1976 'Emerging Role' article – the skill available within the group is limited to the skill of the set members and even when enriched by the tutoring of the set adviser, this may not be enough.

Deep feelings

In practice I often begin to feel that an individual needs to work things out at a deeper level than the set is able to accommodate. Sometimes it becomes clear that someone is about to express deep feelings which they dearly long to express and which they are finding very difficult to handle. Other set members may be aware of this but feel unable to help. Some may consciously or subconsciously contrive to stop the process going any further. They may have real worries about the group 'getting out of its depth' or they may be afraid that once a new level of exposure becomes a group norm, their turn will come sooner or later and the prospect may fill them with dread. So they abort the process. The skill exercised in aborting the process has to be seen to be believed – an innocent request to have a natural break, a throw-away flippant remark, an alliance formed by miniscule eye contact across the group – hundreds of tiny subterfuges like these are employed to break the spell and to sabotage a process which is just getting to the point of usefulness. Only when I twigged the subtlety of what was going on, did I realize that I, the set adviser, was the only person who could help. Simply uncovering the process itself was no use – the process would be denied and argued about – diverting attention even further away from the difficult work to be done.

Let us look at an example. Ted is a solid, competent 54. Proud to be running a £20 million division of a large industrial group. Also proud of having made his way to the top 'off the tools'. For ten years he has turned in more profit each year, on a rising turnover, so that his division has become a model, held up by the group main board as an example to the other divisions – most of which seem to be losing money. Without Ted's reliable performance year after year, the group would be in trouble. This was the picture Ted painted for us – a brilliantly successful career coming steadily to a satisfactory close. Ted talked of early retirement – he mentioned his age frequently. One day I took him on – partly because I could not believe in the perfect success story – mostly because I felt Ted did not believe in it either. Under challenge Ted was soon exposing himself as complacent – not shouldering his responsibility as a member of the main board – turning a blind eye to incompetence elsewhere, remaining safe in the success of his own division. I challenged him in a strong and straightforward way – was he prepared to accept incompetence at group level? Was it right that he should receive the accolade of a successful division managing director when he was clearly abdicating from his group responsibilities? Could he retire from the group without shouldering his responsibility to leave it in a healthy state? The questions all came from me. Every other member of the set sat quite still and silent as a dialogue between Ted and me continued for 20 minutes. He smouldered with anger.

At the next meeting Ted told us that he took the next two days off after this confrontation. He booked a hotel in Bournemouth with his wife and they talked for two whole days. He decided, with her enthusiastic backing, to stand up and be counted in the group. He told us, with a new glint in his eye, that he was the *only* person in a strong enough position and with the personal guts to put things to rights. It would be tough – but he felt young again. 'After all, I'm *only* 54!' he said. Every meeting after that Ted seemed to get younger. He has already achieved great progress (with some help from the set) and he is happier, full of energy and looking forward to the next ten years of hard, uphill fight. For me, the surprise came later – at the final dinner for this set Ted said he owed it all to me; not to the set, but to me. And in my heart of hearts I know he is right. I also know that such a significant breaking out from his own shell could never have happened if I had limited my role to group process work and denied the group my skill as a person-to-person consultant, within the group setting. So this is the fifth task I want to add to the four tasks in my 1976 article:

5   To act from time to time as personal consultant to set members, in the group setting.

The success of failure

Ted's example is one of many. In the past few years, every time I have worked this way with an individual chief executive, within the group setting, I have felt a failure. Because in the intensity of person-to-person work I would totally forget everybody else! What kind of a set adviser was this, totally oblivious to the group processes and stepping outside the classic role of catalyst? And yet, nearly every time I felt compelled to work in this mode, it worked. More importantly, I knew I had helped the individual do some work of importance for him and *that nobody else could have done it*. Typically, it has helped him break free from an imprisoning shell rather than break into other people's shells. Always, there has been pain. This is what Kahlil Gibran meant: 'Your pain is the breaking of the shell that encloses your understanding'. Self-understanding.

The chief executive trap

Are there some characteristics of chief executives, which make them different? Is there some special need that chief executives have in an action learning set, to work things out for themselves at a relatively deep level? Perhaps there is. The chief executive role is acknowledged as a lonely role; is there anything else special about it? I think there is – the chief executive role is very special indeed.

A typical chief executive is a leader in his[3] organization, in his neighbourhood, in his clubs, in his professional bodies, in all his various activities. He is expected to exercise leadership everywhere he goes. And it becomes a self-fulfilling prophecy – no sooner is it known in the golf club that he is the managing director of Brown and Smith, then he gets elected to club captain. His skill at Speech Day prize-giving leads to a seat on the local Magistrates Bench and so on. All this has great benefits for him and his capacity for leadership grows as he gets pushed (however willingly) into various lead roles in different kinds of organizations, in different social settings. But there are great penalties too for the individual human being behind the 'great leader' exterior. It becomes increasingly difficult for him to say 'I don't know' or 'I'm afraid' or 'I need help'. As years go by, many chief executives find they have built up a survival kit which does not contain these phrases. They find another way to survive – and it is more likely to be based on knowing a lot, distributing their wisdom, giving advice, making decisions and telling other people what to do. And they find it works like magic.

Why it works like magic is because the rest of the world colludes in what can be a cruel way. People need to be led, managing directors need to be in place, decisions have to be made, magistrates have to be found and local authorities need to appoint chief executives – so the stage is set for a drama, some aspects of which contain the seeds of tragedy. Once they have a willing leader out front, clever followers can make almost any decision work (very often all that is needed is a decision because many options could be made to work) and when the decision is seen to work, the leader's belief in himself as a decision maker is bolstered falsely – reinforcing his self-image as a leader. The sardonic comment from one chief executive. 'When you are out in front, you are never quite sure whether they are following you or chasing you', is much more serious than at first appears.

And so, over many years, chief executives develop a belief in themselves. They learn to think of themselves as somehow different. People near them begin to flatter as they see opportunity for themselves in the chief executive's growing power and soon a chief executive can become cut off from any trustworthy feedback. That is a very dangerous position to be in. Some get pushed beyond the point where it is difficult to say 'I don't know', 'I'm afraid' and 'I need help' to the point of no return, when they begin to *believe* that they do know, they are not afraid and they do not need help. That is an even more dangerous position.

Little understanding of themselves

I have found on the Ashridge Programme that chief executives often have an insatiable thirst for knowledge and an impatience with ignorance. Most of them have an encyclopaedic knowledge of the world and a well developed forcefulness in projecting their opinions. In contrast, they have little understanding of themselves. They crack avidly the shells of ignorance and find only the rewards of more knowledge. To break out from their own shells and discover something of themselves is so terrifying that some of them cannot even begin to think of doing it. In my five years at Ashridge two such chief executives left the programme altogether – both at an early stage – as soon as they saw the awful dangers which might lie ahead if they once started to chip away at the strong protective shell inside which they had learned to feel safe. These two[4] were exceptions; most participants fully understand the nature of the programme and I believe most of them come because they want to find out something about themselves and see this strange programme as offering that possibility. Naturally enough, when the time comes to crack the shell of pain and come to an understanding of themselves, they are afraid.

They are afraid because their survival kit, carefully built up by themselves and by others over many years, is about to be whisked away at a time when they need it badly. Their colleagues feel afraid too, and hold back. Only the set adviser knows that it is now or never – and only the set adviser has the courage and the skill to sharpen the pick and tell the chief executive just where to tap, if he is to begin the painful process of learning who he really is.

Many chief executives decide to hold back. The opportunity for them may have arisen too late in the programme; they may decide that on balance they need their survival kit as it is; they may be near retirement age and judge that the potential pay-off for them is not worth the investment in pain . . . there are countless valid reasons why chief executives decide not to break the shell of their understanding. For me, as set adviser, the important thing is that the opportunity should be there, if they want it.

The conspiracy of love with truth

So, was Ignatius right or was Benedict right? In a strange way they were both right. Unless the atmosphere is one of trust and love, the chance for self-understanding would never arise, so sets of chief executives need a set adviser able to develop a 'Benedictine' environment. But unless the set adviser is also Jesuitical enough to hold on to his belief that the only way to help at the moment of truth is to push the learner through the shell of his own pain, no amount of supportive understanding will really do the trick. This conspiracy of love with truth is a formidable alliance and a potent source of help.

At this stage my conclusion is that (at least in chief executive sets) set advisers not only have the right to abandon process work from time to time and engage in personal therapy; they have the obligation to do so. Because if they do not, nobody else will.

Over the past ten years I have argued that the set adviser's role should be concerned more with group processes than with person-to-person consultancy. I still believe that. What I have learned from my work at Ashridge – and I thank Ashridge for it – is that to be dogmatic about excluding personal consultancy as one part of the set adviser's repertoire is wrong. As with any other skill used by the set adviser, it is simply a question of choosing when to use it. I also want to thank a good friend – Roger Gaunt knew many years ago what it has taken me ten years to learn.

References and Footnotes

1 Casey, D. (1976), 'The Emerging Role of Set Adviser in Action Learning Programmes', *Journal of European Training*, 5 (3). An adapted version of this article appears as Chapter 20 of this book.
2 Gibran, K. (1926) *The Prophet*, Heinemann.
3 The Ashridge Programme is open to men and women chief executives but in practice all have so far been men. The masculine pronoun is used here only for convenience.
4 Both of these chief executives were 'sent' by their personnel directors. Most participants find the Programme for themselves by reading about it in general management journals or by word of mouth.

26 Continuity in Action Learning

Jean Lawrence

When Action Learning has been introduced in an organization what happens to it? Is it just the latest fad of a management development manager, or the chief executive? Is this first programme repeated appropriately? Do other areas of the organization become a new focus for Action Learning work? Do the managers involved in a first programme introduce new developmental ways of working with their own departments or divisions? Does 'implementation' remain a vital part of the work, or is it steadily diluted until Action Learning fades to some form of project work – or is there a complete reversion to taught programmes?

Other contributors to this volume have already drawn attention to the vital distinction Reg Revans made between 'P' and 'Q', – 'P' being the programmed knowledge that can be systematically taught and learned, with well-defined stages and outcomes, and 'Q' being the complex process of raising and working with fundamental questions that do not admit unequivocal answers.[1] Can 'P' and 'Q' live side by side in programmes or must 'P' precede 'Q' and be separate from it? Does 'P' always drive out 'Q'? What makes it possible to integrate them, and what breaks them apart?

Established courses – and the very word 'course' may indicate a large proportion of 'P' – attract participants over long periods; perhaps through general reputation or inertia? Organizational fathers and grandfathers seem to send their sons and grandsons, and even their granddaughters, to the institutions and to the very same programmes which seemed to help *them*. The programmes will be modified over time but their 'character' may well remain the same. Is this phenomenon based on loyalty to the institution, as for example, with sending undergraduates to colleges in Oxford, or, is it that practitioners in Action Learning are not presenting a variety of high-quality new opportunities persuasively enough to break a habit and generate the energy to accept a challenge.

Action Learning makes many demands on the organization, especially for those embarking on it for the first time. It may be that the complexity of these demands and the fact they they continue into later programmes is largely unrecognized by those organizations and becomes one of the important factors threatening continuity. Action Learning encourages all those engaged in it to learn and change, and demands that they move forward; repetition, old answers to old questions, is not enough. Perhaps the continual challenge to old ideas, and the disruption and reorganization of established systems which may follow, is too uncomfortable. If the challenge comes from the middle of the organization and not only from the top, it may, sooner or later, prove intolerable.

Three stories of 'Q' and 'P'

Let us look at three experiences:

1 An Action Learning programme closely related to taught modules, is well established at senior management level in a large organization. After three years, the head of management development moves to another appointment, a major change occurs in the environment of the company and new appointments are made at the top. Questions are asked, and answered, about the project work. New line managers are concerned about the way the disruption caused by enthusiastic project champions may affect their regular results. There is a move towards safety – the taught modules survive and are extended. There is a gesture towards project work in extended live case studies and group investigations, but implementation is dropped, in spite of the pleas of the training staff involved in the previous activities. New development staff may welcome the

opportunity to change, rethink and promote new approaches.

2 A level of management in an organization is thought by trainers and top management to have deficiencies for which Action Learning may provide considerable benefits. A programme begins after careful preliminaries and is repeated three times in later phases alongside major organization changes. It is guided by a group of senior line managers and is seen to fulfil the objectives, regarded as highly successful, bringing additional unforeseen benefits. The line managers take up a new role in relation to management development in the whole organization. After three years the whole level of management has been through the programme; so, it is said, there is no further opportunity to pursue that way of working. The issues are compounded by the retirement of the person most involved with day-to-day work on the series of programmes.

3 A group of three top managers, each from a different small organization, take part in an introductory week and then embark on a series of six-weekly one-day meetings to support each other in their current problems. They pay three meetings in advance for the meetings, including the help of the facilitator. A fourth manager joins them quite soon, and one of the originals leaves after two years. Now after six years, they are still meeting regularly. Two more people have joined, one of whom has continued (with nine-month gaps) through two changes of organization, industry and location. Attempts, most of them successful, have been made to introduce Action Learning as a way of life in some areas of the organizations represented. There seems to be no reason for this continuous learning to end.

These experiences raise questions which go beyond the information presented, but, taking what is said at face value, we may conclude that there are particular difficulties with internal programmes. In the first of these two examples of internal programmes 'Q' declined and in the second the specific activities ended after about three years. Internal programmes inevitably have a higher component of organization development within them. Concentration on individual management development reduces the threat. It may therefore be more likely that continuity can be maintained when senior or top individuals work on their own development with others outside the organization.

Experience earlier with GEC and recently with district managers in the Health Service gives me the hope that, for example, district to district within the same large region, may provide sufficient differentiation to permit continuity within a large organization. If it is true that individuals must take their problems outside to gain new insights into what is happening and to work on the real issues, perhaps 'outside' can sometimes mean a fairly distant part of the same very large organization. A clearly bounded area of authority appears to be a prerequisite for participation in a successful programme of this kind.

My experience persuades me we should be particularly concerned about programmes within organizations or within parts of very large organizations. The difficulties seem greater but the benefits of success can be dramatic. Results may include a clear move in the culture of the whole organization towards a growth of leadership skills right down the system; developing a questioning innovative approach at all levels; and gaining confidence that whatever changes in the environment occur, the organization will be flexible enough to survive and prosper.

If the benefits can be so splendid and appropriate for today, how can we tackle the difficulties presented by introducing an Action Learning approach within organizations, so that the work is sustained to a point when it becomes 'a way of life'?

Let us take the example of an organization where influential people have come to believe that a commitment to Action Learning will bring important advantages, including improving the bottom line, providing much better service to customers, constituents, and so on. Given this ideal opportunity, what strategy can we adopt to ensure that we keep questioning alive?

An organizational strategy for making 'Q' a way of life

An approach might be:

1 To work with the top management group to define their commitment to a specific approach, and to develop a programme for those senior managers immediately responsible to them. An outside consultant, probably engaged specifically for this role, continues to work with this group.

2 At the same time, workshops are devised to develop the skills of those inside the organization who can work alongside the consultant at the senior management level.

3 Some months later the senior level have had the experience

of set work and the achievement of projects, over a considerable period. They may now be helped to set up their own Action Learning activities in and between their own spheres of influence, involving those immediately responsible to them and those further down the system. The aim will be for line managers to facilitate groups of peers and those reporting to them as they tackle new work, new aspects of their work, or, indeed, as they develop ideas for new work.

4 Internal facilitators, consultants, developers, and trainers who have been involved in the workshops in 2 above, will be available to support this work in appropriate roles.

5 Programmes for developing (not 'training') staff, supervision, first level management, graduate intake, and so on, will be devised and developed on an Action Learning base. Projects ranging from simple quality circle tasks, through to operational and inter-departmental confusions will be tackled as part of the participants' normal roles, but supported by set work and the work of a facilitator. Facilitators will frequently be from among the work group involved, temporarily taking up a new role for this work.

6 A key to keeping 'Q' alive may be the regular, though possibly quite infrequent (one day in six to eight weeks perhaps), intervention of an outside consultant in the work of the top group. An extended board meeting without a regular agenda may be the form the meeting will take. The outsider's job is to work on the linkages within the group and to ensure that nothing is glossed over or taken for granted in the group. Questions will be supported and always treated seriously, listening will be active and acute. Development projects and the development of individuals and the group as a whole will dominate the flow of work. If this top group is continually asking questions of itself others will feel more confident in taking this approach, which otherwise might seem dangerous. The process is liable to get everybody thinking and exploring and unsatisfied by the status quo. Greater demands will be made on management, leading to their development and again the subsequent development of their people.

Many attempts have been made to do most of these things, and it all sounds relatively straightforward as it is spelt out. However, we should remind ourselves that we started with an ideal opportunity. Achieving integration throughout the organization is, perhaps, the most demanding part. There must be some explanation for the degree of difficulty most of us have, and for the evidence all around us of the decline of 'Q' in organizations which courageously begin to work in a questioning way.

Three processes in organizations which increase the difficulties

Let us now try to identify some of the processes which occur both in the organization and in those practitioners concerned to introduce and sustain it, to see how the interruption of the development of Action Learning occurs. There are, it seems, three groups which particularly influence the continuation or decline of 'Q', each of whom encounter problems and difficulties as the activities progress. There is the central powerful group in the organization, individual managers closely involved in the programme, and the practitioners who believe the approach is fundamentally effective and advantageous.

First the practitioners – what are the pressures on us from others and from our own backgrounds and attitudes as we try to introduce and establish Action Learning within an organization?

In Appendix 1 David Pearce has given a detailed account of the steps involved in starting up an Action Learning programme within an organization. These are still necessary steps but many of us find a great deal of difficulty as we follow that path. We may have learned to manage it better, but still we do not foresee all the consequences of early minor decisions and influences. The underlying processes are complex and these early steps may begin a story which is brought to an end after a very few chapters, by the very complexity it generates.

As we negotiate each stage in the development of an agreed programme, we have to remain open to change and modification. It is very unlikely that we will be satisfied with any previous design in these new circumstances. We will initially welcome the opportunity to work with those within the organization on a new joint proposal. But pressures are applied, commitments entered into, while politics and culture are little understood. It feels more like finding angles and loopholes,[2] than following a blue-print. We may well wish we could legitimately sell a product based in experience, and repeatable with only the slightest tinkering – but this would be a 'P' type programme!

As it is we recognize the need to gain commitment by top management before the work begins. Yet it often seems necessary, as the negotiations proceed, to modify the full acceptance of Action Learning, so that we risk losing its characteristic benefits. For example, implementation is not to be emphasized – recommendations will be considered, probably some ideas will be put into action, but the members of the programme may not be involved; or there must be some formal teaching in a, b or c at some point in the programme. If we can integrate the preparation for project work with the 'P' teaching, and ensure that the 'teaching' is as learner-centred as possible, will we keep 'Q' alive throughout the programme? Or will we find eventually that a rapidly moving management game overlaps the slow thoughtful preparation for, and choice of, a project? Inevitably then 'P' will drive out 'Q', as the need to compete and win against tight deadlines in a neat well-designed teaching vehicle takes priority.

At each stage it may all seem very reasonable – 'they need to have better financial skills so an accounting module is needed' and so forth. But at each point we may be allowing the results of the programme to be clouded by less definition of implementation, less clear increase in self-reliance as a taught module takes over, weaker work in the set because there is less at stake. These decisions about what we can afford to let go and on what aspects we must stand firm are very fine matters of judgement. Eventually those monitoring the activities may have considerable difficulty in seeing results, and wonder whether the effort they are making is worth-while. We may, unwittingly, have sold the pass! If, as is often the case, only a 'trial' set or a small group can work at first, assessment may rest on a very small sample activity and the reality of the experience inevitably includes many hazards – our judgement of the risks is crucial. The assessment may only be made at the end of this first limited programme (after, perhaps, six months) so that any second phase may start almost a year after the first. There is a very slow accumulation of experience, on which confidence can be based.

In addition to these difficulties we may experience conflicts about our own role. We may be basically academics, basing our strength in specialized knowledge and analysis. We may then feel that adapting to the roles required for Action Learning is comfortable in the investigation and report writing stage, but we have little experience in implementation. We approach it with little confidence: it seems nitty-gritty, endless, it is not something we want to be involved in. 'P', and variants on 'P', triumph. We can go only so far with 'Q'. So perhaps we are likely to collude with the client and agree too readily that implementation as such is not quite the cornerstone of Action Learning we thought it was. In later programmes 'project work' is included, reports are presented and tactfully praised, but the demanding nature of Action Learning has somehow withered away.

There is a second process that may have a serious effect on the decay of 'Q', located in the managers taking part in the programme and those closely associated with their activities. Usually by the third meeting of the set, members are becoming enthusiastic, questioning and probing the work of the others, offering support, and listening to and questioning the responses they receive as they talk through their own ideas and activities. As the set progresses confusions of role can arise, as they try to balance their normal work role and their project role, working with both a 'boss' and a 'client' each having expectations and deadlines. The 'client' is hoping that the problem he or she has identified will be tackled and some contribution will be made to its solution. If the participant's boss *is* the client *that* confusion is minimized, but the variety of experience available to the participant is likely to be more limited, and the challenge may be reduced. Again, careful judgements at the design stage are required.

If we have all made good decisions at the selection stage we may have flexible enthusiastic participants who will, with the help of their fellows, turn each of these difficulties to advantage and learn from each hurdle as they cross it.

But clients also have their own anxieties. Processes which can stop the development of 'Q' can originate with them. They are seen by others to be committed to this strange activity. Perhaps they had a (secret) conviction about an expected solution and were disappointed when the analysis led the participant in a new direction. Or they may be concerned that if the project 'fails' it may reflect badly on the participant and/or the client. It may be difficult for them to be able to accept that as much – perhaps more – can be learned from an unsuccessful struggle in a demanding project, as from a highly successful, relatively straightforward project.

On the other hand success in a difficult project may mean the participant has tackled and dealt with a problem normally handled at the level of his boss. With renewed confidence has he become a competitor or, at the least, a more demanding member of the team for whom new opportunities have to be found? There might be expectations of promotion with the risk of loss of an experienced resource. Does the client (or the boss) want to support such developments repeatedly? Being good managers, they do, of course, want to develop their people but perhaps the decline of the programme after a while is not altogether surprising.

Thirdly, the most inimical process may be at work within the most powerful group. Influential managers may be in many different roles, and many ways to distort, divert or stop the work of Action Learning have been found. Some are quite conscious, for example, managers complain that their people are unlikely to meet their targets while they are working on the programme. Those who are taking no part in the programme may vary between ridiculing the work in the set, and envying what the members are so obviously learning, and the demanding experiences of clients. They may feel the programme is disrupting the managerial team, or it is too unstructured – the managers need to be more 'educated', they are not learning the latest techniques – 'now if we just put in time management . . .' – all conscious moves that may interrupt the development.

Some of the moves by these powerful people to stop such a programme may, however, be less conscious, and may originate in a desire to hold the organization steady, in fear of dilution or sharing of power. There is a strong need to uncouple, once again, the learning activity, so that learning can be kept safely within the confines of courses and training centres. Thus, the dominant culture, the way of life of those in power, rejects the more demanding aspects of Action Learning, and modifies and emasculates it until it is manageable without effort.[3] Gradually it becomes so structured and repeatable that it might as well be a course.

These are some of the processes at work as we try to establish continuity in Action Learning within an organization. If we are to succeed we must work to integrate the skills and commitments of these three groups.

Some guidelines for safeguarding 'Q'

Perhaps we have now some clues about keeping 'Q' alive.

First, if we have a bluechip opportunity to enter an organization with strong support from the very top, as discussed earlier, we can develop a full programme of activities as outlined. But we must take special care to protect the activities and, most importantly, should avoid expecting the idea to cascade – to flow down the organization under its own momentum. We will have to work at each level and in each area of operation to establish this new way of life.

Second, three ways to reduce risk and anxiety should be carefully evaluated. If the project is defined so that the client is the boss of the participant, there may be less role confusion for the set member. If clients (and perhaps colleagues of set members) are introduced to the programme very carefully so that their roles are fully understood, anxiety may be reduced. And if more than one set is initiated at the start of the programme there is less risk of quick assessment of the programme on little evidence and against a background of change and constructive disturbance of established habits. Anxieties can perhaps be contained.

Third, an understanding of the culture of the organization is necessary at the start. The rapid development of that understanding so that negative processes can be identified quickly, should be given priority as the programme begins.

Fourth, we can establish a steering group for the programme or activity. This steering group of senior managers at client level or above can take responsibility for the start and the progress of the programme. If such a group can be set up at an early stage in the negotiations, it is likely that problems of conflict with the organization culture, and of the roles of individual managers relating to the programme, can be well managed. The steering group will consist of line managers involved in activities recognized as central to organization success, joined by one or two developers, trainers or facilitators. There is an opportunity for development work in the group as they work on the new task of initiating and supporting an Action Learning programme. It will, initially, be concerned with the selection of participants and developing criteria for choice of projects, and choosing them.

It can continue throughout the programme picking up any difficulties in relating to the formal structure. The steering group also can, and usually does, ensure the interest of top management in the programmes. Its last role on any one programme may be to follow up an evaluation and to ensure continuity, if appropriate, by starting a second programme quite soon after the first. Ideally, the second should overlap the first to encourage learning one from the other.

Lastly, careful attention should be given to the structured part of any programme. Here I am referring to the administration in general, which must be watertight, and the timing, length, size, shape and cost of any programme. In both programmes and activities we need a clear understanding of relations with clients or sponsors, who have, themselves, gained a considerable understanding of the opportunities and perceived dangers of the approach. We are providing a boundary to protect the unfamiliar and unplanned activities so that those involved can feel relatively safe to question and criticize, explore their feelings and learn.

In particular, it is, I believe, important to 'end' a single activity or programme and to gain new commitment, a new contract, for further activities, if they are to follow. We should consider carefully, at the start, what we are to mean by 'ending' both the programme, and the projects within it.

With this early work completed we can arrange that participants leave the programme with a clear idea of how it has ended, and how they individually can take their learning further. They are no longer concerned with a programme but free to take full charge of their own futures. They may have completed a project and begun to think how that work can be developed, and by whom, for the benefit of the organization. A new version of 'who knows, who cares and who can'[4] is forming in their minds so that other colleagues may have an opportunity to contribute to a particular development and to learn from it. Or they may be considering how they can use their experience of learning powerfully in this way to develop the learning of their staff; they could start a process of continuous learning together, from the experience of their development activities. Or they may be looking specifically at their own roles, trying to see how to ensure that they individually learn from each task they tackle; and searching for ways to get and be given the support they will need when facing the challenges they can dimly see but are quite convinced lie ahead of them.

Thus, clarity about the structure at the start helps us to be able to work with members of the set with clarity about 'ending', which, paradoxically may mean continuity. They may, being completely released from the first experience, choose to promote another, providing themselves and others with particular opportunities to continue to learn.

I hope it is clear that in discussing the continuity of Action Learning I am considering a different set of issues from those involved in the continuity of successful courses. This continuity of successful courses is to continue to meet a development need of individual managers or groups of managers, who then have to take the responsibility of applying what they have learnt within their organizational roles. The continuity that we seek in Action Learning is to be a part of the actual life of organizations in a process of change, continuing because their contribution to organizational change is to sharpen awareness and to raise the levels of energy and effectiveness in the company of fellow learners.

This is not an exhaustive set of guidelines! The activities have inherent difficulties, but the level of effectiveness is well above any other form of development available now. If we can continue to learn from each other as we pursue these challenging tasks, 'Q' may be kept alive in many more organizations.

References

1 Revans, R. (1983), *The ABC of Action Learning*, UK: Chartwell-Bratt.
2 Heller, J. (1979), *Good as Gold*, London: Jonathan Cape.
3 Morris, J. (1986), 'The Learning Spiral' in Mumford (Ed) *Handbook of Management Development*, (2nd Edn), UK: Gower.
4 Revans, R. (1983), op. cit.

27 Action Learning for chief executives

Ian Cunningham

This chapter is based on research I carried out in 1986. A fuller version with greater detail of the views of participants and the research methodology can be found in Cunningham (1986).[1] The programme was the 'Action Learning for chief executives' course at Ashridge Management College. (The title is abbreviated in Ashridge as 'ALCE' and I shall use that designation here.)

The programme

The ALCE programme has been operating at Ashridge since late 1980. Superficially it is similar to other Action Learning courses. For example, participants meet in sets of about five persons, each with a set adviser. The sets meet for one day at a time at intervals of about one per month for six months or more. I shall comment later on the extent to which this programme differs from other Action Learning courses. Fuller details of the ALCE programme are contained in Braddick and Casey (1981)[2] Casey and Hastings (1983)[3] and Casey (1984).[4]

The research

In the spring and summer of 1986 I interviewed 32 out of the 41 participants who had made up the eight sets run at Ashridge by that time. The remaining nine people were unavailable for various reasons; no one refused to be interviewed. My research assumptions are close to those associated with New Paradigm Research or Post Positivist Research. Central to this stance is the recognition of the limited and partial nature of my analysis and the emphasis that I was not trying to identify some absolute, objective truths. More detail can be found in Appendix II of Cunningham (1986).[5]

I wrote a draft report in September 1986 and circulated it to all the participating CEOs for their comments. I specifically asked them to check that the report reflected the programme, and to tell me if I should change it in any way. Sixteen CEOs replied: 14 said that it was fine as it stood and that I should not change it; one suggested a minor addition (which I have made); and one felt I could reduce the length of it. The latter point was countered by others who said that it should not be reduced. For example, one CEO wrote, 'The report caused me to live through every facet of my experience; don't change it.'

The research was stimulating and enjoyable to carry out, despite the serious logistical and travelling problems it created for me. All the people I met were helpful, prepared to talk and generally keen to contribute to the research.

The people

Of the 41 CEOs who participated in the ALCE the following is an analysis of their organizational bases:

Public sector	8
Family business	8
Part of larger organization (private sector)	23
Own business	2
Total	41

There was no CEO from a large corporation. All participants were male. Their ages ranged from the late 30s to 60. Within the apparent similarities there were also great differences, for example in terms of:

- home circumstances
- place of work (which varied from Belfast, Newcastle and Perth in the north to Bristol, Winchester and Croydon in the south)
- social class

- education
- personality

Main issues

The following is a summary of the main points identified in the research, some of which are elaborated later.

1 Most participants benefited greatly from the programme.

2 Such benefits were often expressed in general or personal terms, rather than about specific things learned.

3 However, there were specific organizational pay-offs for some people (though these were often seen as secondary to personal learning).

4 Self-analysis and personal re-appraisal were central issues for many.

5 One set was significantly less successful than the other seven studied. A number of design and logistical problems were identified by this set.

6 There was a wide variety of sources of recruitment to the programme, and range of reasons why people joined it.

7 The initial set meetings were often felt to be confusing and frustrating. However, this phase was worked through as sets realized how to use the programme to best effect. The process of the set was described in rich detail by participants. For many it was a new experience (and a positive one for most).

8 A number of sets have continued to meet after the formal programme concluded.

9 Four factors in the programme were considered important: management, design, face-to-face activity and theory.

10 The overall design was liked, but there were specific concerns about the mix of participants in a set and the timing and timetabling of meetings.

11 The role of set adviser was regarded as important.

12 The theoretical basis for the programme is supported by this research.

Benefits of the programme

Overall the benefits and pay-offs from the programme were clearly very great. However, in many cases people found it difficult to be precise about *specific* things they had learned. My interpretation is that the ALCE programme provides mainly for the development of what could be labelled more personal learning as opposed to the learning of specific techniques of management. At the same time, people did indicate some specific pay-offs, and before going back to elaborate the more personal learning, I will quote here some examples of organizationally oriented benefits:

> It helped me a lot. It helped me to have a very close relationship with customers. They are interested in what we think. They felt that something was being done to make me a better senior manager of a business they had a stake in.

> Certainly the ability of myself and my chief executive to communicate has dramatically improved since I went to Ashridge. I don't lose my temper as much as I used to. I try to keep the discussion sensible and constructive.

> I suppose that is really one of the principle things I have learned in terms of a 'skill'. The art is how to ask questions rather than give answers.

> What I got out of it was some real help and guidance during a very, very difficult transitional process which enabled me, frankly, to make better decisions in running the business. That is a true statement. That's all I can say about it.

> It really does bring home to you the problems that you have. The real ones, not the superficial ones.

> I must say that since I have come back I have often, consciously, quite consciously, done a bit of that with my own people. They have had a problem and because one of the things I learned was to listen I was able to stand back from all the problems (and not problems which required an answer now). And the 'phone goes and I pick it up now. Before I would offer solutions straight away. Now you see I say 'Oh dear. I wonder what do you think?' . . . because not all problems are things which require me to decide today. If somebody rings up and says we have got to take a decision 'now', then I take the decision now – right or wrongly – I don't want to ask anybody. But if it is something that is going to hit us in a day's time or two days' time or four days' time, when there is time, you can alter your approach to the problem and the person who has got the problem. And I find more and more I don't find a solution at all – what I do is manoeuvre the people so they find

their own solution. And it leads to a somewhat more pleasant working situation.

Other specific pay-offs mentioned included:

- one person re-structured his organization as a result of discussions in the set;

- people talked of 'broadened horizons', 'making me more aware and keener to do things', 'made me question more things';

- some CEOs did 'collect tools and techniques from other members of the set'. For example, a local authority CEO decided to use ideas from marketing and market research for the first time;

- two people commented that they had been prompted to go and read more as a result of the influence of the set.

In some cases people commented on their colleagues in the set, for example:

> X talked a lot about the value he got from it for himself, and of course the promotion which he has now got which he did feel was assisted by his involvement within the set.

> He certainly said that he had changed and, I think, felt more relaxed – I can't remember the words he used. I don't know whether it was relaxed but certainly gave the impression that he had thought about a lot of the things that had come up in the set.

Re-balancing

For many people, the development seemed only to come after self analysis and re-appraisal of their situation. This then gave them an opportunity to re-balance their lives, for example in dealing with both the rational/thinking aspects of their work and the emotional/value based dimensions.

As one person commented:

> I was able I think to keep a very balanced view of that which I might not have otherwise done. I would have been very – I think – potentially depressed about it and it would have shown through more than it actually did. The other evidence is the fact that my wife used to say to me: 'Are you going on your course? Are you going for your group therapy this week?' and I would say: 'yes' or 'no', as the case may be and she would make the comment: 'Well I think you had better go and have your group therapy because it enables you to be a far better human being and get all the pressures

and problems off your shoulders.' So, yes, I think it did make a difference.

Well, I'd say that I know it was totally unique to me. Totally outside my experience and it was a lot more than group therapy but frankly it was an opportunity to air things, concerns, problems and issues with other people and get their input, which enabled me then to make practical decisions and better decisions than I might otherwise have made. That's what I got out of it. The added benefit was that it was a real opportunity to get it off your chest. So all right it helped me. It was a group therapy in that sense and if that's group therapy I don't give a stuff.

Others commented on the supportive value of the set, for example:

It helped me enormously. I owe my sanity to the set.

It helped me over a hole.

A boost to flagging morale.

It put the whole thing in perspective and I stopped worrying about it then and just got on with the job and focused on what I should have been doing all the time.

Helped me through difficult personal circumstances.

You go for a day and come back revitalized and feel you have learned something. And maybe that faded after a while and then you sit back and think: 'Well, did it actually help me?' Perhaps my wife has commented more than anyone . . . she found that it was very good for me, that I came back . . . really more enthusiastic and feeling envigorated, I think really. Particularly some of the sessions more than others. I think it is traumatic for most people in some way or other because it usually makes you face up to some fairly large problem.

The people here have not said 'Oh, Ashridge has made a difference to you'. They don't see any real difference. I probably find a difference. I remember once ringing one of the lads up [in the set] because I felt particularly depressed and fed up and was dying to talk to him about why I felt depressed. And he told me about his problem and I talked to him about his problem for quite a while and didn't talk about mine at all. And I thought 'Mine wasn't such a big problem after all'.

I keep struggling with the word 'self-realization', which is awful really, but it is probably the nearest I can get. I think it changed me from being put in a job where I didn't know how to do it and being a little bit worried that I not only didn't know how to do it but that the devils had got their knives out ready to carve us into little bits. I think it helped to get me through a period where I certainly realized that probably nobody ever knew what to do anyway – you make it up as you go along. The fact that you get a title like MD shouldn't actually mean that all the answers are there.

There are a variety of further quotes which indicate the richness and value of the programme:

You are actually not learning how to manage or about a specific subject, you are actually learning about yourself. Not really about the theory of management or accounts or whatever course you are on. You are actually there analysing yourself. It was interesting from my point of view to see these different types of people, different areas, different backgrounds, we all have the same problem. Basically the problem is always the same . . . ourselves. Our not understanding the problem.

I don't think there is any doubt [there is a pay-off], but I feel it is entirely subjective. One of the things I have got out of it was it helped make me a general manager rather than just a guy who had been put in the seat. Now it could have been that the company could have done ten other things to do that. I rub shoulders and have become part of a group of people called managing directors; I got great personal kudos out of saying to the guys who worked for me: 'yesterday I spent the day with the guy who runs the X Group . . .' etc. Now I got a lot out. What it did to my ego to find that those guys didn't have magical answers to everything and that my views on some of those things seemed to be as important to them as theirs were to me. Not on their own, but when one of those was seeking views or comments they were looking to four people. They never said to me 'we are not interested in your views' so I was able to feel I was contributing to a group of people that I respected because they ran successful businesses.

You really question 'was I doing the right thing?' 'do I really want to do it any more?' 'should I be doing something entirely different?' So I came to the conclusion that this job, considering I have been here 14 years, was not really giving me self-satisfaction and I got to the stage where I was coasting to some extent because there was, perhaps, a lack of challenge or even, perhaps, a lack of involvement because the more efficient you make the organization and the better you can make the people, the more you can pass the decision-making. In actual fact the less you become involved yourself. The conclusion I had come to was that the job wasn't fulfilling any longer. Some of the problems of the business here and some of the problems was that I wasn't able to think like that and that's something Ashridge has done for me. But there again it takes you away from the work. If you sit in an environment every day you never actually think about it. You have got to be taken away from just sitting there and listening to other people's problems. They are all actually similar and the conclusion we came to was most of our problems were more than 50 per cent self-created by not facing up to something or whatever.

It's mainly finding out about yourself. Once you can handle yourself then, for the most part, you can handle the rest. Because things start to become fairly obvious if you once understand how you're reacting to it.

I don't think there is any question of that. I found it a tremendous benefit. The hard part is actually saying where, how and why. It is very difficult to specify what do I do differently now? What change have I made? It had a tangible effect. I find that extremely difficult to put forward. I think the others find it equally so. Some of the others have even asked 'what's it done for you?' Nobody can actually answer the question though. One of the surprising things is the very strong group loyalty. A very close bond. I mean my wife had difficulty in understanding why I have such a strong affinity to this group of people I didn't know five months ago. They are from all round the country and I only see them once in a blue moon. And why, for instance, we had to rearrange our holiday last year, at considerable inconvenience, because there was a meeting. That's very difficult to understand.

Lack of pay-off?

One set was markedly less successful than the others, and I want to comment on that group separately. However, even in successful sets there was a minority of people who felt that they had not benefited greatly. In two cases people left the programme before its completion; in others people stayed to the end. However, in *all* cases the CEOs concerned could see the value of this approach to learning.

The set that didn't work so well

Let me give some quotes from people in this set in order to give some background:

I think my immediate feeling at the end of the series was that it was a bit of a waste of time, but I knew I would revise that feeling after a bit and sure enough I have, after a couple of months, and it was worth the time spent, but it could have been a lot more worth it. I think it is a combination of things, including getting the atmosphere right, including getting everybody there. But just as importantly the chance combination of people concerned, where I don't think we hit it off in the way other groups did, which was a pity because I think they have got a considerable amount more out of it than we did.

I am terribly aware now that all of the potential that I saw in the technique I have done almost nothing to benefit from since the end of that – it's how long ago now? It must be getting on for a year.

I don't think it was really fulfilling a need. Maybe there was a need that I had not recognized. But I certainly didn't find that when I attended the course that it was very stimulating.

I asked most people in the set if they would recommend the programme to other CEOs or not. They indicated that, with provisos, they would. For example:

I think my approach would be two ways. I think I would only want to recommend him to go on it if I thought he was going to actually be a positive part of that group. So that I would be interested to try and find out what it was he thought he was going to get out of it and what he was going to put into it. But yes, I mean unless I interpret him as being negative in terms of the effect he would have, and therefore somebody who would feel it was a failure because he wasn't prepared to accept the basic discipline of the thing. Then yes, I would recommend it.

Despite the problems with this set, some people did get positive things out of it. One person reorganized his management structure, commenting:

It emerged. I couldn't say I left the last meeting saying 'Eureka I have it!' I began to realize there was something I could do.

Others positive comments were:

I think I have definitely made some improvement actually in the way I use my time. I think in a sense I have got more determined to make certain I spend more of my time on what I think is important.

What did I get out of it? I got several things. First of all a commonality of problems. An awareness that at chief executive level you do run out of places to go for, not necessarily specific advice, but for an exchange of views with your peers and that I came away from the set with the feeling that my problems were really not entirely different from those of other people.

The reasons offered by participants in this set as to why it had been less successful included:

1 Not everyone attended each meeting (and one person left the set completely). Attendance by everyone at each meeting was seen as desirable.

2 The day meetings were usually not a full day because of travel problems for some people – this didn't give the set time to gell.

3 The set, unlike some others, didn't meet up the night before. Other sets have commented on the value of a night-before get together to unwind and re-connect to colleagues.

4 Some felt that the mix of people wasn't right: that somehow the 'chemistry' didn't work. This may have contributed to a feeling that there wasn't a high enough commitment to the set. This also meant that people didn't open up as much as in the other sets.

5 The gaps between meetings were seen as too long (they went longer than 4 weeks often). This didn't give enough continuity to the set.

6 Some felt the set might have worked given longer, and given that logistical problems could have been sorted out. The rigid six meeting format was seen as a disadvantage.

Design issues

To quote one CEO:

> The design is superbly simple. When you look at what we actually did, all we did to start with was agree some dates and send one another information about the businesses we ran and a little bit about ourselves. The set adviser talked for about ten minutes worth of what it was all about and we took it from there.

In broad-brush terms this statement is valid. However, when one looks at the detail there are some complex issues to consider.

1. Preparatory work

This varied from people who had thoroughly checked out the idea and felt enthusiastic about it to those who were pushed into the programme by someone in their organization. A number of CEOs expressed specific concerns that they came to address, for example: 'I wanted to broaden my horizons'; 'my business wasn't going how I wanted it to'. Others felt that their preparatory thinking was inadequate or shallow, and that they made the decision to attend on poor information. In some cases they felt that better briefing from Ashridge would help. In other cases CEOs blamed themselves for not checking out the programme more.

Participants usually saw written material before attending (for example, Ashridge prospectus, articles about ALCE). Such written material was generally seen as helpful, though often participants felt it did not give a full enough picture of the programme. Many participants spoke to someone from Ashridge before they signed up. In some cases these were telephone conversations, in others, someone had visited the CEO in his office. Some who had only spoken on the phone said they would have preferred a visit from someone from Ashridge.

In general, because of the unusual nature of ALCE (to many CEOs) there was a feeling that the college might invest more on pre-programme contact, though people recognized the time and cost factors in this. By and large they saw that this would need to be one-to-one contact (presentations were not particularly favoured).

2. Initial set meetings

Comments about the initial set meetings varied from the practical and factual to the more critical. For example:

> I didn't understand, or didn't recognize it as I should, that it was very much about me. It is, it's me as a person. . . . Get to know me as a person. Get to know my strengths and weaknesses. What I want is some help as a person rather than a business. One tended to come and talk about the business. But it's me really . . . and it took me, certainly a couple of, you know, visits to really get to understand that. And that may be me. I don't necessarily blame the course.

A number of CEOs commented that the initial meetings were 'tense' and 'uncertain' and some felt that this early less-productive phase could have been moved through more rapidly with more assistance from set advisers. Others were not sure and felt that the early struggles to get to know each other and understand the process were inevitable. A positive suggestion from some was that perhaps the first meeting, which was mainly around fixing dates, could have been extended to include an overnight stay (so that more ice-breaking could occur).

3. Getting going

In moving from the initial meetings to making the set work people sometimes expressed concerns about how the course was turning out. It was 'a bit of a shock' (to quote one CEO who had expected a taught course). Others felt frustrated because they did not know where it was going and what (if anything) they were learning. However, such views usually changed after a time. Comments from participants included the following:

> I think we might have got a lot more out of it if what we were trying to do had been better explained. I went in, I read the literature when I went in but I was really groping . . . I was tending to flounder a bit over the first two meetings until the set adviser gradually, as his catalyst role was, caused us to stop and think a little bit more about what was happening. I think if we had been briefed on that a little better I think that might have helped to get us on the road a bit quicker. Yet, here again when I say that, for me personally, the others may not have felt the same because some of them had already had some background to this. Some had some experience of group work in this field; I hadn't. So for me, while they weren't floundering, maybe over the first couple of meetings I was.

> At the beginning of the course, we found it very difficult to accept views, or even suggestions. All we were particularly interested in was telling people our problems. And I think most of us had fairly fixed ideas how we would solve them. And it was only later on in the course, and subsequent meetings, where, certainly I for one have been quite noticeably impressed by the change of attitude of the others over the progression of time. As you become more familiar with the individuals and begin to realize that, yes, they can brainstorm . . . and can give you a number of other ideas that you may well have kicked out. I think Ashridge for me taught me to listen a lot more; you know, rather than talk.

> I think it is a funny sensation because the first day we were there we got pretty concerned with a person who doesn't like to talk about his problems. And he also keeps his business life and personal life completely separate if possible. When I went there on the first day not having any idea what they expect and got involved in another chap's very personal life on day one I thought, God, this is not for me! On the way back, I drove back in the evening, I sat for two and a half hours in the car. I had time to think about it and I thought it is not so silly. Your personal and business problems are interwoven and you probably do not realize it unless you sit down and actually think about it. So I decided to go back for the second day and the second day worked pretty well. It was fairly intense and tiring and then when I was due to go for the third day I had been at X Co and had a fairly difficult day and almost got to the stage of packing up there and then, so I had arranged to stay overnight to go on the Ashridge course and I did, in fact, consider not going. I thought I would go home and forget all about it. However, I went on the course and told my fellow colleagues what had happened the day before. That was very

interesting to hear the different reactions from the other four individuals.

After the first meeting I came away from I didn't feel any relationship really with anyone else in the group, because they were from different backgrounds. And I thought: What do I really have in common with these people? And it took, I think, about two meetings to really establish that we all had problems. They were all different. I really don't know how that happened. How the group sort of welded together but by about the third meeting people were being very open and very frank and very positive. They were all contributing. No one sat back as a passenger. People wanted to participate. People were very honest. Now what the magic ingredient was I don't know. I can only put it down to the chemistry and the maturity, the commitment. And the fact that the people wanted to be there. They all wanted to learn. They wanted to participate.

4. The set in operation

Again quotes from course participants illustrate some of the richness, power and excitement of the process:

The big thing about it I think, from the point of view of somebody who is Chief Executive of a company, is that in a group like that you are actually able to talk and talk honestly about your problems and feelings. I think it is virtually impossible to do that with anybody else. You can't do it with people you know in the company because you're always defensive or you are always maintaining your position in relation to . . . directors and . . . board members. You are not as honest to them I think as within a group of people outside . . . I don't think the same course would work really with people for example from within the same group of companies. I would be very sceptical.

That's the main thing I think, opening up. Yes. People are not used to doing it are they? . . . Men in this society particularly are not used to doing it.

Listening to the way that they tackled those problems, telling them about mine, comparing notes in a very free atmosphere after the first two sessions we were able to talk about things that I wouldn't dream about talking to a colleague and, frankly, I would even hesitate to talk about to my wife in some cases because a very strange relationship developed in that set. And I expect this is so with all the sets, where you haven't actually got any close interrelationship at all and that enabled you to be very open and free in what you said to one another. Also indiscreet furthermore.

I think the greatest thing you have, with this group of four other

guys, who are in the same sort of scrapes I am in every day of
their lives. Some of them have been in scrapes I have not been in
and there are some scrapes they are going into that I have been
in and they haven't. And that's what helped. I think that is the
thing that the group has to sell. I don't think it teaches you an
awful lot – it's not like going on a course – like to learn about
VAT or something. It is just not like that. The group gives you
this support group that you can use or find comfort in and I think
if you are the head of a substantial patch in any business it's a
good thing to have. A place to go to. A place where you know
you are not going to get beaten up. I mean that is the thing it
gave me more than anything else. This sort of comfort. And the
fact that you could honestly feel that you had helped other people
with things you may or may not have said. And also that feeling
of privilege that other people talk to you as an individual or as
part of the group about their problems and allowed you into their
problems and to express your views and to question their views.
This helped me greatly.

5. Supporting and confronting

Part of the value of sets clearly comes from the 'supportive
confronting' environment, where participants are cared about
sufficiently for them to be challenged in quite a powerful way.
People talked of the set being 'brutal' at times, and experienced
themselves being 'nailed'. Yet this was balanced by the support
provided.

Comments exemplifying this factor included:

> I think one of the values of taking five or six total strangers with
> no business relationship whatsoever has a lot of merit because you
> can actually talk fairly openly. We came quite close on a couple
> of times to falling out . . .

> We did a lot of that right back to the bare bones of soul stripping.
> We didn't hold back anything.

> You get a lot of pretty clear observations as long as you are
> prepared to open yourself up.

> It's a sign of weakness (in my company) to seek advice . . . you
> could store up problems to bring to the table because you know
> you could get a truly honest view.

> A progress meeting . . . if you hadn't implemented (what you said
> you would do) by the time you got back to the next meeting you
> had better have a good reason why. Because otherwise you go
> through the whole rack again.

> Now, in the work situation one of the Chief Executive's problems

is too often he can solve things by power rather than technique. I think because of the pace of things very often he has to solve them by power . . . But it can become addictive – I think is one of the dangers, and I think one of the important things about that group as an Action Learning Set is it actually does most Chief Executives good I would think. Certainly I felt it did me good to be in a situation where you weren't God. You know, you were facing problems with people who would actually disagree with you and you would have to accept they had every right to a different view. Whereas there is a danger in a line management situation, that you assume when people disagree with you it's because they are wrong. I don't mean it quite as strongly as that but you can always solve it by rank if you are not careful.

That really I think probably sums up the nature of the set really; that you feel it is supportive. It may be very critical and absolutely stop you in your tracks but it is supportive in the end . . . in a way that you probably would never get within your own organization.

And again we eventually pinned him down. Actually nailed him and it took us some time to nail him.

And he was a very difficult guy to get through to. Every time one put up a suggestion, X would knock it down by saying: 'Yes, we thought about that.' I personally didn't feel I was getting through to the guy because every time I said something, he said: 'Yes, yes, we thought about that. That's a good idea but we have thought about it' or 'we have tried it'. And again it took – it was about the fourth meeting with this particular guy. Then he came clean and what he had been worried about essentially was the fact that the overall business in which he was a part . . . was getting into some difficulty, and the guy running it wasn't really sort of aware of it and no one else seemed to be too concerned about making him aware of it and making him do something about it. He had got sufficiently wound up by one of the group meetings where we all had a go at him. About what he should be doing, etc, etc, etc. And he came back the following month and said: 'Well thanks for your advice. I did what you said and these are the changes that are going to happen, I think.' So we are all watching now to see what happens. So I think we really helped that guy. But again he was going through a personal crisis as well as a business crisis and he didn't know quite how to handle it. He was able, I think, despite the fact that he said 'Yes, well we tried that and we tried this.' I think we were registering with him in his sub-conscious to the extent that he was able to get guidance and went away and did it.

This latter point is an important addition to earlier comments. It seems that people for all sorts of reasons don't recognize at the time what needs doing. And the group might feel it's failed.

However, the message may well get through at a more unconscious level, helping the person to take action at a later date.

6. After the formal course has ended

A number of sets have continued to meet after the formal course
has ended. This has been more a facet of later sets (the early
sets have not continued to meet). In some cases people feel that
their set is going better now than it did when it was under
Ashridge's wing. It's as if the first six meetings helped the set to
bond in such a way as to allow them now to go further. In other
cases people are less sure of the value of continued meetings,
or they see the set becoming more of a social gathering than a
learning event.

Some comments include:

> Well he [the set adviser] is not there now but I think we have got
> through the process of knowing each other. Of being able to say
> to each other precisely what we think at any point in time and we
> tend – now obviously we listen a lot more than we did before.
> And we are more prepared I think to accept suggestions than we
> were before and really the set adviser's role isn't needed now.

> When we have met we have had good sessions, but it has to be
> said that I don't think we have had a complete session which
> everybody has turned up to. I think people felt the formality of it
> was over and it was more of a social gathering.

> Where we have all got together and out of six of us I think there
> has always been at least four of us there, sometimes five sometimes
> six. It was more difficult I think to get us all together when we
> were trying to organize a date after the formal dates that we had
> fixed than obviously it was when we had the formal dates fixed.
> But we do talk to each other . . . there is still quite a lot of
> discussion goes on backwards and forwards. So we try to keep
> ourselves up to date with what's going on out of interest.

> We have meetings – we have had one meeting since and are due
> to have another one this week. And the meeting that we had
> worked very well. In fact I think, that is having had all the sessions
> at Ashridge, that worked very well. It wouldn't have worked in
> the early days; it wouldn't have got anywhere without a catalyst
> really. And I think the nature of that catalyst is very important.

The role of the adviser

A key argument about the set adviser role is whether one needs
one at all. The views of ALCE participants concur with my own

research evidence (Cunningham, 1984)[6] in supporting the need for such a person. The quotes that follow below are very clear on this. One CEO commented:

> I clearly think the group at the outset needs a focus. So it has got to be there at the outset. You have got to have someone to set it up, run it, who can sort of act as moderator, if you like, and be the stimulus for questions and also to bring people back to order and to guide people. Without those two guys there I don't think it would have got off the ground. I think there is no question about that.

The most used metaphor for the set adviser role was that of catalyst. For example:

> The set adviser played a very minor role. He played the perfect role for whatever he was supposed to be, a lead, a catalyst, I don't know what. But what he said was well worth listening to.

> It would be totally impossible to do that without a set adviser to start with. And it was a very necessary ingredient certainly for four or five meetings. Perhaps if X had been able to come consistently from the beginning we might have got to a sort of self-reliance point a little quicker. But we couldn't have done it for less than four. Basically because you are finding out about people and you're finding out things about people that people don't admit to themselves. So there's little chance of them admitting something to a total stranger unless there's a catalyst to do so. We admitted things to each other but there are not other people in this world who actually know that. Things we would never dream of telling our friends, our business colleagues or even our wives. Another thing is – it's a lot to do with the sort of common bond. We know things which are very, very personal. Or very, very private, I probably think would be [more appropriate]. But without that catalyst, as I say, you couldn't have done it.

'Catalyst' is perhaps too limiting a description. One role he did fulfil was that of an 'infill', that is he filled in and did what nobody else was doing; for example:

> I mean he obviously did quite of lot of filling in of gaps when silences descended because I suppose in effect we'd lost our way. We'd run out of steam or – and occasionally when people were pushing a bit too hard. Yes, for all of us there came a time when you reach a sort of breaking point, when you feel like standing up and walking out. And generally he managed to sort of pull it back from doing damage to somebody.

> He came in at times – I think when he thought there was an element of confusion. Then he joined in. He then joined in because

I think he had always got something tracking at the back of his mind and he wanted to feel that the consumers, us, were getting value for money and he didn't want us trailing off into things which possibly were wasting time and weren't sort of moving the experience on. So he would come in then but he was quite unob-trusive. You know, he seemed content to sit around. I mean he used to have to guide it. I mean the way the process worked in there was that each one of us would talk about something. Talk about ourselves, about problems. And he used to have to prod that. But after the first two meetings, by the time it came to the third and fourth meetings, we were deciding what we were – who was going to talk, and who we would allow to talk and sort of developed a sense of fairness.

The use of the term 'guide' in the above correlates with another person's comment that the set adviser would 'guide and steer'. Here are some relevant quotes:

So the set adviser steered it and he didn't want the conversation to degenerate. Some of the things he pointed out in the early stages were when you know somebody would talk about a problem he had got and other people didn't question to enable the person who had got the problem to question himself. They question for themselves only and then started suggesting specific answers for the guy. We soon learned that that wasn't the way to help the other fellow.

I think the most fundamental aspect would be that he taught us to ask questions. When we stopped asking questions and started proffering solutions, he would stop us and bring everything back down to earth, and get it pointed in the right direction. Because all that's happening when you start offering advice – I mean I know nothing really about those other people's work. I don't know their mode of operation. I don't begin to understand the types of customers they have and so on. I don't really know – well not really enough to be able to go and say: 'You should be doing this.' And that's what was tending to happen. It would be; 'Well, why don't you do such and such? If you do such and such – ' it started trying to get detailed solutions . . . from people who really weren't in a position to know and understand. So he'd bring it back and he'd turn it into a question sort of – it's difficult to describe actually.

It is useful to have somebody there who actually intervened. He wasn't just sort of an observer who took pressure off people when they were under pressure. It's sort of a responsive way and the way he played it was actually to intervene in a positive sense and say: 'Hang on, that's not the way to do it. What you need to do is not to give opinions but to ask questions.' And he kept on reminding us that the way in which we were going about our work wasn't very productive.

This description of the set adviser's role implies that he was 'directive about attention' but not 'directive about action'. He clearly, according to the CEOs, didn't just make comments about the process of the set; he confronted issues in order to direct people's attention to what they were doing and what they (in his opinion) should be doing. However, what I did not get from CEOs was any hint that he was teaching people (in the way in which that term has come to be used).

This directiveness element links to what some CEOs saw as the ground rules for working. For example:

> Firstly the ground rules which the set adviser established that – the first one was that . . . when you start with one person's problem everybody else wants to chip and get their oar in. And he said from the very beginning that you must let one person ask a question and then develop that idea before the next person will ask his question. Otherwise . . . you are all trying to score a point . . . Develop ideas and see where they get to. And the other ground rule he said was that you must not make suggestions on how the problem's going to be resolved. You can ask questions. I presume other people have identified those two points? Because they were clearly stated at the beginning.

Interestingly, some people saw that once they had worked through the early problems in the set, they would get into advice giving (and see it as useful). One set that was carrying on after the programme was clear that it disagreed with their set adviser on this.

Theory issues

I want initially to make the simple point that the theoretical assumptions underpinning ALCE seem vindicated from my research.

A quote from someone who left the programme after one meeting is interesting here:

> I actually think it is a better method at all levels. I don't really believe that taught courses do a fantastic amount of good at the end of the day regardless of the content. I am not totally happy with the effect they have on other people within the company . . . we send some to Ashridge and they all come back determined to get things moving but I think that any course done in isolation for an individual or even a group of individuals, cannot really work

unless the environment is already receptive. But I think far too many people come off courses and are not about to apply what it is they have learned. But I also believe that on many of the courses that the case studies or actual teaching itself is in itself a little bit divorced from reality.

Others made similar comments. The value of this approach is also confirmed in a Local Government Training Board report. They studied the ALCE programme and other programmes that provide for CEOs. Their conclusion was:

It is apparent that the Action Learning programme had the greatest impact on the participants and, even more significantly, these were permanent changes in behaviour applied directly to their work and which are still continuing.

It is interesting to counterpose this with some of the earlier quotes about the benefits of the programme. People could identify a change, but often found it difficult to articulate why this was so. My interpretation is that they were trying to make conscious learning that was often unconscious and trying to comment in linear, linguistic form about learning that hadn't taken place in a linear, sequential mode. If you ask someone how they learned a subject in a classroom they can usually tell you the sequence by which they were instructed. If the teacher is a skilled presenter such an analysis by the learner will correlate reasonably well with the syllabus the teaching was working to. In Action Learning there is no syllabus and no teacher (in the sense of a skilled presenter). More importantly it seems that people learn different things from Action Learning than they do from a taught course.

A useful formulation of this difference is by Nomme (1986) and his colleagues who distinguish between 'static competence', which relates to context specific knowledge and skills (eg finance/accounting skills) and 'dynamic competence', which is much more about abilities and qualities which transfer across contexts.[7] A good example of developing 'dynamic competence' is in the following quote from a CEO on the programme:

I recognised that if I was ever in an environment that was quite different I could probably survive. Which I hadn't previously had . . . It gave me confidence . . . that I could open out a bit more. I could pursue other courses of action for career development.

Let me take the example of 'listening' to show the difference between 'static' and 'dynamic competence'. One can deal with this at the 'static competence' level as is often done on so-called inter-personal skills courses. In this approach the trainer might give people advice on listening, provide role plays or simulation, use 'drills' or whatever. The notion of listening here is of a surface, mechanical skill.

On ALCE, CEOs commented about listening in quite a different way. They related to a deeper level of engaging with other people. Here are two sample quotes:

> It developed quite a good attitude in myself, listening to other people rather than trying to jump in and solve – give the answers. Which is what I had always tended to do in the environment I was in. I hadn't got the time to bother to listen to the other guy. We had to take action and the best action to take was *my* action because I hadn't got the time to think about anybody else's.

> I hadn't realised how little I actually listen to people who were trying their very best to contribute. I always felt I listened a hell of a lot to people coming in here asking me questions and so on. Yet, because I was asking questions of the bits that I wanted to know I wasn't really giving them an opportunity to contribute, other than what I wanted them to contribute. In other words: 'Answer the question please; I don't want your views on anything else, I just want the question answered.' And I think that was the big benefit to me and I think we all tumbled to that at various stages; and once we had tumbled if we asked a question and they went off onto something else, we tended not to say: 'Oh, the hell, I don't want to know about that.' We let it go. And I think we all found that at different times.

A key element of the Action Learning approach is also to address problems participants bring rather than offer pre-packaged solutions, and this again correlates with a 'dynamic competence' model. This links to points made by some CEOs that the problems were eventually seen as themselves. Thus the set, if it works well, causes people to face their own beliefs, values and feelings. This makes the process quite different from a solely cognitive learning model. However, for some people working on problems wasn't enough, for example:

> I think perhaps I would very much like to learn more how to actually deal with those problems identified; how to solve them as well as realizing I've got them. I'm not sure I actually found that out at the end of the day. If you like, I'm still struggling with the problem.

The basic notion of working on problems before working on solutions seems valid. Yet if solutions are not eventually addressed perhaps the course is missing something. In the early days of its inception there was the idea that participants would use the set as a base from which to access other learning resources in Ashridge (academic staff, books, sessions on other courses, and so on). This does not seem to have happened. Yet it could be added back into the programme (and there are successful programmes in other colleges that do this). This would indicate that, having worked on 'dynamic competence', some 'static competence' development might be a useful supplement. Such changes would move the programme further from an Action Learning mode into something which is potentially richer and more sophisticated.

References

1 Cunningham, I. (1986), *Developing Chief Executives*, Ashridge Management College.
2 Braddick, W. and Casey, D. (1981), 'Developing the Forgotten Army' in *Management Education and Development* **12** (3), pp. 169–80.
3 Casey, D. and Hastings, C. (1983), 'Day Release for Chief Executives' in *Personnel Management*, June.
4 Casey, D. (1984) 'Lifeline for Lonely Bosses' in *Chief Executive*, September.
5 Cunningham, I. (1986), op. cit.
6 Cunningham, I. (1984), *Teaching Styles in Learner Centred Management Development Programmes*, University of Lancaster.
7 Nomme, R. (1986), Address to University Executive Programme Directors Conference, Ashridge, March.

28 Action Learning: an evaluation

Mark Easterby-Smith and John Burgoyne

When we were first asked to write a chapter on the evaluation of Action Learning, it seemed a most attractive proposition. 'Evaluation' is a topic with which we both have some experience, and Action Learning is a most worthy object of evaluative activities. But once we started work, we rapidly ran into trouble!

For a start, there is no common agreement about what constitutes a valid evaluation. But from a welter of definitions and viewpoints[1][2][3], we might distinguish for our present purpose two distinct definitions: evaluation as *judgement*, and evaluation as *development*. The former definition implies an attempt to assess the value, or worth, of an activity or programme against certain explicit or implicit criteria – usually in order to decide whether to continue funding and resourcing the activity in question. The latter definition tends to assume the continued existence of the programme, and therefore implies adoption of various procedures and processes to enable the programme to become better.

The second problem is that of deciding just what is to be evaluated. The extraordinarily wide dissemination of Action Learning causes some difficulty here since it is evident from this book, and elsewhere[4][5][6], that the nature of Action Learning can vary greatly with the context in which it is applied and according to the different approaches of those who initiate it. Each may bear a greater, or lesser, resemblance to the forms and nature

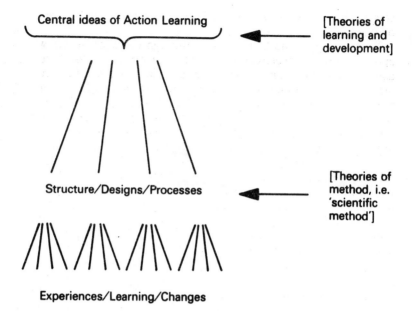

Figure 28.1   Action Learning: some levels of analysis and alternatives

of Action Learning as developed and propounded by Professor Revans. Indeed, Revans's own approach to Action Learning varied somewhat over time according to the different constraints of the context within which he was operating. Apart from these variations in the nature of Action Learning according to context, one may also view any particular Action Learning intervention from a number of different perspectives, in simplified form, these are illustrated as a hierarchical 'tree' (see Figure 28.1)

The figure indicates that there are a number of alternative structures and designs which may be used to facilitate Action Learning; that on one hand they are based on a fairly consistent body of ideas regarding the essence of Action Learning, and on the other hand these structures and designs may be experienced in a whole variety of ways by those who participate in Action Learning. At the two higher levels it is possible to identify theories which have influenced Action Learning practices. Thus, the central ideas of Action Learning are related closely to the views of John Dewey and his associates about the need to establish a linkage between thinking and acting; similarly the desirable processes within Action Learning rely heavily upon scientific methodology.[7]

Those readers who have worked through the book so far will appreciate that 'development' is a concept central to the theory and practice of Action Learning – at least in the sense of improving situations and increasing the capacities of those who manage these situations. Thus the notion of evaluation as development is very close to the central philosophy of Action Learning and we shall therefore comment in the following section upon how evaluation may be seen as an integral part of any form of Action Learning procedure. This does not, of course, negate the value of, and the need to make, some wider judgements about Action Learning. Indeed, judgement (or audit, as Revans calls it) is an important feature of the Action Learning cycle (System Beta), and we shall therefore discuss in the final part of this chapter the various attempts that have been made to assess the impact, and value, of Action Learning.

Developmental evaluation: making it better

Many of the central ideas of Action Learning have been tackled in the first part of this book. It would appear that there is rather less diversity of opinion amongst writers and practitioners at this level if only because those approaches which deviate markedly from the central tenets are rarely accepted as being 'genuine' Action Learning. Nevertheless, there is still a certain amount of divergency, and despite being rather abstract, some of the ideas may be examined empirically. For example, Revans discusses a number of theoretical questions about the way learning takes place within an Action Learning framework.[8] Does learning occur suddenly or in small increments? Is learning a single factor of a multi-factor process? And so on. These are questions about the nature of Action Learning and of the theories underlying it. Based on his own experience, Revans has his own view about the answers; and no doubt other practitioners might be in a position to draw their own, and differing conclusions. At this level, there may therefore be some role for evaluation, either in examining the validity of some of these theoretical ideas, or in attempting to refine and develop such concepts. Either way, Revans probably has a marked advantage in these areas, since his book (1971) represents one of the first attempts to think through some of these issues in relation to managerial learning.

At the next level, the *structures/designs/processes* whereby

Action Learning ideas may be implemented within a particular context, there is obviously an enormous amount of variation. The breadth of these variations may be deduced from the range of applications described in Part II of this book, and some of the relevant variations are summarized in chapter 16 by Alan Lawlor. In judgemental terms it would seem that evaluation may not have much to offer at this level, since it is obviously extremely difficult to generalize about the 'ideal' features of an Action Learning design. Indeed, one of the main messages of this book is that those involved in initiating Action Learning must be able to adapt the basic concepts and processes in order to meet the specific requirements of the particular problems being addressed. A 'developmental' evaluation may have far more to offer, since within any programme there may be many points at which it is worth reviewing whether the particular procedures adopted are appropriate at that point in the life of the programme, and thus for making the necessary adjustments to facilitate individual and group learning processes. For example, in Action Learning-based programmes run as CSML the ideal 'set' size varies greatly. When members of the set are engaged in exploring and developing ideas about their future action, it is often beneficial to have at least five or six members within a set; once they get involved in implementing specific actions in their work, the ideal set size may be no more than one or two members; but when they come to review their experiences, far larger groupings may be appropriate (ten to twelve). Some participants appear to have marked preferences for smaller sets; others prefer larger sets. Similarly, the particular teaching style of the set adviser may lend itself to larger or smaller groups.

The primary role of evaluation when looking at the structural and design aspects of Action Learning processes must therefore surely be to assist with the right adaptation to the particular needs of the people involved at that point in the history of the Action Learning intervention. It implies that evaluation should be seen in developmental terms, or as 'short-cycle' evaluation. Clearly it is consistent with the philosophy of Action Learning to place the problem and responsibility for conducting this evaluation with the participants involved in the exercise. But this is more than a 'process review' being conducted at the end of each session; it requires some detailed thinking about wider design and structural issues and may require clear decisions and action to be taken as a result of this. There are a number of ways of organizing this kind of do-it-yourself evaluation. For example, buzz groups might be asked to develop lists of issues concerning the operation of the set, and these are then reported back to the rest of the group in order to collate feelings about particular issues raised; alternatively the tasks might be delegated to one or two individuals who would take on the responsibility of interviewing the other members of the group in a fairly unstructured way before reporting back to the group as a whole. Naturally it would be unwise to prescribe ideal procedures in cases such as this; all we are implying is that Action Learning processes should be deliberately designed in such a way that the people involved can learn about how they might operate more effectively.

This leads into our third level at which Action Learning might be considered: that of the *experiences, learning or changes* that take place within, and as a result of, an intervention. In effect, the preceeding paragraph has suggested that through understanding the experiences of participants in Action Learning processes, it may be more possible to take decisions leading to the improvement of the structure or design of Action Learning. It is in terms of learning and change that a *judgemental* evaluation must primarily be formulated; but there is still room for *developmental* evaluation at this level too. Since the former is rather a large topic, we shall consider it in the subsequent section of this chapter, and confine our comments at this stage to developmental evaluation.

In some respects, Action Learning is concerned less with experiences of individuals than with the learning and change that results from these experiences. The structural considerations that we have discussed above are intended to promote more effective learning and change in general, but are seen primarily as the responsibility of set advisers (if any) and of the group as a whole. Learning and change must be seen primarily as an individual responsibility, and the concern of developmental evaluation should therefore be to help individuals become more aware of their own learning and change processes in order that this might be facilitated. Personal learning diaries are now used quite frequently on post-experience courses for managers, and some companies have initiated developmental diaries which managers are expected to record their own processes of change and development. There are a range of other techniques available whereby individuals might examine their own learning progress and process.[9] Although we are not aware from the literature of such self-evaluative approaches being used within the context of Action Learning, we would not be surprised if there are many examples, in practice, since firstly the notion of individual responsibility for action and learning is a central tenet of the philosophy of Action

Learning. Secondly, reports of such processes are less likely to find their way into the literature which is more likely to be concerned with structural considerations or with success stories at a collective level.

Judgemental evaluation: the impact of Action Learning

The impact of Action Learning may be assessed at the level of its effect on individuals, the apparent outcomes from specific projects, and programmes, and in wider terms, upon management education as a whole. The notion of conducting 'scientific' evaluations on the learning of individuals being given an Action Learning treatment in comparison with the learning of individuals through more traditional vocational approaches seems rather far fetched, and has rightly been strongly criticized by Parlett and Hamilton.[10] Perhaps the best approximation to a scientific evaluation of Action Learning's impact on individuals would be to consider each individual as a unique case study. Thus, we might consider whether Joe Bloggs has learnt more effectively as a result of an Action Learning programme, compared to previous educational methods that he has encountered. Unfortunately no one has yet attempted to collate such individual experiences in any rigorous manner and the evidence must therefore remain rather anecdotal.

It is clear that a small portion of people do not relish their encounter with Action Learning: this may be something to do with themselves, or with the particular variant of Action Learning involved, or with the general ideas underlining Action Learning; but which of these three is by no means clear. However, the majority of people who encounter Action Learning (and allied educational methods) do seem to take to it quite enthusiastically and subsequently adopt many of the ideas and principles from Action Learning within their normal working lives. We suspect that this is not merely a matter of following the latest cult; it is indeed quite deep rooted.

There have been a number of specific Action Learning projects which have taken place within the last two decades and which have become quite widely known. Of these, it is the Hospital Internal Communications (HIC) project (Revans 1981), the Inter Universities project (Revans 1971), and the G.E.C. project (Casey and Pearce, 1977) that are most widely quoted. With the exception of the HIC project, these, and various other projects that have found their way into the literature, have been written up by people who played a major role in them. There is thus a rather uncritical flavour in much of the literature, which occasionally borders on the evangelical. This is not to say that it is not of value; most of it is very penetrating and absorbing, but those who believe in the ideal of objective evaluation might be disappointed in it.

One interesting exception is that of the HIC project which was evaluated by George Wieland, an American who spent several years studying the programme. He conducted a rigorous and exhaustive evaluation of that particular project which concluded that the project actually had very little effect on the hospitals involved.[11] Changes were observed amongst scattered individuals, but not in the more important organizational variables. No changes in patient care could be detected with the measures used, nor was there any general increase in morale as indicated by absenteeism and turnover figures – in fact absenteeism increased slightly over the period of the project. Curiously enough, he revised his views several years later, commenting more favourably on the impact of the programme, particularly with regard to reductions in the average length of patient stay in comparison with other comparable hospitals. He accounted for this turn-around on the grounds that it had taken a number of years for the impact of the Action Learning programme to work through to the basic performance criteria by which the effectiveness of the hospitals were measured. So much for scientific evaluations.

At the wider level of management education as a whole, one is tempted to speculate about what the state of management education would be like (especially in the UK) if there had been no Revans or Action Learning. Clearly there would have been no programmes specifically labelled Action Learning, but these seem to remain a fairly minor portion of the existing programmes in further and higher education (only a handful of Polytechnics have attempted to establish Action Learning MA programmes, and this with limited success). Within companies there have been quite a large number of programmes entitled Action Learning, but these have usually taken place within a rather experimental format, and have rarely become institutionalized within the normal management development procedures. Perhaps rightly so.

But the major impact of Action Learning has, we believe, been an indirect one. Action Learning, as an approach and as a philosophy, has generated a very great deal of interest within management education and development. It has also inspired a great deal of activity, if only through attempts to incorporate some of the principles of Action Learning within the framework of more traditional educational methods.

On occasion this has no doubt led to mis-application of the central principles, but it would be churlish to reject a certain amount of eclecticism and pragmatism as being 'non-genuine'. There are some who feel that Action Learning programmes cannot be given the genuine label unless personally vetted by Revans himself.

Finally, however, perhaps one might judge the impact of Action Learning by the way some of its basic terms have found their way into the everyday language of trainers and developers – to the extent that Action Learning is no longer seen as anything special or unusual by most people, whether or not they are able to make their practice conform to its ideals.

References

1 Cronbach, L. J. (1963) 'Course Improvement through evaluation', *Teacher's College Record*, **64**, pp. 672–83.
2 Scriven, M. 'The methodology of evaluation' in R. W. Tyler, R. M. Gagne and M. Scriven (eds) (1967), *Perspectives of Curriculum Evaluation*, Chicago: Rand McNally.
3 Easterby-Smith, M. (1981), 'The evaluation of management education and development: an overview', *Personnel Review*, **10**, (2) pp. 28–36.
4 Casey, D. and Pearce, D. (1977), *More than Management Development*, Aldershot: Gower.
5 Revans, R. W. (1981), *Action Learning*, London: Blond and Briggs.
6 Precious, W. (1982), 'Flush doors for the 80s: a case study of action learning', *Management Education and Development*, **13** (2).
7 Revans, R. W. (1971), *Developing Effective Managers*, London: Praeger.
8 Revans, R. W. (1971), op. cit., pp. 117–18.
9 Pedler, M., Burgoyne, J., and Boydell, T. (1978), *A Manager's Guide to Self-Development*, London: McGraw-Hill.
10 Parlett, M. and Hamilton, D. (1972), 'Evaluation as illumination: a new approach to the study of innovatory programmes', *Occasional Papers* 9, Centre for Research in Educational Sciences, University of Edinburgh.
11 Wieland, G. F. and Leigh, H. (eds) (1971), *Changing Hospitals*, London: Tavistock.

Appendix 1 Getting started: an action manual

David Pearce

Editor's note
This Appendix is David Pearce's attempt to explain in a simple and logical fashion how to start an Action Learning programme. Inevitably therefore it re-states and summarises many of the points made in the book by other contributors.

Is Action Learning what you need?

This manual is intended:

1 to help you recognize some situations where Action Learning would be appropriate
2 to help you set about getting it started
3 to give you some ideas about how to manage it once it is started.

Action Learning is a well-tried way of accelerating people's learning so that they can handle difficult situations more effectively. It does this by creating a situation where relevant people get together to solve the problems of today in such a way that everyone learns explicitly and powerfully from the experience – building capabilities while making considerable progress on the problems being treated.

So, how is it different from everyday life in most organizations? Surprisingly it isn't very different. Yet people who have experienced Action Learning will tell you it is. It is mainly to do with the facts that:

1 problem areas and potential opportunities are highlighted

2 conditions are created where people really want to see results

3 a new mixture of people are brought together to work on the problems and opportunities

4 at least one adviser usually works with the group to help it function best in its job of doing relevant work to achieve the necessary output, while accelerating each person's learning of how to be more effective

5 it is allowable to admit ignorance

6 people learn that problems are solved by asking the right questions rather than trying to impose favoured solutions

7 the Action Learning situation is more demanding and testing than many day-to-day situations, but it is also more supportive in a tough but realistic way.

You will recognize elements of day-to-day management, strategy management, project teams, group dynamics, problem solving and decision taking, and so on. They are all part of it.

Action Learning's uniqueness lies in the fact that it does not prescribe any one solution as best, or any one way as the correct way. It creates the conditions where people can learn the best way to achieve results within the constraints which are imposed. In doing so each person discovers and tests out his strengths and develops new ones.

Action Learning creates favourable conditions to enable people to 'learn best with and from each other by tackling real problems'.

Action Learning is unnecessary if solutions have already been found and tested. It is also of no help if some powerful individual or group is presenting a solution and has the weight to implement it.

Action Learning is of use if:

1 no one knows the solution to the problem

2 no one knows the way out of the complex situation (of course there will be different opinions about the best way)

3 there aren't enough people who can pose the right questions in situations of uncertainty

4 there aren't enough people who will take the risk in difficult situations, and will produce good results

One thing is certain, you won't get a feel for Action Learning or understand it until you try it – just like golf.

Forget Action Learning when:

1 answers are already known

2 the learning is programmable

3 it can be done more cheaply by other means

4 the conditions are stable and are likely to remain so

5 systematic analysis can give the solution

6 the top man, or a group of top people, is determined to go their own way regardless of the outcomes.

Deciding whether Action Learning is applicable

Ask yourself the two questions in Figure A1.1 simultaneously, and follow the arrow directions from there.

How to begin

Starting Action Learning is similar to starting training activities, but there are some significant differences:

1 the programme participants will need real problems/opportunities to work on

2 important people will need to be prepared intellectually and emotionally to accept that the programme will bring about changes to the ways things are done

3 people who do not consider themselves as participants on the programme will be involved, i.e.
    (a) the person(s) who own(s) the problem/opportunity
    (b) individuals and groups who are significant in the problem/opportunity
    (c) departments which have a bearing on the problem/opportunity

4 line management will need to be involved in deciding the

forms of the programme because it involves them and their business. It cannot be left to functional experts.

Types of Action Learning programmes

Because Action Learning is concerned at one and the same time with people and problems/opportunities, programmes can be aimed at differing levels of complexity.

Least complex

People		**Problems/opportunities**
Individual	M	Own job
Pair	O	Highlighted project at same
	R	level
Small team	E	Highlighted project at higher
		level
Large team/department		Team project in one department
More than one department	C	Team project in more than
	O	one department
The whole organization	M	Project involving the whole
	P	organization
More than one organization	L	Project involving the whole
	E	organization plus its sup-
	X	pliers, its customers, the full-
		time trade unions, the
		government, etc.

Most complex

Most Action Learning management development programmes start with the people. A simple matrix can show the types of situations that can be created for the learners (see Figure A1.2).

Type I *Own job* tends to be useful for developing an individual's current competence and future capabilities. It also clarifies his role and problems related to the job.

Type II *Highlighted projects* These can be valuable for increasing a person's vision and abilities in a bigger organizational context, and can achieve progress on a problem/opportunity.

Type III *Same job* done elsewhere. This tends to be the least effective in developing managerial problem solving because of its overconcentration on technical puzzle solving.

Type IV *Project in a stranger organization* tends to be highly

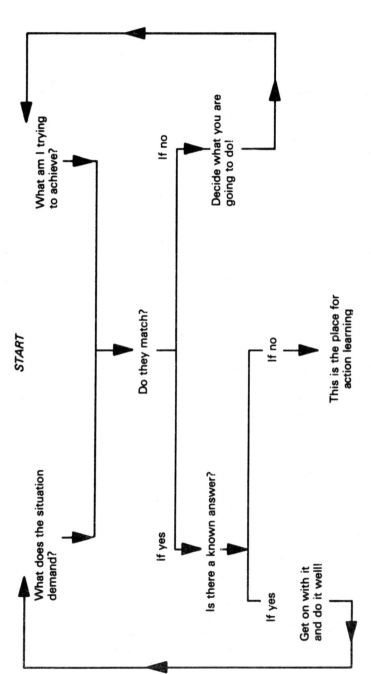

Figure A1.1 The Action Learning decision process

effective for significant personal development and helping the client organization to learn to value different experiences and views.

SITUATION	**TASK** Known	Unknown
Known	Own job I	Highlighted projects II
Unknown	Same job in another part of the organization or in a different organization III	Project in another part of organizaton, or in a different organization IV

Figure A1.2 The learning matrix

All sorts of possibilities for personal and organizational development can be produced using the options in the matrix. Combinations of types I to IV can be incorporated into one programme. On the other hand, if you are a senior manager looking for quick significant results on an important problem/opportunity, you may wish to consider team based management development activities.

Deciding the type of Action Learning programme

See Figure A1.3. Start by asking the question, What is the problem/opportunity? and follow the appropriate arrows to guide you through the appropriate action path.

Steps in setting up an Action Learning programme

Decide you really want to do it

↓

Start explaining why and what you are doing

↓

Gain some support and commitment

↓

Agree the people and problems/opportunities that it is aimed at

↓

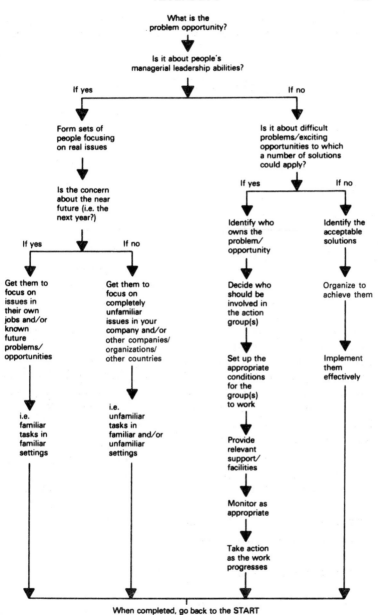

Figure A1.3 Deciding the type of Action Learning programme

Produce a basic outline of the programme, i.e. objectives, estimated (or fixed) timings, costs, resources, activities, etc.
↓

Try to produce a cost/benefit analysis (in operational terms and as far as possible in financial terms)
↓

In some cases produce a prospectus explaining the programme
↓

Agree a budget (try to get an allowance which the participants can manage.)
↓

Recruit resources internally and/or externally, i.e. set advisers, etc.
↓

Get participants and problems
↓

It is particularly important that you spend lots of time and energy briefing *everyone* you possibly can, but particularly: participants, the problem/opportunity owners, participants' bosses, your personnel/training colleagues, and your boss(es)
↓

Bring the appropriate people together for a start-up activity. Involve participants advisers and try to involve problem/opportunity owners, and participants' bosses.
↓

GO!

The set

In most Action Learning programmes participants work in small groups of 4–6 participants plus one or two advisers. This group has become known as the set. (See Figure A1.4)
Each participant brings to the set:

1 a problem/opportunity

2 which is owned by a client

3 the problem/opportunity is in an organizational context

4 the participant brings himself (i.e. his own particular experiences and mental frameworks, etc.)

The adviser has the general role of helping the set to work on the projects and on the learning.
Sets tend to meet regularly. The frequency and duration varies

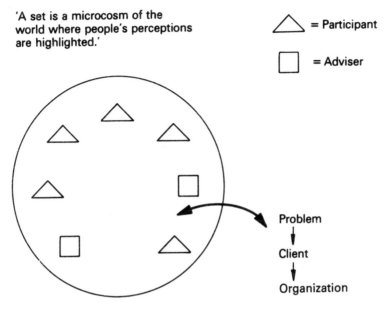

'A set is a microcosm of the world where people's perceptions are highlighted.'

△ = Participant

□ = Adviser

Problem
↓
Client
↓
Organization

Figure A1.4 The set

with the circumstances. A typical way is for the set to meet for a whole day once a week, a fortnight, or sometimes once a month. All sorts of other variations are possible.

> a project set is a temporary system with a strong problem orientation, and it results in cohesion, shared involvement, and a sense of purpose, which are similar phenomena in a task force. . . . Adherents say an action learning set is not a task force because a task force seldom has a learning objective.[1]

What happens in a set

There is no one way for a set to operate. It depends upon the mix of the particular adviser(s) and the delegates.

In practice the early stages are often dictated by the set adviser's preferences. This can vary from high structure (chairmanship) to virtual abdication (laissez-faire). If you are an adviser, you need to decide what you are likely to do best while taking account of the needs and expectations of the set members.

If the set is to become mature it will need to work through a process which is common to all new groups.

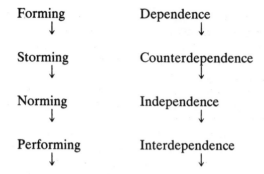

Forming	Dependence
↓	↓
Storming	Counterdependence
↓	↓
Norming	Independence
↓	↓
Performing	Interdependence
↓	↓

Typically, each participant in turn presents the problem/opportunities he is grappling with while the other set members and adviser(s) listen, pose questions and offer advice and suggestions. This process tends to cause the presenter to rethink his position and approach. This leads to further thoughts and ideas to be tested in action during the intervening periods between set meetings. The results are then presented and discussed at a later set meeting.

The presentation in the set of organization problems/opportunities leads the discussion and action into the full range of managerial activities, e.g. strategy and tactics, finance, negotiations, getting things done through others, marketing, internal and external politics, organization, managing change, etc.

The set's reason for existence is to improve work performance. Once that is established, it releases the legitimacy to talk about anything and everything else from metaphysics to high technology. But it is always anchored in the reality of action; because each client is expecting results from his participant.

Each set and each individual takes a different path depending on previous experience and current pressures. This is one of the most difficult things for people who have not tried it to come to terms with – particularly trainers who have been steeped in systematic training principles, and personnel people who are accustomed to the tight control of industrial relations.

There is a tendency to believe that there is a common core that can be given to everyone and is right for everyone. At the level of skill and knowledge for doing certain tasks it is true. At the level of managerial action in conditions of uncertainty, it is patently not true. Each person must find his own way of being successful in difficult situations.

At various stages, relevant people can be invited to join the set. These can be clients; people who have a potentially useful expertise; people who have expressed an interest, etc. But the set tends to become very protective of its territory creating a series of strong norms in the early bonding stage of its life. The set adviser can help to prevent the set becoming too inward looking. It is useful to get sets to visit each other's place of work. Most sets like to draw a lot of flip charts. But a number of set advisers have commented on the reluctance of typical members to produce effective written material. Also getting sets to read things, even newspapers, is often quite a challenge.

Like all human activities which are dealing with difficult problems, the pace varies a great deal from frenetic excitement to abject dejection – but rarely boredom.

Outline of a typical own job (Type 1) programme

Setting up the programme

Time likely to be taken 2–6 months

1 Getting delegates (usually quite time-consuming).

2 Course organiser/set adviser interviewing each delegate and his sponsor (usually his boss), plus any other interested parties, such as personnel specialists, training managers or management development advisers.

3 Agreeing the project the delegate will treat on the programme, i.e.
   (a) current job
   (b) selected parts of job, that is, an area which requires special attention because it is a problem or because it has never been properly tackled for whatever reason
   (c) a special part-time project devised by more senior management. With this option it is vital to ensure that the project is real and sufficiently important.

4 It is useful if each delegate is asked to do a simple write-up to create a bench-mark of where he is. It can help later to judge progress.

During programme

1st Meeting
Preferably dinner on the first evening and a short session after-

wards. It is useful if sponsors can attend this session. Next day the set works a full day with the set adviser(s).

At this first meeting the business is:

a The set adviser describes Action Learning, the aims of the programme, the format of the programme, the role of the set adviser, the facilities available, i.e. budgets, and so on.

b Each delegate describes his job/project as he sees it, what he is trying to achieve, and how he hopes to achieve it.

Professor Revans's questions are useful at this stage: What am I trying to do? What is preventing me from doing it? What action am I going to take?

2nd to 5th Meeting
1 day every fortnight (i.e. months 1 to 3):

1 Working on projects

2 Working on delegates' needs/skills; supporting and criticising

3 Visiting one another's companies – as a set and individually

4 Dealing with whatever arises

6th or 7th Meeting
(i.e. months 3 or 4)

1 Invite clients and/or sponsors to the set for lunch and an afternoon meeting:
    (a) to explain what has happened
    (b) to answer their queries
    (c) to show progress
    (d) to learn from one another

7th/8th/9th Meeting
(i.e. months 3½ to 5)

1 Continue working on projects, particularly on action

2 Continue working on members' needs of skill/knowledge development, support and critiques

3 Visits as appropriate

10th Meeting
(5th month)

1 Review activity $<$ programme successes and low-spots
                           personal progress

2 Decide how to handle unfinished business, that is, how to
   continue with activities which still need handling, by working pairs, and so on.

People and projects

Participants

Participants on Action Learning programmes have been very
diverse. What they have had in common is that they have wanted
to improve the situation they found themselves in. Are there
some guidelines to follow? Perhaps the following points may be
of some help:

People who have jobs with one or more of the following:
   a large amount of discretion
   a lot of ambiguity
   a great deal of problem solving
   a co-ordinating role
   a need to innovate
   a complex reorganization to handle
   technological change; including computers
   introducing new systems
   complex politics within the company and/or in relation to
   suppliers, customers, trade unions, government agencies, the
   community.

When is an appropriate time?
   at the very start of a completely new job
   in preparation for a promotion
   in the early stages of a first managerial appointment
   when complex change (as outlined above) needs to be handled
   at the crucial point in a high-flier's career
   when a good man has lost some impetus
   when there is uncertainty about the way a good performer's
   career should develop
   when it is vital for two or more significant people to have to
   work together
   during reorganizations

during and after takeovers
during business crises

It is an advantage if each of the prospective participants wants to develop significantly as a risk-taking achiever.

Projects

Throughout these notes the term 'project' implies a real management task/problem/issue on which action must be taken. Any academic interpretation of 'project' must be avoided.

The first thing about an Action Learning project is that it must be a piece of demanding work. Also, at least one significant person must want results from the work. In order not to waste time tackling purely technical or relatively simple aspects of work, it has been found useful to keep in mind the difference between puzzles and problems.

Problem

Where there are a number of possible solutions on which reasonable men can disagree.

Puzzle

Where there is a right answer provided the right resources are applied to find them.

The following areas may present Action Learning problems/opportunities:
  a complex managerial job
  introducing change
  a problem which concerns more than one department
  a new business opportunity
  motivation and productivity
  problems of relationships with suppliers, customers, trade unions, government, the community
  handling a foreign culture
  reorganisation
  introducing a new technology
  expansion or contraction

For an individual, action projects can be:
  coming to grips with a new job
  delegating current responsibilities while preparing for a new one

pairing with a manager in another department and both helping each other to improve the situation
doing an action project in addition to one's own job either in
your own part of the business
or in a different part of the business
or at a higher level
or in a different company
doing a full time action project (like those above)

Clients

A client is someone who owns the problem and wants the participant to work on it.

Gaining a client's support is essential in effecting change. Programme organizers need to be very sensitive in their handling of
clients during the setting-up stages, otherwise they may store up
problems for the participants.

Clients should also be built formally into the programme wherever possible, i.e. at the first meeting of the programme, at the
mid point and at the end.

During the programme a participant may decide that his original client it not the right person, and may negotiate a change.

In own-job projects the client is sometimes difficult to decide.
At one and the same time, it can be the participant, his boss,
all sorts of other people who are involved in part of his job.

Sponsor

The person who puts forward a participant for the programme,
and who feels responsible for his progress.

The set adviser

At its simplest, the set adviser's role is to help the set and its
members to work on the problems and on their own learning.
His secondary objective should also be either to make himself
redundant as quickly as possible, or to become a full, equal
member of the set with his own declared project.

The set adviser's first job may be to brief the participants,
their bosses and their clients as a preparatory stage before the
programme starts. This is a crucial phase that needs to be done
well. However, it does not necessarily have to be done by the
set adviser.

The set adviser needs to start working with the set from its very first meeting. This is the time that the bonding of the set takes place, and the important norms are established.

Each set adviser will need to decide his own preferred way of operating. Each set adviser does things differently as a result of personal preference and previous experience. It has often been found useful to gain practice in the role *either*:

by being a set participant before trying the set adviser's role, *or*
work with an experienced set adviser, *or*
take your courage in both hands and try it.

It is useful to remember the things you are *not* there to do:

provide solutions
be an expert on everything – omniscient
control everything – omnipotent
be a teacher/chairman/leader/tutor

but you can do all of the above at certain times – just like every other set member can.

You are there to:

help the set work effectively
help the set to work on the projects
help create the conditions where participants can learn to be more effective
either become redundant as quickly as possible
or become a completely equal interdependent member of the set.

I try to do the following when I act as a set adviser:

1 Act as I really am, bringing into the set all my limited but rich experience.

2 Try to respond honestly and openly at all times – very difficult!

3 Work with the set on the problems/opportunities and to find ways to meet skills and knowledge needs.

4 Work on the group processes.

5 Try to get each set member to understand and face up to himself – all that he is in his many roles, of which being a worker/manager/superior/shop steward is only part.

6 Work on Action Learning processes, that is, posing ques-

tions, gaining an overall view of the problem, stages in a project, gaining support, risk, and so on.

7 Introduce ideas.

8 Try to get people to see the connections between ideas, people, events, problems, the environment, etc. Try to get something appropriate done about the realizations and perceptions.

9 Work with individual set members, if it seems natural and appropriate to their needs and the situation.

10 Work on organizing specific formal or informal learning experiences to meet needs.

By its very composition, the set will create the conditions where each individual will be pushed fairly forcibly towards a search for a greater understanding of himself – but it is possible to resist if one wishes. After all, each participant (and the set adviser) is trying to be effective in a series of difficult tasks.Each set member is in the same boat and is probably trying desperately to help each of the others. The fear of failure creates sufficient conditions for each person to try their hardest.

Personnel and training specialists

The steering of an Action Learning programme is a complex online activity in its own right. The personnel and training function often acts as the initiator, but not always. Line management itself can, and does, run Action Learning.

The personnel/trainer who decides to introduce Action Learning is leaving the safety of courses where there is total control in a classroom environment. One becomes involved in the real dynamics and politics of running the enterprise. There are risks, but the rewards can be high. Skilful use of appropriate Action Learning activities can lead to improved performance at all levels, and to a shift in the way the organization operates. Your task is to help management, at all levels, see the possibilities which can ensue from involving their people in the real problems and opportunities of the organization. This may not be easy for some managers to accept. They may need support in learning to do things differently. The Action Learning approach of high support and high critique is helpful.

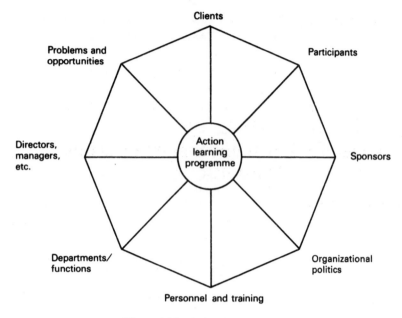

Figure A1.5 **Action Learning web**

The Action Learning web

The instigators of Action Learning programmes are inevitably caught up in a web of activities which involve a large part of the organization. Once an Action Learning programme is started all sorts of people are involved, and the interaction between different functions and systems are highlighted and affected.

It is vital to be aware of Action Learning's interactions in the web of organizational interests (see Figure A1.5). Managing the situation is a mini general management role.

Reference

1 Foy, N. (1977) 'Action Learning Comes to Industry', *Harvard Business Review*, **55** (5).

Appendix 2 A bibliography of action learning

Nelson F Coghill

Action Learning Projects International (ALPI) (1978), 'A self-development programme for managers through Action Learning'. ALPI.

Ashmawy, S and Revans R. W. (1971) *The Nile project: an experiment in educational autotherapy*. ALPI.

Bailey, J. (1980) 'Action learning for small firms', *Training Officer*, **16**, 174.

Baquer, A and Sundaram, C. (1978) 'The use of action learning in evaluating the Family Planning Programme in India', *Social Change*, December, p. 24.

Boddy, D. (1980) 'An action learning programme for supervisors', *JEIT*, **4**(3), 10.

Boddy, D. (1980) 'Some issues in the design of action learning programmes', in Beck, J. and Cox, C. (eds), *Advances in management education*, London: Wiley.

Boddy, D. (1981) 'Putting action learning into practice', *JEIT*, **5**(5), 2.

Boisot, M. and Fiol, M. (1987), 'Chinese boxes and learning cubes: Action Learning in a cross-cultural context', *J. Managt Dev*. **6**(2), 8.

Boulden, G. (1988), *Organisational values and style – the barrier to individual and organisational performance improvement*, Rugby: Action Learning Associates.

Boulden, G. and Lawlor, A. (1987), *The application of action learning: a practical guide*, Geneva: International Labour Office.

Bourner, T. (1987), 'Spontaneous combustion and the diffusion of grassroots action learning', *International Foundation for Action Learning (IFAL) Newsletter*, **6**(1), 28.

Boydell, T. (1976), *Experiential learning*, Manchester Monograph No 5, Dept Adult Education, Manchester University, 1976.

Boydell, T. and Pedler, M. (eds) (1981), *Management self-development: concepts and practices*, Aldershot: Gower.

Braddick, B. and Casey, D. (1981), 'Developing the forgotten army – learning and the top manager'. *Managt Educ. Dev.*, **12**(3), 169.

Brix, V. H. (1983), 'Action Learning and control theory', *Omega*, **11** (5), 491.

Brix, V. H. (1984), 'Cybernetics in management: Action Learning analysed by control theory', *Indust Managt Data Systems*, March/April, p. 25.

Burgoyne, J. G. (1977), 'The set adviser role', Lancaster University, February.

Casey, D. (1976), 'The emerging role of set adviser in Action Learning programmes', *J. Europ. Training*, **5**(3), 3; Also see Ch. 22.

Casey, D. and Pearce, D. (eds) (1977), *More than management development: Action Learning at GEC*, Farnborough: Gower, 1977

Coghill, N. F. (1980), 'The role and training of set advisers. Report of an Action Learning Trust (ALT) workshop', *ALT Newsletter* No 7, p. 4.

Coghill, N. F. (1983), 'Summary of the work of an Action Learning set examining the problem of disruptive behaviour in schools', IFAL.

Cortazzi, D. and Baquer, A. (1972), 'Action learning: a guide to its use for hospital staff, based on a pilot study in co-ordination in hospitals for the mentally handicapped', King Edward's Hospital Fund for London, THC 72/736.

Crout, E. (1975), 'The theory and practice of Action Learning. Project evaluation by Action Learning', (ALT) IFAL, November.

Cunningham, I. (1986), *Developing chief executives – an evaluation*, Report of the Action Learning programme for chief executives at Ashridge Management College, Ashridge College, November.

Foy, N. (1977), 'Action learning comes to industry', *Harvard Business Review* **55**(5), 158.

Fryer, N. P. (1987), 'Action Learning by degree – management development: a personal perspective', *IFAL Newsletter*, **6**(3), 15.

Garratt, B. (1983), 'The role of the learning group adviser: a process of phased redundancy?', *Managt Educ. Developt.*, **14**(3), 201.

Garratt, B. (1986), 'Action Learning in the Middle Kingdom', *IFAL Newsletter*, **5**(1), 16.

Garratt, B. (1987), 'Learning is the core of organisational survival: Action Learning is the key integrating process', *J. Managt Dev.* **6**(2), 38.

Gilbert, R. V. (1979), 'Action Learning down under comes out on top, *Educ. and Training*, **21**, 315.

Gilbert, R. (1981), 'Youth, vandalism, anti-social behaviour and security in Flemington and Kensington high-rise estates (Melbourne)', (ALT) IFAL.

Hall, S. and Dingwall, R. (1984), *Management training and development – practical approaches: a case history*, Blyth Valley Borough Council: development and member participation. TM. 73.00. Local Government Training Board.

Harries, J. M. (1981), 'The role of Action Learning set advisers (and some implications for their training)', *Training*, **7**(2), 7.

Hughes, P. J. R. (1987), 'The security of learning', *IFAL Newsletter*, **6**(2), 9.

International Foundation for Action Learning (IFAL) (1987), 'What is Action Learning?' IFAL.

Kirkwood, W. G. and Pettitt, S. J. (1987), 'The spirit of

entrepreneurship. Action Learning methodology for small business starters: an English experience', Paper given at the 32nd Annual World Conference, International Council for Small Business, Vancouver, British Columbia, June.

Lawlor, A. (1985), *Productivity improvement manual*, Aldershot: Gower.

Lawrence, J. (1986), 'Experience in Action Learning', Discussion paper for the World Congress on Management Development, London, June.

Lessem, R. (1982), 'A biography of Action Learning'. in *The origins and growth of action learning*, by Revans, R. W., Bromley: Chartwell-Bratt.

Lessem, R. (1987), *Action Learning and the drama of enterprise*, Graduate Business Centre, The City University.

Lewis, A. and Marsh, W. (1987), 'Action Learning: the development of field managers in the Prudential Assurance Company', *J. Managt Dev.*, **6**(2), 45.

Morland, J. (1982), *Quality circles*, Revised edn, London: The Industrial Society.

Morris, J. (1987), 'Action Learning: reflections on a process', *J. Managt Dev.* **6**(2), 57.

Musschoot, F. (1973), *Action Learning in small enterprises*, ALPI.

Paine, L. (1974), *Co-ordination of services for the mentally handicapped*, King Edward's Hospital Fund for London.

Pedler, M. (1981), *The diffusion of Action Learning*, Sheffield City Polytechnic Occasional Paper No 2.

Precious, B. (1982), 'Flush doors to the 80s: a case study of Action Learning', *Managt Educ. Dev.*, **13**(2), 89.

Rapier, E. (1976), 'Action Learning in Sweden: an attempt at an evaluation', Ekonomiska Forskningsinstitutet, Stockholm, Working Paper No 6073, August.

Revans, R. W. (1966), *The theory of practice in management*, London: Macdonald.

Revans, R. W. (1971), *Developing effective managers: a new approach to business education*, London: Longmans.

Revans, R. W. (1971), *The response of the manager to change*, (ALT) IFAL.

Revans, R. W. (ed.) (1972), 'Hospitals: communication, choice and change – the Hospital Internal Communications Project seen from within', London: Tavistock.

Revans, R. W. (Ed.) (1976), *Action Learning in hospitals: diagnosis and therapy*. London: McGraw Hill. [Contains the substance of *Standards for morale: cause and effect in hospitals* by Revans, R. W. (1964), London: Nuffield Provincial Hospitals Trust/Oxford University Press.]

Revans, R. W. (1977) 'Action Learning and the nature of knowledge', *Educ. and Training* **19**, 318.

Revans, R. W. (1978), 'Action Learning and the nature of learning', *Educ. and Training* **20**, 8.

Revans, R. W. (1980), *Action Learning: new techniques for management*. London: Blond and Briggs.

Revans, R. W. (1981), 'The nature of Action Learning', *Omega*, **9**(1), 9.

Revans, R. W. (1981), 'Management, productivity and risk – the way ahead', *Omega*, **9**(2), 127.

Revans, R. W. (1982), *The origins and growth of Action Learning*, Bromley: Chartwell-Bratt.

Revans, R. W. (1983), *The ABC of Action Learning*, 2nd edn, Bromley: Chartwell-Bratt.

Revans, R. W. (1984), '"Meadium": on the learning equation in 1984', *Managt Educ. Dev.*, **15**(3), 209.

Revans, R. W. (1984), *The universality of Action Learning*, (ALT), IFAL.

Revans, R. W. (1984), 'Action Learning: its universal application'. Address to the World Congress on Management Development, London, June.

Revans, R. W. (1985), *Confirming cases*. Revans Action Learning International (RALI).

Revans, R. W. (1986/7), 'Our search for identity', *Bull Educ. Dev. Res.*, Newcastle upon Tyne Polytechnic. Winter, p. 3.

Revans, R. W. (1989), *Management, management talent and*

society, Lecture delivered at the Manchester Business School on 8 February, part of a series on *Vital Topics*, Manchester: Manchester Action Learning Exchange (MALex).

Rowell, W. H. M. 'Initiating Action Learning programmes'. A discussion paper for the Training Services Division of the Manpower Services Commission.

Segal-Horn, S., McGill, I., Bourner, T. and Frost, P. (1987), 'Non-facilitated Action Learning'. Brighton Polytechnic Working Paper in Business Management No 15, May.

Sutton, D. F. (1973), *Learning by doing*, ALPI.

Sutton, D. (1977), *Action learning in hospitals for the mentally handicapped*. A summary of the work carried out in the Whittington Hall Unit of North Derbyshire Health District by the staff of the Unit in collaboration with ALPI Ltd, October.

Sutton, D. (1987), 'The problems of developing managers in the small firm', *Training and Management Development Methods*, MCB University Press, **1**(1), 1.05.

Weekes, W. H. (1985), 'Action Learning and organisational change', Third organisational and Policy Development Conference, University of Louisville, USA.

Wieland, G. F. and Bradford, A. (1981), 'An evaluation of the Hospital Internal Communications (HIC) Project' in Wieland, G. F. (ed.) *Improving health care management*, Ann Arbor, Michigan: Health Administration Press.

Wills, G. and Day, A. (1984), 'Buckingham's Action Learning business school – How well does the theory work?', *JEIT*, **8**(6), 3.

Copies of the items in this bibliography, except books, may be obtained at cost (post free) from the librarian of the International Foundation for Action Learning (IFAL), address: Nelson Coghill, 28 The Grove, Ealing, London W5 5LH; phone 081–567 1072. The IFAL library contains some 800 items and a full list of these is available from the librarian (£5.00; £3.00 for members of IFAL); and also a selected list (£1.50; free to members of IFAL). These prices include postage. A (free) book list is also available. These lists are updated yearly.

Enquiries about the library, and about specific items and subjects, are welcomed by the librarian, who can give information about publications dealing with particular aspects of Action Learning.

Appendix 3 People and organizations involved in Action Learning

The picture is changing and being added to all the time so this list is known to be partial and incomplete. My apologies to those who are not included and should be, and also to those whose details are incorrect. Despite these problems I hope the list serves its purpose – to provide starting points for those thinking about embarking on Action Learning and to widen the network of those already engaged.

The International Foundation for Action Learning (IFAL)

IFAL is a registered educational charity which includes a network of practitioners, but which also maintains a library, bibliography service, holds workshops, provides advisory services, publishes a newsletter and otherwise disseminates information about Action Learning.

Membership is open to organisations and individuals and details can be had from the Secretary:

Krystyna Weinstein,
26 Harcombe Rd.,
London N16 O5A

United Kingdom

London and the South

Tom Bourner	Brighton Polytechnic, Brighton
Norman Brown	20 Cunningham Avenue, St Albans, Herts
David Casey	108 Chelmsford Road, Shenfield, Essex CM15 8RN
Nelson Coghill	28 The Grove, Ealing, London W5 3SH
Ian Cunningham	Roffey Park Management College, Forest Road, Horsham, West Sussex RH12 4TD
Bob Garratt	3 Beresford Terrace, London N5 2DH
J M Harries	Local Government Training Board, Arndale House, Arndale Centre, Luton, Beds LU1 2TS
Julie Hay	7 Oxhey Road, Watford, WD1 4QF
Ronnie Lessem	7 Michael Fields, Forest Row, Sussex RH18 5BH
Alec Lewis	The Old Rectory, Church Road, Bream, Burnham-on-Sea, Essex
Peter Ormerod	25 Lonsdale Rod, Bournemouth BH3 7L
David Pearce	36 Station Road, Woodbridge, Suffolk IP12 4AU
Alan Mumford	IMCB, Hill House, Castle Street, Buckingham MK18 1BS
David Sharman	55 Mayhill Road, London SE7 7JG
John Talbot	EMAS, Southover House, Rusper Road, Crawley, Sussex RH11 0LN

The Midlands and the North

George Boulden	ALA, 83 Bilton Road, Rugby CV22 7AE
John Burgoyne	CSML, Gillow House, University of Lancaster, Lancaster LA1 4YX
Mark Easterby-Smith	CSML, Gillow House, University of Lancaster, Lancaster LA1 4YX
Brian Hague	10 Portree Drive, Croco Park, Holmes Chapel, Cheshire CW4 7JB

Martin Hughes	11 Southbourne Court, Drury Lane, Dore, Sheffield S17 3GG
Bill Huddleston	Thrang Lodge, Chapel Stile, Nr Ambleside, Cumbria
Jean Lawrence	The Development Consortium, 6 Parkhouse Lane, Prestbury, Macclesfield, Cheshire, SK10 4HZ
John Morris	The Development Consortium, 6 Parkhouse Lane, Prestbury, Macclesfield, Cheshire, SK10 4HZ
David Newton	Department of Management Studies, Manchester Polytechnic, Aytoun Building, Aytoun Street, Manchester M1 3GH
Mike Pedler	Rivelin Cottage, Hollow Meadows, Sheffield S6 6GH
Reg Revans	8 Higher Downs, Altrincham, Cheshire WA14
Tony Winkless	Selwood House, Park Avenue, Wisbech, Cambs PE13 3AQ

Scotland

David Boddy	18 Duchess Park, Helensburgh, Dunbartonshire G84 9PY

Northern Ireland

Gavin McWhinney	University of Ulster, Shore Road, Newtownabbey, Co Antrim, N Ireland BT37 0QB

Europe

Desmond McAllister	The Development Consulting Group, Square Robert Goldschmit 22, B–1050 Brussels, Belgium
Noel Mulcahy	National Institute of Higher Education, Limerick, Eire
Rolf Th. Stiefel	Dufourstrasse 30, CH–9000 St Gallen, Switzerland
Lennart Strandler	Langakersvagen 906, 12241 Enskede, Sweden
Joel Tillhammar	Mellangartan No 3, 951–38, Lulea, Sweden

Australasia

Roy Gilbert

Charles Margerison

Warwick Rowell

127 Ross Street, Port Melbourne, Victoria 3207, Australia

50 Carmody Street, St Lucia, Brisbane, Queensland 4067, Australia

20 Onslow Road, Shenton Park 6008, Western Australia

Rest of the World

Action Learning Network

B K. Bakhshi

Samir Mahomed Fahmy

C Jackson Grayson

Zhou Jian-Hua

Graham Williams

c/o Nancy M Dixon, Department of Human Services, The George Washington University, Washington DC 20052 USA

Indian Oil Corporation, Janpath, New Delhi, India

9 Sheik Seddik El-minshawy Street, Qubea Gardens, Cairo, Egypt

American Productivity Centre, 123 N Post Oak Lane, Houston, Texas 77044, USA

30 Zuo Yuan Li, Zao Zhan Xin Cun, South Gate, Wuxi, Jiangsu, China

City Polytechnic of Hong Kong, Argyle Centre, Tower II, 700 Nathan Road, Mongkok, Kowloon, Hong Kong

Index